BASIC ORGANIZATIONAL PSYCHOLOGY

Terry A. Beehr
Central Michigan University

Allyn and Bacon
Boston • London • Toronto • Sydney • Tokyo • Singapore

Vice President/Publisher: Susan Badger
Editorial Assistant: Erica Stuart
Executive Marketing Manager: Joyce Nilsen
Production Editor: Catherine Martin
Editorial-Production Service: Ruttle, Shaw & Wetherill, Inc.
Cover Administrator: Suzanne Harbison
Composition Buyer: Linda Cox
Manufacturing Buyer: Aloka Rathnam

Library of Congress Cataloging-in-Publication Data

Beehr, Terry A.
    Basic organizational psychology   /   Terry A. Beehr.
      p.   cm.
    Includes bibliographical references and index.
    ISBN 0-205-14811-5
    1. Psychology, Industrial   2. Organizational behavior.
    I. Title.
    HF5548.8.B365   1996   95-17938
    158.7—dc20   CIP

Printed in the United States of America
10 9 8 7 6 5 4 3 2 1   00 99 98 97 96 95

With love, to Dana, Matthew, and Alison

CONTENTS

PART V *Applied Organizational Psychology*

PREFACE

Organizational psychology, like any discipline, can be described in many different ways. One way is to consider the values that seem to be inherent in the discipline. Although organizational psychologists might try to be objective and discover objective reality about organizations, they do not and cannot seriously consider all aspects of an organization in their work. Neither, for that matter, do professionals from any other disciplinary perspective. Thus, we find economists and accountants focusing on monetary variables, marketing experts on product image and customer reactions, engineers on the physical production processes, and so forth. Even within the social sciences there are different emphases: Personnel psychologists focus on matches between peoples' characteristics and job characteristics, organizational sociologists on various aspects of organizational structure, and vocational counselors on the nature of individuals' careers. Each organizationally oriented discipline attempts to integrate what it knows about the topic of its primary focus or interest with other organizational topics, but there are usually themes in what and how they study in organizations and implement applied programs.

I argue here that these themes, which the repetition of similar models, theories, variables, and methods have represented over a course of decades, provide clues about what people of a discipline tend to value and believe is important. If we did not think something were important, we would not keep talking about, studying, and working on it. Chapter 1 identifies four such themes or values in organizational psychology, and subsequent chapters illustrate the manner in which these values are inherent in our work as organizational psychologists.

Organizational psychologists have frequently divided the field into three so-called levels of thought, inquiry, and action. The individual level, the group level, and the organizational level progress from "micro" to "macro" concepts in organizational psychology. Although these three levels sometimes make somewhat arbitrary distinctions, there seems to be a tendency for each organizational psychologist to find a preferred level at which to think and work. I use these levels to divide the book into sections, but similar themes and values sometimes cross the boundaries from one level to another, binding the parts of the field together. While I explicitly indicate this in many places, I urge the reader to accept the challenge of finding these bindings. Doing so should help the reader to understand the psychology of organizations over all.

In addition to the workspace, colleagues, and library resources at Central Michigan University, my summer appointments at the Lincoln Research Institute in Lincoln, Michigan, notably aided me in the completion of this book. The relative time, peace, and quiet were instrumental to getting this work done, in spite of the occasional distractions of looking out the window at the lake and of my membership in our little five-person organization (and assorted pets).

I would also like to acknowledge the helpful comments of the following reviewers: Clayton Alderfer, Rutgers University; Robert Baron, Rensselaer Polytechnic Institute; Jerry Greenberg, Ohio State University; Ira Kaplan, Hofstra University; Jason Shaw, University of Arkansas; and Robert Vecchio, University of Notre Dame.

1

INTRODUCTION TO AND HISTORY OF ORGANIZATIONAL PSYCHOLOGY

Social organizations are fascinating for their diversity and unpredictability, yet they are the epitome of stability and conformity. How can this be? First, one must recognize that social organizations do not refer to organizations with social goals but to any organizations composed of people or social groupings. What are they made of? They are composed, not actually of whole people, but rather of people's activities and patterns of relationships that are aimed at achieving some goals or purposes. While the activities and patterns of relationships in the organization seem aimed at a common set of goals, all the members of the organization may not share the same aim. In other words, what appear to be an organization's goals may not be commonly shared by all of the organization's members.

Contrary to some traditional definitions of organizations, not everyone who is a member of the organization shares the goals toward which the organization seems to strive. The slave ship of a former time, for example, may have been a very tight organization, but the slaves were not likely to share the goals of the masters. They may even have harbored goals that would almost have destroyed the organization. Similarly, but on a much less obvious scale, all members in a large business organization today are unlikely to share many goals completely and with the same passion. The owners' primary goal might be profits, the production workers might favor high wages and benefits, some professionals in the organization might wish to maximize the use of their valued skills to feel a sense of accomplishment, some managers might want to work on one flashy project for a few years to get a better job at another company, and so forth. The possible goals of people in the organization are almost endless. Why then do the members seem to cohere and work together, making up a single organization? Only by studying the various subtopics within organizational psychology can one begin to glimpse some of the complex answers to this question.

The goals of any company are typically those of the members of the organization who have the power to bend the organization's actions and employ its resources in the direction of their own goals for the organization. This dominant coalition of powerful people can change over time, but for a while they rule and get their way. While the actions of and patterns of relationships among people in the organization may be highly organized, not everyone shares in deciding how such organized behavior comes about.

Organized behavior is necessarily limited behavior. That is, the organizationally relevant behavior of each individual member is constrained. It is certainly not random behavior; instead, people's behavior in organizations is restricted within boundaries so that, if the restriction is successful, the behaviors of all the different members of the organization will mesh to accomplish some goal, for example, the production of a hamburger (or billions of hamburgers). A simple example of this restriction of behavior is work schedules. Employers typically require their employees to be present and working during certain hours of the day. If large numbers of them are absent because they have not constrained their behaviors to the one acceptable behavior (coming to work), the dominant group's goals will not be met.

A set of people develop the constraints on organized behavior, as well as the goals of the organization. Employees comply with the constraints, regardless of whether these people are present. This is the essence of social psychology, that is, the influence of people, whether present or not, on each other (e.g., Allport, 1985). Because of this, one can consider organizational psychology to be the social psychology of organizations. Social psychologists have typically been interested in topics such as attitudes and beliefs, motivation and emotion, people's attributions about causality, personality, conformity, and groups. Organizational psychologists are also interested in these subjects, but the difference is that organizational psychologists are interested in these things in the context of organizations. Sometimes the context can change things.

THREE LEVELS OF
ORGANIZATIONAL PSYCHOLOGY

Other than to say that organizational psychology is the social psychology of organizations, it is probably easier to describe organizational psychology and list the topics that it includes than it is to define it in a single sentence. One approach to organizing these descriptions is to categorize the topics into three "levels," as this book is. The three levels are the individual, the group, and the organizational levels.

Organizational psychology at the individual level, sometimes labeled the micro level, concerns differences in individual members of organizations and in individual jobs in organizations. Individual differences can be relatively stable, such as personality differences, or they can be differences that work situations more readily influence, such as attitudes toward one's job or employer. These will differ from one person to another.

Organizational psychology at the group level focuses on the behaviors and attitudes of people in groups within organizations. Such a group consists of more than one person, but fewer than all people in the organization, who have systematic interactions with each other over a period of time. The groups can be formal ones that might even appear on an organization chart (e.g., the psychology department of a university), or they can be informal ones. Of course, all sorts of social influences abound in these groups.

At the organizational or macro level, organizational psychology focuses on the broadest elements of the organization and their impact on the behaviors and feelings of people in the organization. Examples include the structure of the whole organization, the technology it uses, and even the size of the organization. In addition, one can consider the interactions between two or more of the organization's groups as organization-level phenomena.

The field of organizational psychology examines these three levels, but a quick study of the literature quickly shows that all levels are not equal. Organizational psychologists have studied some much more than others. One might guess, as psychologists they seem to have a penchant for the individual, and they have studied and worked at the individual level much more than at the other two levels. As one result of this, one may surmise that this book's descriptions of theories and phenomena at the individual level rest on more voluminous research, and therefore, on more solid ground than the information regarding the other two levels.

OTHER RELATED FIELDS

It would be a mistake to think that organizational psychology knowledge, research, theories, and practice all come from and are limited to psychology. Instead, the field is interdisciplinary. Some of what we know comes from psychologists, some from sociologists, some from political scientists, some from business experts, some from experts in communications fields, and so forth. Of course, to ignore information that is relevant to organizational psychology just because organizational psychologists did not discover it would be folly. Instead, the field freely adopts information as its own, regardless of source. To make things a little more confusing, there are many experts, educated as psychologists, who are working in locations that are not psychology locations—business schools being probably the most frequent location. The same is true of people trained in sociology and other disciplines. Perhaps these are among the truest interdisciplinary people, and they have contributed heavily to the knowledge base of organizational psychology. We cannot really understand the behaviors and feelings of people in organizations without considering many viewpoints.

There are a few fields that are especially closely related to and even overlap with, to varying degrees, organizational psychology. As Figure 1.1 indicates, these include personnel psychology, organization development, organization theory, organizational behavior, and organizational behavior management. At the risk of oversimplifying, I describe these only briefly here with an eye toward showing their most obvious relationships to organizational psychology.

Personnel psychology is related to organizational psychology more due to its combination with organizational psychology in formal college courses and graduate programs than to its overlap in concepts and topics. For example, colleges commonly offer a single course in industrial and organizational psychology, and such courses include both organizational psychology and personnel psychology—usually covered quite separately in different sections of the book. There are also many graduate programs in industrial and organizational psychology, and there is a division (Division 14) of the American Psychological Association titled Industrial and Organizational Psychology. Personnel and organizational psychology are the two largest segments of this field of "I/O" psychology.

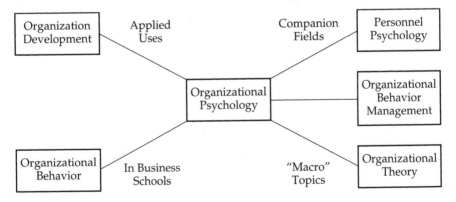

FIGURE 1.1 Relationships between Organizational Psychology and Other Fields

Although personnel and organizational psychology seem to mix frequently, they rarely blend well. The mixture is similar to an unusual dish, called peas and peanuts, which restaurants frequently serve in my hometown. They are mixed together with a small amount of sauce. Regardless of how well the chef stirs the combination, it doesn't take a culinary expert to see which are the peas and which are the peanuts. Mixtures of personnel and organizational psychology don't actually blend them but simply put them in the same bowl. The personnel peas are still usually quite distinguishable from the organizational peanuts.

If one can consider organizational psychology the social psychology of organizations, then one might label personnel psychology the measurement psychology of personnel departments. It usually relies heavily on psychological measurement technologies and concepts such as reliability, validity, and the many siblings and cousins of these two concepts. Personnel psychology then applies these measurement technologies to personnel problems, most notably job analysis, employee selection, performance appraisal, and training.

Organization development, on the other hand, can have overlapping content with organizational psychology. It consists of changing organizations for the purpose of improvement of the organization's functioning as well as for the betterment of the individuals within the organization. Such changes are planned. It is usually recommended that they occur organization-wide, and the changes have a basis in behavioral science knowledge, theories, and technology.

Organizational psychology is one of the behavioral sciences that provides a basis for these changes, and therefore sometimes one can see organization development as applied organizational psychology. Some examples of this are in the applications section of this volume.

Organizational theory is concerned with macro-level issues such as organization structures, processes, and outcomes (Gerloff, 1985). It is more focused on organizations as entities than organizational psychology is. When organizational psychologists examine such organization-level variables, they are more often interested in how those variables affect the individuals or groups inside the organization. Even so, these differences between macro organizational psychology and organization theory are only in degree and not absolute boundaries, never to be crossed by researchers, practitioners, and theorists in each discipline. One of the landmark books in organizational psychology, *The Social Psychology of Organizations* (Katz & Kahn, 1966, 1978) clearly shows this. That book covered a substantial amount of macro organizational psychology that overlapped with organization theory. Macro level organizational psychology can "learn" much from organizational theory, and at times it unhesitatingly borrows from it.

The field of *organizational behavior* has virtually no clear differences from organizational psychology. It is the term that usually describes the same field in management departments of universities rather than in psychology departments. The term *organizational behavior* occurs in psychology settings many times. For example, when the *Annual Review of Psychology*, obviously a psychology-oriented publication, publishes chapters on organizational psychology, it titles them "Organizational Behavior" (e.g., Cummings, 1982; Ilgen & Klein, 1989; O'Reilly, 1991; Schneider, 1985). In another telling example, the American Psychological Society, in its annual convention, lists organizational behavior as one of its categories for presentations. Psychology seems to be adopting the title of "organizational behavior" in some settings.

One of the reasons for the small difference is that some of the people who teach and conduct research in organizational behavior learned their craft in psychology departments, and, of course, they teach what they know—organizational psychology. Of the people with whom I attended graduate school in organizational psychology and who later obtained jobs in academia, about 90 percent of them are in management departments rather than in psychology departments. Of course, what they teach as organizational behavior and what I teach as organizational psychology is not much different, because we learned the same things in graduate school.

I find interesting that organizational behavior seems to have developed a larger following in business schools than organizational psychology has found in psychology departments. Because the market for books is therefore larger in management departments, most authors have chosen the title more familiar in that setting. Textbooks in organizational behavior frequently include chapters on learning and motivation, perception, group dynamics, and many other psychological-sounding topics. As management departments teach these topics over a number of decades, it will be interesting to see how the two fields that are now so close, organizational psychology and organizational behavior, might eventually diverge.

One of the differences now often seems to include style of teaching. It is difficult to say why, but, for example, organizational behavior classes seem to use more fully experiential approaches to teaching than organizational psychology courses do. This could give it a stronger skill-development orientation. Organizational psychology courses, on the other hand, seem to focus more on research methods than organizational behavior courses do and seem more willing to settle for teaching theory and research than management skills. When all is said and done, however, these two disciplines are more different in name than in material. Perhaps like twins, they spring from very similar beginnings, but their experiences and environments will make them more different over time.

The final related area is *organizational behavior management*. Organizational behavior management's root is the psychological school called behaviorism. It is the study and application of behavior modification principles to management problems (O'Hara, Johnson, & Beehr, 1985). Operant conditioning principles including the use of antecedent and reinforcing stimuli are the focus in efforts to alter job-relevant behavior in organizations.

All of these fields—personnel psychology, organization theory, organization development, organizational behavior, and organizational behavior management—are related to organizational psychology. Furthermore, organizational psychology unabashedly borrows from each when there is something valuable to be learned. In fact, it would be odd to do otherwise. How could organizational psychology pretend to know about employees' motivation to perform their jobs if it ignored the fact that systematic reinforcement can alter job behavior? If organization theory were to show that organizations' cultures affect employees' attitudes, how could anyone pretend to know about organizational commitment without knowing about culture? These fields necessarily overlap, sometimes greatly and sometimes only a little. Occasionally people refer to them globally as the organizational sciences.

THE VALUES OF ORGANIZATIONAL PSYCHOLOGY

Sometimes one can infer people's values by observing what they do. In the case of a discipline such as organizational psychology, one can make inferences about the basic values of the field based on the nature of the research over many decades. If organizational psychologists study the same thing over and over again, then they probably have a basic belief that this thing is important in some way. By observing what they have done, said, and written the most about, the following seem to be four common values of the field (Table 1.1): (1) the person is as important as the organization, (2) people have high abilities and are trustworthy, (3) interpersonal activities are important, and (4) research and theory have value. This might seem to contrast with a common view of science that scientists should be objective to the point of even being valueless and not let their values influence their work. While scientists must be objective in conducting research so that its results will be accurate rather than biased, the interests, beliefs, and values of the researcher often influence the choice of topics to study.

TABLE 1.1   Basic Values of Organizational Psychology

The person is as important as the organization.
People have high abilities and can be trusted.
Interpersonal activities are important.
Empirical research and theory have value.

The Person Is as Important as the Organization

Personnel psychology is an older, longer established field than organizational psychology, and it is more oriented toward enhancing the welfare of the organization. Organizational psychology, by contrast, is more concerned with the individual than personnel psychology is. The history of the study of job satisfaction in organizational psychology is instructive in this issue. Personnel psychologists are much more likely to show interest in performance appraisal and in validating employee selection programs using job performance as a criterion. These are organizationallly relevant criteria, that is, outcomes that are more directly of interest to the organization than to the person. In organizational psychology, on the other hand, job satisfaction has been one of the more frequently studied variables. Locke estimated that there were easily thousands of studies already in 1976. Satisfaction is more directly important to the individual than to the organization.

This does not mean that organizational psychologists ignore the welfare of organization. To do so would be to miss important variables in the work place, to risk employment by business organizations, and to appear irrelevant to many people in the workplace. Business owners and managers often tend to be suspicious that psychologists would like to simply make all employees happy and ignore productivity. While this is not actually true of organizational psychology, the field does tend to value *both* the individual's welfare and the organization's welfare about equally—and this is not what organizational representatives are usually looking for when they hire someone. Instead, because the organization does the hiring, it wants the organization's welfare to be first and foremost. While the organizational psychologist may work on the organization's criteria as part of the job, the theories and research in the field show that there is at least an equivalent interest in the welfare of the person. For this reason, managers sometimes may not entirely trust the organizational psychologist, characterizing him or her as too soft-hearted (or soft-headed). In general, however, a basic value of organizational psychology seems to be that the person and the organization are both important.

People Have High Abilities and Can Be Trusted

A second value that one can infer from studying organizational psychology is that the person has high ability and is trustworthy. These are really two separate beliefs about the nature of people. The first is based on the observation that organizational psychology seems to assume that the person has a greater ability than the typical organization allows on the job. The theories and research are replete with recommendations that the person have a chance to use more skills, for example, by taking jobs requiring a wider variety of and higher level skills than the typical organizational job allows. Sometimes these recommendations have gone under the rubric of Theory Y, sometimes as job enrichment or job enlargement, sometimes as participative management, sometimes as empowerment, and so forth. Even though nearly all of us probably believe that there are individual differences in abilities, organizational psychologists seem to have traditionally acted as if the more important belief is that organizations generally underestimate these abilities.

The reader might note that the related field of personnel psychology has paid more attention to the idea that people differ in their abilities (i.e., more traditional personnel psychology areas such as job analysis, selection, performance appraisal, and training usually make individual differences a primary concern). While organizational psychologists probably know better, they have not paid as much attention to individual differences in abilities as they have in their underutilization. Perhaps this is because the personnel psychologist has done such a good job in selecting and training the organization's members that this has reduced the individual differences by the time the organizational psychologist encounters them!

The second part of the assumption is that people are trustworthy. That is, not only does organizational psychology often maintain that people have more ability than their current jobs allow them to use, but it also seems to maintain that they will use their abilities in service of the organization if the organization trusts them to do it. Allowing people more responsibility, empowerment, decision making, and so forth assumes that people both have high abilities and are trustworthy to use them for the good of the organization. Approaches to management that do not take this position, such as the well-known Theory X (McGregor, 1960), show a distrust of people by supervising them closely, monitoring their activities, and punishing deviance. One can infer this to be a common value in organizational psychology.

Interpersonal Activities Are Important

Because organizational psychology is known as the social psychology of organizations, it comes as no surprise that those in the field have an interest in social or interpersonal activities. Topics such as leadership and group interaction have always been prominent in organizational psychology practice and research. Here once again, the very fact that these have been topics of study so often in the field suggests that they must be important and valuable. This is another value that seems to be inherent in organizational psychology.

Empirical Research and Theory Have Value

A final value of the field is that organizational psychology values empirical research in searching for answers to its questions and solutions to the problems it encounters. Its link with psychology in general may contribute to this, and its link with social psychology in particular reinforces it. The field seems to prefer the systematic gathering of data in the form of quantifiable observations. The reader can infer that the field does not, however, strongly share social psychology's emphasis on laboratory experiments as a form of inquiry. Instead, organizational psychology tends to emphasize research in real organizations, no doubt out of a concern that the results of the research will generalize to real organizations. As will become apparent in the next chapter, doing true experiments in the field is far more difficult than it is in the laboratory, and because of this, a great deal of the research in organizational psychology is nonexperimental. A sign that this tendency to favor field research over laboratory research has been a serious one is that a journal, *Organizational Behavior and Human Decision Processes,* came to be in large part to provide a publication for people doing laboratory experiments in organizational psychology. Prior to the founding of this journal, publication of even a well-done laboratory experiment was much more difficult in this field. Regardless of the form of the research design, however, systematic, quantifiable data with reproducible results is a basic value of the field.

In addition to empirical research, organizational psychologists tend to believe in the value of theory. Research in the field tends both to guide and be guided by theories. There is a preference for research that tests theory and for theories that are consistent with existing research. Aside from its link with research, however, theory seems to have more general value. In the applied parts of the field, where theory might seem to be irrelevant, theory still has value. Kurt Lewin's (1951) well-known maxim, there is nothing so practical as a good theory, is widely believed. In fact, practitioners who promote specific organizational practices on the grounds that they will result in better organizations usually do so on the basis of theories, even if the theories only consist of their own implicit set of assumptions about the way that people behave in organizations. In the history of the larger, umbrella field of industrial and organizational psychology, when organizational psychology came along, one of the things it brought to the field was an emphasis on theory. Before that, the field was primarily personnel psychology and was more atheoretical.

Certainly there are organizational psychologists, including ones whom I respect a great deal, who do not agree with one or more of the four values as I have stated them here. For example, some influential people who work in certain applied areas explicity reject the last one regarding empirical research (as one can infer from reading the chapter on applications). Nevertheless, interpretation of much of the mainstream work and writing in the field is generally consistent with the values. Therefore, recognizing that organizational psychologists are not all alike, I offer these values as a guide for readers to understand and interpret the topics in this book. As one progresses through these topics, these values will be apparent, even where they are unstated, by what I cover and by the nature of the theories and practices. Astute readers will be able to recognize them creeping in from time to time.

HISTORY OF ORGANIZATIONAL PSYCHOLOGY

Some of these values are even apparent in a brief accounting of the field's history.

The Backdrop: In the Beginning There Was Bureaucracy

To be blunt, much of the theory, research, and practice of organizational psychology consists of efforts to overcome the problems of bureaucracy. While everyone today likes to complain in general about "bureaucratic red tape," one may argue that bureaucracy is actually a relatively specific way of organizing, which came about because it was more efficient and more fair than other known ways. Compared to organizational styles that were dominant before the emergence of bureaucracy, such as feudal societies, bureaucratic regulations and rules were more fair because they were impartial and put limits on the organization's and leader's authority over organizational members (Weber, 1947).

Bureaucracy tended to institute meritocracy to replace the aristocracy of feudal times. Partially as a result of hiring, placing, promoting, and rewarding people based on their competence rather than on their birth and favoritism, bureaucracy resulted in more productive organizations. Nevertheless, as everyone acknowledges today, bureaucracy has its own shortcomings. The focus of some of its problems is the failure to implement its principles successfully. Personnel psychology constantly strives, for example, to improve personnel decision systems that have not completely eliminated favoritism in the workplace. Organizational psychology, on the other hand, sometimes seems to focus on improving organizations that have too fully embraced the impersonality bureaucracy advocated. This is apparent in attempts to make leaders more responsive to individual's needs, to improve job satisfaction and reduce occupational stress, and to promote the smooth functioning of interacting groups of people. Sometimes the aims of personnel psychology and organizational psychology seem to diverge, with personnel psychology techniques promoting the status quo or improving the bureaucratic organization in its current structure and with organizational psychology trying to make it less bureaucratic.

Besides impersonality, personnel decisions based on competence, and formally limited authority, bureaucracy also advocated the now familiar hierarchy of authority in which each job is under the control and supervision of a higher one and in which the people in the top jobs (managers) are separate from the ownership of the means of production. This means that the people at the top of the hierarchy run the organization but do not own it. Weber (1947) noted this principle of bureaucracy in his observations of the church and the military; however, it applies today to many corporations in which stockholders own the organization, but managers and executives actually run it. The thought then was that this allowed bureaucracies to be more impersonal. The owners, if they actually ran the organization, might be too inclined to make decisions based on personal outcomes; managers, on the other hand, could be more objective and impartial by not being so immediately and personally affected by their decisions. One may easily see, however, some of the problems if impersonality is taken too far. Bureaucratic organization theory and its spinoffs sometime have the labels of machine theories or mechanistic organization theories, because they seem to consider the organization as a mechanical device or machine with the parts (people) all very uniform and replaceable with no problem should they break down or leave (e.g., Katz & Kahn, 1978).

In summary, bureaucratic styles of organizations set the backdrop for organizational psychology, because many programs of practice and research in organizational psychology are reactions to the abuses and shortcomings of bureaucracy and other "classical" theories of organizations.

Taylor and Scientific Management: Setting the Stage

Bureaucratic theory described organizations from a broad perspective, that is, it looked at organizations from the point of view of the organizational level mentioned earlier. There is not much that is very directly psychological in it. A movement called scientific management developed principles that were more clearly psychological and that focused more on individuals, and its principles meshed very well with those of bureaucracy. Frederick Taylor (1911) was one of the earliest proponents of scientific management, and today his name is probably more closely connected with it than anyone else's. Other famous people working in scientific management around the same period include a husband-and-wife team, Frank and Lillian Gilbreth. Two of their children, who wrote a book on their life with a father who tried to run the family using scientific management principles (*Cheaper by the Dozen;* Gilbreth & Carey, 1948), provided a humorous look at scientific management.

Two of the basic themes of scientific management were work simplification and piece-rate pay systems. Work simplification advocated finding the one best way to arrange the work on the job. Efficiency experts conducted time and motion studies using stop watches and determining which ways of doing the job resulted in the most production over a given period of time, such as a workday. They conducted nearly all of the applications of scientific management on lower-level production jobs, but Taylor (1911) specifically noted that the principles were meant to apply to jobs of all sorts and at all levels. Interestingly, the decision makers, the managers of the organization, tended to accept these principles as appropriate for lower-level jobs but not for their own. The application of scientific management to these lower-level jobs tended to result in jobs requiring very simple physical labor, hence the term *work simplification* used here. As with bureaucracy, these historical principles are still very important for understanding today's workplace, because they have not disappeared. The field of industrial engineering does similar things today, and manufacturing organizations frequently use these historical principles.

In making the work simple, scientific management indirectly addressed the individual's abilities. While scientific management strongly advocated the principle of hiring the worker whose skills precisely fit the job, in practice its efforts toward work simplification seem to have overpowered its hiring principle. After all, if the work is always very simple, the company is always likely to find many applicants whose skills are at least adequate to perform the job. One may argue, however, that the skill requirements of these simple jobs were so low that the company would unlikely find enough workers whose skill levels were low enough to precisely fit the job. Some of organizational psychology's principles and practices today seem aimed at overcoming this problem, for example, some current job redesign strategies. At any rate, making the jobs simple also made it easier to replace people who might leave or prove unsuitable for any reason, and this easy replacement of the parts of the organization fit neatly into classical organization theory.

The second theme of scientific management, piece-rate pay systems, is scientific management's means of motivating people. A strict piece-rate system meant that the employee received a certain amount of pay, for example, one dollar, for each piece of work produced. Because pay for performance was already a tenet of classical organization theory, this principle of scientific management also fit very well into classical, bureaucratic theory of organizations. By producing more pieces, therefore, the person would earn more money. This obviously worked best for jobs in which the work output was easily quantifiable, for example, production jobs in which there were products that one could count. Out of a self-interested need for money, therefore, management expected the employee to be motivated to perform at high levels. As with bureaucratic principles and work simplification, this and similar systems of paying employees still exist today. Furthermore, as I show in a later chapter, they are more or less consistent with various psychological theories of motivation. These pay systems sometimes have led to problems in organizations, however, causing organizational psychology to develop other approaches to motivating employees.

The Hawthorne Studies: The Organizational Psychology Reaction Begins

The now famous Hawthorne studies of the 1920s and 1930s are probably the first prominent examples of an organizational psychology reaction to and against the bureaucratic and scientific management themes. Ironically, these studies began in a manner entirely consistent with the scientific management approaches to organizations. They ended, however, by touting some principles that appear to be in the organizational psychology domain. They are easy to criticize as their research methods were quite primitive by current standards, but their historical impact on theories and trends in all of the organizational sciences is difficult to overestimate.

The Hawthorne studies and the primary reports of their results continued for more than a decade. Researchers from the Massachusetts Institute of Technology and Harvard University conducted the studies, in the Hawthorne Works of the Western Electric Company in Chicago. As with the typical industrial engineering approach in the workplace, the researchers intended to examine the physical conditions of the workplace and the effects these conditions had on the production of lower-level workers. A series of experiments, actually quasi experiments, investigated lighting, rest pauses, temperature, humidity, hours of sleep, and diet as potential causes of productivity. The researchers apparently hoped to find some simple relationships that would account for productivity differences (Roethlisberger, 1989).

After obtaining very confusing results, the researchers changed course and started investigating other potential causes of productivity. They did this, in part, by trying to determine the meaning of work situations to the workers themselves. This required interviewing them and asking them directly how they saw things. This was not ordinarily done in prior organizational research—perhaps on the grounds that a good experimenter would experiment *on* subjects (people) rather than *with* them. After all, using physical science models of research, the researcher would not ask supplies or equipment any questions; therefore, a behavioral scientist also would not ask subjects for information. Doing so, however, led to the examination of new variables, new ideas, and eventually to the development of the field of organizational psychology. Asking employees about their perceptions of the workplace is commonplace in the field today, and it is probably somewhat responsible for the popularity of today's cognitive psychological approaches to understanding people in organizations.

Social psychological variables and hypotheses came to the fore in these studies, and these "illumination" studies culminated by illuminating concepts such as human attitudes and social influences in the workplace. Researchers finally recognized employees' social sources of motivation as important, in addition to the monetary motivation scientific management advocated. Employees' job satisfaction became as interesting and as important to researchers as employee productivity had been. The studies emphasized the importance of people as human beings, in contrast to the bureaucratic theories about organizations that advocated impersonality. The organizational psychology that eventually took root and grew, although only after some halting steps, was a reaction to the problems that seemed to be inherent in the classical theories of organizations and of the people in them. Furthermore, because the "classical" bureaucratic and scientific management principles have not disappeared but still play an important role in organizational practices, one may still view some of the current theories and practices in organizational psychology today in this light—that is, as reactions to classically styled organizations.

The Hawthorne studies thus brought to prominence the ideas of social influences on employees, individual's attitudes as having importance, and research methods involving asking workers' opinions about things.

Post-Hawthorne Writers

From around the time of the Hawthorne studies until World War II, there were influential writers of two sorts: those who elaborated on classical theory of organizations without changing it in any significant way and those who pushed along the type of organizational psychology inroads the Hawthorne studies initiated. Those who adhered to the first and dominant approach often labeled it the administrative management approach, while the minority approach struggled along namelessly in those days. The second, minority approach, however, later led to modern organizational psychology.

Administrative Management

Administrative management authors generally took bureaucratic principles and added some details to explain the way they thought the designs of organizations should be for maximum effectiveness. The audience was managers. The writing style was notable for its lists of important points, at times almost resembling the Ten Commandments by saying or implying that a manager should follow these principles in designing effective organizations. One of the best known of such lists became immortal as a nearly impossible-to-pronounce acronym, POSDCORB, standing for planning, organizing, staffing, directing, coordinating, reporting, and budgeting (e.g., Gulick & Urwick, 1937). These were the functions of a manager and the things a good manager must do. The lists usually described in some detail something approaching the one best way to do each.

Administrative management recommended specifics regarding span of control (how many subordinates each supervisor should have), how to organize staff (advisory) and line (production) functions, shapes of organizations (tall or flat, depending on the average span of control throughout the organization), and other features of the internal structure of the organization. Along with bureaucracy and scientific management, administrative management continued the dominant influence of classical theory of organizations until World War II.

Forerunners of Modern Organizational Psychology
In those early years just after and even during the Hawthorne studies, there were some notable reports that, along with the Hawthorne studies, foreshadowed what was to become organizational psychology. Three examples are the writings of Mary Parker Follett, Chester Barnard, and Kurt Lewin and his colleagues.

Follett (1982), in the 1920s and 1930s, went against a prevailing view among organizational scholars of the day by maintaining that working in organizations, even in the lower-level jobs of large industrial organizations, was unnecessarily debasing and dehumanizing. Instead, she argued that good human relations practices could result in the integration of the individual's needs and the organization's requirements for efficiency and effectiveness. The employer and the employee have some interests in common as well as some that are different. Their common interests could lead them to work together for the benefit of both if they try creative approaches.

Most of her contemporaries, however, tended to focus on the principles of classical theories, such as a belief in the need for some people to control others in order to make them work toward organizational goals. Contrary to this, Follett proposed the wide use of participation in organizations, that is, letting individuals have more power over their own work than classical theory advocated. She argued, for example, that giving controlling orders to other people cannot take the place of good training. All the management orders in the world will not make an untrained employee do a good job. Instead, organizations need well-trained people who want to do a good job, and they need to encourage these people to use their own judgment regarding how to get the job done. Furthermore, Follett noted that the way of giving orders could lead to resistance rather than to good work. These arguments fit quite well with the themes emerging from the Hawthorne experiments.

Barnard (1938) echoed Follett's call for more participative management styles, although he focused on responsibilities and activities of top-level management of the organization. In identifying executive functions, he did not list the ones from administrative management and classical theory, in particular controlling. Instead, he maintained that the executives or top managers of the organization need to develop a system of organized communication within the organization, to work on getting the needed effort from people, and to determine the purposes of the organization. Specifically regarding getting people's effort, Barnard considered recruiting and selection very important. Just as Follett noted that controlling or giving orders could not overcome lack of training, neither could it overcome poor personnel selection. Having obtained good, capable, and trustworthy people, an organization could then allow them the kind of latitude Follett advocated, and the work would get done very well. Thus Barnard and Follett both argued against overly detailed controlling that might result from adherence to classical organization theories.

While Follett and Barnard wrote generally about promoting participative techniques among business managers, Kurt Lewin wrote about and dealt with business organizations less directly. He was a refugee from Nazi Germany just prior to World War II, and he and his colleagues conducted somewhat politically oriented studies of leadership and social influence. Of particular interest at this point were their studies of three leadership styles labeled authoritarian, democratic, and laissez-faire (Lewin, Lippitt, & White, 1939). There can be little doubt that the international political situation of the time probably influenced the choice of these topics to study. This is also a good example of values playing a role in organizational psychology. It would be easy to imagine, given Lewin's personal situation, that he might strongly desire to show that democratic leadership was superior to the authoritarian situation from which he had recently escaped.

Lewin studied the three styles of leadership with adult leaders of after-school boys' clubs. The autocratic adult leader determined all activities of the group, determined the way the activities were carried out, gave no advance notice of what would happen next, and was quite personal in praising or criticizing the boys. The democratic leader encouraged and assisted the boys in deciding these things and tried to be objective and focused on facts when giving praise or criticism. The laissez-faire manager, on the other hand, did very little other than provide materials for group projects and answer questions. A quick summary of the results follows, with an eye toward generalizing to adults in a workplace. Autocratic leadership tended to result in good performance, low satisfaction, some hostility, and a dependence upon the leader in order to continue performing well. Democratic leadership tended to produce good performance (although not quite as high in quantity as autocracy did), high satisfaction, cooperation and enthusiasm, and an independence from the leader—that is, people would perform well even if the leader were not present. Laissez-faire leadership was not very effective in any particular way at all.

Although quantity of work performed was actually greater in autocracy than in the democratic leadership groups, this and an associated study was taken as evidence for the effectiveness and even superiority of democratic leadership styles. Furthermore, it was assumed that these results reinforced the participative management styles that Follett and Barnard advocated. The organizational psychology value and belief that people have high skills and are trustworthy shows clearly in the early enthusiasm for these works.

Post–World War II Themes

After World War II, organizational psychology research and theory entered an explosive growth period. Three themes in particular were leadership, groups, and internal psychological states such as motivation and satisfaction.

Leadership

Perhaps due to experiences in World War II, the U.S. government, or at least the military, seemed to be particularly interested in leadership. Perhaps there was a belief that certain battles, or even the war itself, were won because of the leaders. At any rate, federal grants funded several research programs on leadership soon after the war. Some of the most prominent ones were at the University of Illinois, the University of Michigan, and Ohio State University, and they lasted for many years.

The former writings about participative, considerate leadership as an alternative to directive, controlling leadership found its way into these postwar research reports. Although the research programs at all three universities had important differences in the way they operationalized things, they used similar language to describe what they did. At Illinois, led by Fiedler, one heard about relationship-oriented versus task-oriented leaders; at Michigan, the labels were employee-centered and production-centered leadership; while at Ohio State it was consideration and initiating structure by the leader (Schein, 1980).

Although the terms used to label leadership styles sounded somewhat similar, there were three very important differences in the theories and research. First, the Michigan and Ohio State approaches dealt most directly with the behaviors of leaders, as their subordinates observed and reported, while the Illinois studies used what seemed to be a psychological test of leadership style, perhaps a trait, given to the leader. Second, the Ohio State program allowed and even advocated the principle that a leader could show both leadership styles, even simultaneously. The Michigan and Illinois approaches did not allow for that, because their measure of leadership style required the leader to be more of one and less of the other type of leader. The Michigan researchers eventually decided that a leader could do both types of leadership behaviors; at that point, their approach was no longer very different from the Ohio State studies. The older leadership approaches of controlling versus participation seemed to be necessarily opposites, that is, to be both controlling and participative seems impossible. After World War II, however, the participative stream of thinking became, in part, being nice to people as much as allowing them to have more control over their work situation.

The third major difference in these approaches to leadership was that the Michigan and Ohio State approaches tended to argue that there was one best leadership style (at Ohio State, for example, it was to be both considerate and initiate structure), while at Illinois, Fiedler led the way into contingency thinking in leadership by arguing that the most effective leadership style was contingent upon or depended upon the situation. This basic idea is common thinking in leadership today.

Finally, a little longer after World War II, French and Raven (1959) took a very different approach to leadership. In essence, one can infer that they investigated followership, asking why people follow leaders and do what leaders want them to do. Reasons for following and being influenced by others are bases of power, and they identfied five of them. Reward power refers to a situation in which one does what another person says because the other person has control of potential rewards, while coercive power means that the other person can punish. Legitimate power derives from concepts of social norms and roles; in this case, one does what the other person wants because it is correct role behavior to do it. In organizations, for example, part of one's job (role) might be to obey certain orders from a supervisor. Referent power is based upon identification with the other person. Applied to the workplace and leadership or supervision, it might mean the workers like the supervisor well enough to emulate him or her by doing things that the supervisor might do. This is a form of influence that a leader could employ. Finally, expert power operates when workers perceive the other person to be an expert regarding the task at hand; therefore, it makes good sense to do the task the way that expert says to do it. These bases of power can describe social influence in any situation, but if they describe why a subordinate follows a supervisor in the workplace, they are relevant to leadership.

In general, the research conclusions were that expert and referent power are superior to reward, coercive, and legitimate power because of their relationships to various employee behaviors and attitudes (Podsakoff & Schreisheim, 1985). There were, however, consistent methodological weaknesses in the studies, making it difficult to embrace strongly these results.

Groups

Although there had been some interest in groups earlier in this century, there was a rapid growth in social psychological research on groups after World War II, and funding for such research was widely available, compared with former times (Cartwright & Zander, 1968). In fact, researchers conceived and tested many of the theories of leadership as much on groups as they did on leaders. After all, a leader and his or her followers can be assumed to be a type of group in most cases.

Several themes regarding groups emerged during the post–World War II era, including three especially influential ones: (1) group cohesiveness and deviation from group norms, (2) group problem-solving processes, and (3) communication patterns within groups. Most of these themes are still alive today in group research in organizational psychology.

Group cohesiveness means that the members of a group stick together, stand up for each other to outsiders, and help each other when necessary (Seashore, 1954). In some ways deviation from group norms is related inversely to group cohesiveness, because conformity, rather than deviation, is the hallmark of cohesive groups. Most of the studies of group dynamics, as the field came to be called in those days, were not directly conducted on groups in organizations. An exception was a study of group cohesiveness that showed that groups whose members stick together tend to conform to a productivity norm (Seashore, 1954). That is, the members of cohesive groups are all likely to produce about the same amount, while members of noncohesive groups have greater variation in their levels of productivity. While the organizational psychology values regarding trust and ability of people and regarding the intrinsic worth of interpersonal activity might have led organizational psychologists to hope that group cohesiveness would result in higher average levels of productivity, that did not happen. Instead, sometimes there appeared to be a high productivity norm and sometimes a low or medium productivity norm in cohesive groups. Whatever the norm, however, there was a tendency for members of cohesive groups to abide by it.

While group cohesiveness has always been a major interest in group dynamics, one might argue that deviance from group norms is merely the opposite side of the same coin. Deviant members of a group are those who do not abide by the group norms in conforming to the important group behaviors. By definition, the greater the average cohesiveness is, the less the average deviance in a group should be. A good example of a post–World War II study examined deviance among male college students in laboratory-created groups. It showed that for someone whose behaviors deviate from group norms, the group rejected, did not like, and did not nominate that person for committee assignments. Furthermore, at least for a while, the group members tended to direct more communication to the deviant members than to other members, presumably because they were trying to persuade the deviants to conform better to the group norms (Schachter, 1951).

Group processes, specifically those in interactions between group members while they are solving problems, also were the focus of extensive examination during these years. Most systematic observations of small groups engaged in problem-solving categorized the members' behaviors into two broad categories with labels such as task and maintenance behaviors or task and social-emotional behaviors (Bales, 1950; Benne & Sheats, 1948). These were behaviors that serve one of two functions, either accomplishing the group's task or keeping the group happy and together. It is noteworthy that these are very similar also to the two major functions that many leadership theories thought a leader should perform.

The group-process analysis theme especially seemed to find its way into applied organizational psychology, the field that soon became known as organization development. Related to this and at about the same time, there were studies of conflict among people in groups and among groups themselves (e.g., Deutsch, 1949). Various theoretical ways of reducing such conflict arose, and practitioners in organizational psychology tended to adopt them quickly.

Communication networks, or communication patterns within groups, also received a great deal of attention after World War II, with most of the studies occurring in laboratory experiments (e.g., Leavitt, 1951). Such patterns were the structure of communication or even the structure of the groups. Researchers often considered the results of these studies for their possible relevance to the structure of organizations. The studies tended to restrict the flow of communication in small, non–face-to-face groups of people who were solving a problem. When communication structures were more restricted, that is, when communication was forced to flow along a only a few lines to reach all group members, problem solving was often more difficult and group members did not find it as enjoyable as when there was less restriction on the direct flow of communication among all people. Researchers often assumed this to support the use of less hierarchically and less rigidly structured organizations.

Motivation and Satisfaction

A strong theme of interest in internal psychological states of organization members also was apparent after World War II. The two states receiving the most consistent interest were probably job satisfaction and work motivation. Although motivation and satisfaction variables are sometimes part of a single theory, they are different variables. Unfortunately, in those early years (if not still), writers often seem to have confused the two variables. Motivation is, by definition, a propensity to act or to behave in some relatively specific way, or more specifically, an explanation of the way that behavior is aroused and energized, directed, and maintained (e.g., Steers & Porter, 1975). When organizational psychologists use the term *motivation* by itself, it usually means motivation to engage in productive behavior on the job. Satisfaction, on the other hand, is more simply a pleasurable state. Quite some time ago, reviews of the research consistently established that there is little overall, consistent relationship between job satisfaction and productivity (e.g., Brayfield & Crockett, 1955; Herzberg, Mausner, Peterson, & Capwell, 1957; Vroom, 1964).

Regarding satisfaction, researchers often used need theory to advocate that job satisfaction equates to the satisfaction of needs on the job. Herzberg's (1968) dual-factor theory argued that the characteristics of work that make people satisfied are different from the characteristics that make them dissatisfied. The satisfiers, he thought, were characteristics of work that some people would consider "intrinsic" to doing the work itself, while the dissatisfiers were more extrinsic things that occur independently of doing the work itself (e.g., physical working conditions). Unfortunately, he also began to label the satisfiers in the workplace "motivators" and to claim that they motivate people, even though his studies were not explicitly looking at motivation. If satisfaction and motivation were not already confused with each other, this well-known theory insured that they would be confused on and off for decades to come.

McGregor (1960) explicitly used Maslow's (1943) well-known need hierarchy theory to develop a theory of treatment of workers called Theory Y. Theory Y assumed that American employees of the day probably had their basic lower-level needs (e.g., physiological and safety needs) already satisfied by good working conditions and their social needs satisfied by good human relations practices in their place of employment. Therefore, their higher-level needs, such as esteem or status and self actualization should be strongest. Theory Y maintained that workers would best be motivated by trying to get them to satisfy their higher-level needs through working on the job, and a work motivation theory emerged.

The social psychologist, Kurt Lewin (e.g., 1951), meanwhile, had been focusing on expectancy theory. A decade later, this became the dominant motivation theory in organizational psychology, after Vroom (1964) detailed it in work-related terms. At its most basic level, the theory is cognitive and rational. It maintains that people's thoughts direct them to engage in behaviors that they think will get rewards and avoid punishments. If these behaviors are related to work performance, they will be motivated to perform.

The favorite motivational approach of organizational psychologists, based on the amount of research and theory they devote to it, is probably the motivation of employees through the work itself, that is, finding ways to make just doing the work a reward in itself. If doing the work is rewarding, then people will try to do it. This is consistent with McGregor's Theory Y based on Maslow's need theory and with Herzberg's "motivators." Turner and Lawrence (1965), in another historically important study, started the study of a set of specific job characteristics that are thought to make the work itself motivating. Some of these job characteristics, notably variety and autonomy, survive into today's organizational psychology in modern job redesign theory of intrinsic motivation.

Landmark Historical Events

No history would be complete without the citation of a few specific landmarks. Sometimes events are so important that they either are signposts indicating a significant change occurring in a field, or they are the events that actually cause or shape a new era. Such events are few but important. The founding of influential organizations and key publications especially fit into this category.

Historically Important Organizations

In 1937, the American Psychological Association (APA) experienced a rift in which psychologist practitioners, primarily industrial-organizational and clinical psychologists, formed their own separate organization, the American Association for Applied Psychology. They apparently believed that the purely scientific researchers, the experimentalists, who did not value or even negatively value the application of psychology, were too dominant in the APA. This split symbolizes the organizational psychologists' commitment to applications of psychology. About fifty years later, in 1986, many organizational psychologists joined with the more purely scientific psychologists to form the Assembly for Scientific and Applied Psychology

(ASAP). Apparently, many of them believed that clinical psychologists who did not value the science of psychology enough had become too dominant in the APA. This split symbolizes the commitment of the field to research and science. Aside from these splits, indicating that maybe organizational psychologists have trouble getting along in any organization, these two actions are consistent with the idea that organizational psychology has both a scientific and a practical side, and that it takes both seriously.

In 1987, the Society for Industrial and Organizational Psychologists (SIOP) formed, and it is the primary professional organization for many organizational psychologists. It had been and remained Division 14 of the APA, but its incorporation as a separate entity allowed it more autonomy and allowed it to have a separate membership from the APA if members deemed that desirable. The next year, in 1988, the former ASAP became the American Psychological Society (APS). Soon after, SIOP developed a membership rule that its members must belong either to APA or to APS but need not belong to both.

Aside from SIOP, the other major organization of interest to organizational psychologists, which enrolls many of them as members today, is the Academy of Management, founded in 1936. Many organizational psychologists are members of its Division 3, the Organizational Behavior Division. These formal associations have an important impact on the science and application of organizational psychology. They help to set standards for education and training in the field, publish some of its most important journals and books, and represent its principles and interests to outside groups.

Other than professional societies, some other organizations are important enough historically to deserve mention here: the Institute for Social Research (ISR), the National Training Laboratories (NTL), and the Tavistock Institute. Rather than large societies with the potential to encompass all organizational psychologists, these organizations are institutes whose aim is research or practice or some of each. A group of leading social scientists founded the ISR in 1946 in Ann Arbor, Michigan. This group included Rensis Likert, an organizational psychologist famous for developing the Likert scale of measurement, promoting organization development, and studying participative management forms. The ISR now includes, as one of its subdivisions, the Research Center for Group Dynamics, which Kurt Lewin founded at the Massachusetts Institute of Technology but moved to Ann Arbor in 1948. The ISR has a reputation for its wide-ranging research in the social sciences, including organizational psychology.

The National Training Laboratory for Group Development formed in Bethel, Maine. It later became the National Training Laboratory Institute of Applied Behavioral Science and is commonly known as NTL. NTL has always focused on group dynamics, including the uses of group dynamics skills in organizations. Compared with ISR, it has a reputation more for application than for research, and it has had a strong impact on organization development techniques. These two organizations have had a strong and continuing impact on organizational psychology.

Tavistock Institute, in England, began as a clinic focusing on psychotherapy, including the use of psychoanalytic theory, which is very unusual in organizational psychology today (French & Bell, 1984). An early theme at Tavistock, before working on organizations, was to note that patients did not seem to get better without working with the social setting in which they lived—the family. It eventually used some of Lewin's notions about social psychology and showed how groups in which people worked were important in their motivation and satisfaction.

Historically Important Publications
In addition to formal organizations, some publications have also had a strong impact on the field. Several books have been either landmark events in the field or have shaped the field for some time following their publication. In 1911, Frederick Taylor published *The Principles of Scientific Management,* which advocated the principles of work simplification and standardization through scientific study and motivation through piece-rate pay systems. While some notable good effects occurred, one could argue that organizational psychology has tried to undo the adverse side effects of scientific management ever since. In 1913, Hugo Munsterberg, sometimes considered the father of industrial and organizational psychology, wrote *Psychology and Industrial Efficiency,* outlining the use of psychology in industry.

Jumping all the way to 1965, James March wrote the *Handbook of Organizations,* the first attempt to summarize everything that the social sciences knew about organizations. Along those lines, In 1976, Marvin Dunnette edited *The Handbook of Industrial and Organizational Psychology,* summarizing much the same things, updating them, and explicitly focusing on the field of industrial and organizational psychology. From 1991 to 1994, Dunnette, Leaetta Hough, and Harry Triandis edited the second edition of this handbook, now expanded to four volumes. The intent of these two editions (Dunnette & Hough, 1991) was to "play an important role in reflecting the nature of the growth and development of industrial and organizational psychology during the last 35 to 40 years of this century" (p. xxi).

Aside from the handbooks, two books are probably better known for outlining organizational psychology than any others of their day. The first is Katz and Kahn's *Social Psychology of Organizations,* published in 1966 and revised in 1978. This book both summarized, and more importantly, advanced organizational psychology by bringing open systems theory to it and by addressing the field all the way from the individual level to the organizational level. The original edition had such an impact at the time that many people informally referred to it as the "bible" of organizational psychology. The second book was smaller and did not have as big an impact on the field. It was the first book to have the title *Organizational Psychology* (Schein, 1965), however, and it has became a widely used primer in the field. It has gone through several updates and is still in use.

There are also several journals in which most of the groundbreaking research in organizational psychology has first appeared in print. The *Journal of Applied Psychology*, begun in 1917, publishes research in any area of applied psychology except clinical, but I/O psychology research has dominated its pages. In each issue, a few of its articles are usually specifically on organizational psychology. In 1956, *Administrative Science Quarterly* began publication. It seems to focus on the macro or organization level of organizational psychology. A year later, the *Academy of Management Journal* began publication. Its domain includes all of management, and a few of its articles in each issue might be on organizational behavior or organizational psychology. *Organizational Behavior and Human Decision Processes*, begun in 1966 as *Organizational Behavior and Human Performance*, is devoted to organizational psychology topics, but studies using the laboratory research method dominate its pages, a preference of the journal. In 1976, the *Academy of Management Review* began publication. It publishes reviews of literature on any management topic, including some reviews of organizational behavior or organizational psychology. Finally, in 1977, the *Journal of Organizational Behavior*, originally *Journal of Occupational Behaviour*, was born. It is entirely devoted to organizational behavior or organizational psychology. The most influential original research in organizational psychology tends to appear first in these journals. Although there are other sources, if one is interested in high quality, up-to-date research, these are good sources. Much of the information in this book originated from studies in these journals.

REFERENCES

Allport, G. W. (1985). The historical background of social psychology. In G. Lindzey & E. Aronson (Eds.), *Handbook of social psychology*, Vol. 1. New York: Random House.

Bales, R. F. (1950). *Interaction process analysis*. Reading, MA: Addison Wesley.

Barnard, C. I. (1938). *The functions of the executive*. Cambridge, MA: Harvard University Press.

Benne, K. D., & Sheats, P. (1948). Functional roles of group members. *Journal of Social Issues, 2*, 42–47.

Brayfield, A. H., & Crockett, W. H. (1955). Employee attitudes and employee performance. *Psychological Bulletin, 52*, 396–424.

Cartwright, D., & Zander, A. (1968). Origins of group dynamics. In D. Cartwright & A. Zander (Eds.), *Group Dynamics* (3rd ed.). New York: Harper & Row, 3–21.

Cummings, L. L. (1982). Organizational behavior. In M. R. Rozensweig & L. W. Porter (Eds.), *Annual Review of Psychology, 33,* 541–579.

Deutsch, M. (1949). A theory of cooperation and competition. *Human Relations, 2,* 129–152.

Dunnette, M. D. (Ed.) (1976). *Handbook of industrial and organizational psychology.* Chicago: Rand McNally.

Dunnette, M. D., & Hough, L. M. (Eds.) (1991–1992). *Handbook of industrial and organizational psychology,* Vol. 1–3, (2nd ed.). Palo Alto, CA: Consulting Psychologists Press.

Follett, M. P. (1982). *Dynamic administration: The collected papers of Mary Parker Follett* (2nd ed). New York: Hippocrene Books.

French, J. R. P., & Raven, B. H. (1959). The bases of social power. In D. Cartwright (Ed.), *Studies in social power* (pp. 150–167). Ann Arbor, MI: Institute for Social Research.

French, W. L., & Bell, C. H. Jr. (1984). *Organization development: Behavioral science interventions for organization improvement* (3rd ed.). Englewood Cliffs, NJ: Prentice-Hall.

Gerloff, E. A. (1985). *Organizational theory and design.* New York: McGraw-Hill.

Gilbreth, F. B., & Carey, E. G. (1948). *Cheaper by the dozen.* New York: T. Y. Crowell.

Gulick, L., & Urwick, L., Eds. (1937). *Papers on scientific administration.* New York: Columbia University, Institute of Public Administration.

Herzberg, F. (1968). One more time: How do you motivate employees? *Harvard Business Review, 46,* 53–62.

Herzberg, F. H., Mausner, B. M., Peterson, R. O., & Capwell, D. F. (1957). *Job attitudes: Review of research and opinion.* Pittsburgh: Psychological Service of Pittsburgh.

Ilgen, D. R., & Klein, H. J. (1989). Organizational behavior. In M. R. Rosenzweig & L. W. Porter (Eds.), *Annual Review of Psychology, 40,* 327–351.

Katz, D., & Kahn, R. L. (1978). *The social psychology of organizations.* New York: Wiley.

Leavitt, H. J. (1951). Some effects of certain communication patterns on group performance. *Journal of Abnormal and Social Psychology, 46,* 38–50.

Lewin, K. (1951). *Field theory in social science.* New York: Harper.

Lewin, K., Lippitt, R., & White, R. (1939). Patterns of aggressive behavior in experimentally created "social climates." *Journal of Social Psychology, 10,* 271–299.

Locke, E. A. (1976). The nature and causes of job satisfaction. *Handbook of industrial and organizational psychology.* Chicago: Rand McNally, pp. 1297–1349.

Maslow, A. H. (1943). A theory of human motivation. *Psychological Review, 50,* 370–396.

McGregor, D. (1960). *The human side of enterprise.* New York: McGraw-Hill.

O'Hara, K., Johnson, C. M., & Beehr, T. A. (1985). Organizational behavior management in the private sector: A review of empirical research and recommendations for further investigation. *Academy of Management Review, 10,* 848–864.

O'Reilly, C. O. (1991). Organizational behavior: Where we've been, and where we're going. In M. R. Rosenzweig & L. W. Porter (Eds.), *Annual Review of Psychology, 42,* 427–458.

Podsakoff, P. M., & Schreisheim, C. A. (1985). Field studies of French and Raven's bases of power: Critique, reanalysis, and suggestions for future research. *Psychological Bulletin, 97,* 387–411.

Roethlisberger, F. J. (1989). The Hawthorne experiments. In J. S. Ott (Ed.), *Classic readings in organizational behavior*. Belmont, CA: Brooks/Cole.
Schachter, S. (1951). Deviation, rejection, and communication. *Journal of Abnormal and Social Psychology, 46,* 190–207.
Schein, E. A. (1965). *Organizational psychology*. Englewood Cliffs, NJ: Prentice-Hall.
Schein, E. A. (1980). *Organizational Psychology* (3rd ed.). Englewood Cliffs, NJ: Prentice-Hall.
Schneider, B. (1985). Organizational Behavior. In M. R. Rosenzweig & L. W. Porter (Eds.), *Annual Review of Psychology, 36,* 573–611.
Seashore, S. E. (1954). *Group Cohesiveness in the Industrial Work Group*. Ann Arbor, MI: Institute for Social Research.
Steers, R. M., & Porter, L. W. (Eds.). (1975). *Motivation and work behavior*. New York: McGraw-Hill.
Taylor, F. W. (1911). *The Principles of Scientific Management*. New York: Harper.
Triandis, H. C., Dunnette, M. D., & Hough, L. M. (1994). *Handbook of industrial and organizational psychology*, Vol. 4, (2nd ed.). Palo Alto, CA: Consulting Psychologists Press.
Turner, A. N., & Lawrence, P. R. (1965). *Industrial jobs and the worker*. Boston: Harvard University Graduate School of Business Administration.
Vroom, V. H. (1964). *Work and motivation*. New York: Wiley.
Weber, M. (1947). *The theory of social and economic organization* (translated by Henderson, A. M., & Parsons, T.). Parsons, T. (Ed.). New York: Free Press.

2

WAYS OF STUDYING PEOPLE IN ORGANIZATIONS

Organizational psychologists study people in organizations because of both scientific curiosity and practical concerns. As I noted in the first chapter, there is a basic value in the field regarding empirical research and theory. Organizational psychologists believe in the value of both research and theory as guides in their work. Empirical research means research based on direct observation; that is, the researcher who wants to know about something tries to observe it to see what it is like, how it works, and so forth. If we would like to know about people in organizations, we try to gather some information through observations of them. Sometimes it may not seem as if we are observing them, but in principle we are observing in some form or other. For example, if an organizational psychologist asks employees in an interview or in a questionnaire to describe the nature of their jobs, the employees are acting as "observers" for the researcher by reporting about the jobs—as they have observed them. Typically in empirical research, researchers gather information or data from some sort of observations and quantify it by turning it into numbers. Jobs that have more variety in them, for example, might be assigned a higher number than other jobs on a variable labeled variety. The numerical data then are subject to statistical analysis in most research studies.

People entering any field usually do so at least in part out of an intrinsic interest in the topic. It can be fun to discover how people think, feel, and behave in various organizational situations. The best way to make such discoveries is through systematic research, that is, research that is systematic enough so that (1) we can be relatively sure about the meaning of the results and (2) we can believe that the results apply generally to many or most people in organizations and not just the few studied. Presently we will see how these two concerns translate into principles about causality and generalizability.

Aside from natural scientific curiosity, the systematic study of organizations also is useful for practical purposes. An organizational psychologist working for an organization might have the task of improving productivity, morale, or job satisfaction or the task of reducing absenteeism or turnover rates. Based on knowledge of past research and theory and of local opinions about the specific organization, some plausible causes of the problem will probably come to mind quickly. For example, the psychologist might suspect supervisors' leadership styles, the design of the tasks people do, or the nature of the reward system as the cause of the problem.

By briefly studying these theoretical causes systematically within the organization, the organizational psychologist can rule out some of these potential causes, while others remain as viable explanations for the organization's problems. This "diagnosis" is a study or form of research. Let's say that leadership styles seem to be the most likely problem. The organization might try solutions such as leadership training or new ways of selecting supervisors. If the problem disappears, then it seems likely that the solution worked. Determining whether it "worked" requires another systematic study in the organization. Thus, for both scientific and practical or applied reasons, systematic study is valuable.

RESEARCH DESIGN OR METHODS IN ORGANIZATIONAL PSYCHOLOGY

Research methods or research design refers to what the researcher does to study a topic, regardless of whether the study is done for pure research purposes or for practical reasons. The researcher might, for example, manipulate variables (change things), measure things (observe them), or both. Furthermore, these activities might take place in different kinds of settings.

The Twin Aims of Organizational Psychology Research

There are two important aims or goals of scientific study in organizational psychology: causal inference and generalizability. Sometimes the researcher seems to have one of these goals uppermost in mind and sometimes both. Readers should be able to conclude by the end of this chapter that when these two aims are in conflict, organizational psychologists have tended to opt for generalizability over causality, although this is by no means universally so. Causation is an assumption or attribution that people make; they do not see it. For example, when a croquet ball hits another and the other ball then moves, one usually infers that the first ball hitting the second one caused the second one to move. We did not see causation, but we inferred it or attributed it to the situation. In this example, just about everyone would be satisfied with this causal inference. In some studies in organizational psychology, however, the inference is more questionable, weaker, or takes a larger leap of faith. While we would like to make strong inferences about causation, the design of some research makes strong causal inferences safer or more plausible than other designs.

Earlier, I proposed supervisors' leadership styles as causes of problems in an organization. Before the organizational psychologist satisfies scientific curiosity about leadership or is sure that leadership changes can solve the organization's practical problem, he or she must be able to make the strongest possible causal inference.

The second aim of studies in organizational psychology is generalizability. That is, one usually wants to have confidence that the results of the study will apply to or generalize to situations other than the situation in which the study was done. For scientific purposes one then might have helped to establish a general principle in a theory of leadership. For practical purposes, generalizability helps us to be sure that a similar solution might be workable in another setting or at a future time when problems occur again.

Basic Research Methods

Figure 2.1 on page 32 illustrates two of the most basic dimensions of research design in organizational psychology: the technique, or how the study is done, and the setting, or where the study is done. In principle, these are two separate dimensions, and a study could fall into any of the four main cells of the figure. In practice, however, most studies tend to use methods from only one of two cells: laboratory experiment or nonexperimental field study. The two dimensions (technique and setting) are particularly important, because they are related to the twin aims of organizational psychology research, causal inference and generalizability. The setting and the technique are not important themselves, but they matter because they have implications for these two important aims.

The Setting

In principle, the setting is a relatively simple concept. One often thinks that psychological research is done either in the field or in the laboratory. A laboratory is not in a permanent organization, is usually a place in which people are aware that the setting is not a normal part of their lives, and is the creation of and is in the control, to the extent possible, of the researcher. The term *field* usually means that the setting, so the researcher believes, is the

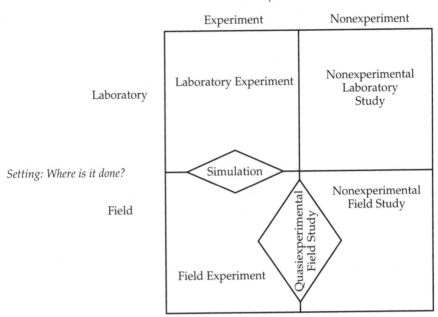

FIGURE 2.1   **Basic Research Methods in Organizational Psychology**

individual subject's normal environment. This is sometimes called the "real world," as if to emphasize the advantage of the field over the laboratory as a setting.

   If the techniques in Figure 2.1 are the same in both a field and a laboratory study, then the field has an advantage over the laboratory. If an equally well-done experiment took place in both the laboratory and in the field, the field would have an advantage. This advantage is related to one of the twin aims of organizational psychology: generalizability. If one wishes to know whether a research result applies to many parts of the real world, it makes sense that results a researcher obtained in the real world are more likely to apply there than are results obtained in the artificial world of the psychological laboratory. At a minimum, the field results from one organization are certainly applicable to that one organization in the real world. One cannot say the same as confidently of research done in a laboratory.

The Technique
The technique refers to how the research is done. It can be done either experimentally or nonexperimentally. The reader should note that the word *experiment* is not synonymous with the word *research*. Research can be an experiment, but nonexperimental research is also common. For the purposes

of separating experimental from nonexperimental research, the concept of manipulation is critical.

Experiments.   In an experiment, the experimenter changes or manipulates something in the subject's environment. The thing the experimenter alters is called the independent variable. To study leadership, for example, the experimenter (this term does not technically apply to a researcher using nonexperimental methods) might expose the subject, or person being studied, to a specific leadership style. The leader or supervisor might allow the subjects to help decide how to go about doing a task, rather than telling them in detail exactly how they must do it. One might call this participative leadership style.

One might want to know whether this leadership style makes any difference in the subjects' task performance, the dependent variable, and therefore one should measure task performance. To know whether the participative leadership style affects task performance, however, one needs to compare it to something else—task performance under some other leadership style. This is usually done in one of two ways. Usually, the researcher randomly assigns many subjects to experience either this leadership style or some other one—perhaps the directive style of telling people exactly how to do things and allowing them no influence over it. The experimenter then compares the difference between the performance of the two groups of subjects. The second way is to give all subjects both types of leadership styles but only one at a time. This way, one can compare all subjects' performance under one leadership style with their performance under another leadership style. Instead of a between-subjects comparison as in the first technique, this would be a within-subjects comparison.

The experimenter wants to be sure that the independent variable (leadership style) is actually what caused the changes in the dependent variable (task performance). Perhaps something else really caused the observed performance differences. Maybe, in the between-groups technique, all the people in the participative leadership group had more skill than the people in the directive leadership group. To avoid this or the effect of other such individual differences, the researcher randomly assigns the subjects to the two leadership groups. On average, therefore, one can usually assume abilities and other individual differences to be equal between the groups. This is a way of "controlling" individual differences. While the experimenter manipulates the independent variable to make the experience between the groups different, he or she must control all other variables and keep them equivalent between groups.

In addition to random assignment to control individual difference variables, there are other ways of controlling other variables. For example, adjusting the thermostat controls room temperature to the same reading for every subject. By doing the experiment in the same room each time, the size of the room, the color of the walls, and so forth are the same for everyone. By having all the subjects do their tasks at the same time of day or night, the experimenter controls the effects of time.

By controlling these extraneous variables, by holding them constant for each group of subjects, they will not be possible causes of differences in the dependent variable. Any differences in the dependent variable then, can only be the result of the independent variable, or at least the experimenter is willing to assume that this is a strong causal inference. This is the strength of the experiment. If the setting of two studies is equal, for example, the studies are both done in the field, the experiment has an advantage over nonexperimental research. The advantage is relative surety about causation; one can make a strong causal inference.

Nonexperimental Studies. By comparison, the nonexperimental technique relies on measurement only—it does not manipulate any variables or control any others by physically controlling them or by randomly assigning people to groups or experimental conditions. To study the same topic, participative leadership, a nonexperimental study would usually examine an existing leadership situation in some organization or organizations. The researcher would identify many supervisors, each probably having several subordinates, and measure their leadership styles. The researchers would do the measuring or observing by literally watching the supervisors and watching the subordinates' responses to the supervisors' leadership styles.

These observations would best be done systematically, for example, by sampling at various times of the day to try to get representative supervisor behaviors instead of just behavior that is idiosyncratic to one specific time (e.g., Jenkins, Nadler, Lawler, & Cammann, 1975). These types of observations are very costly and difficult to do; therefore, another type of observation is more common. In this case, the researcher contacts people who have been in the situation for a long enough time and have made these observations already, although informally and unsystematically.

The subordinates, in the example of a study of supervisors' leadership styles, have an excellent "view" of the supervisors' leadership behaviors; therefore, researchers often ask them, in systematic ways, about what they have observed. This can be done either with interviews or questionnaires. To measure performance, the researcher might obtain access to the organization's personnel records, in which there might already be ratings of the subordinates' job performance. These ratings are someone's (usually the supervisor's) observations of the performance of the employee. These observations were made for a different purpose from the researcher's, but they can also work well as research variables for the study.

After measuring the variables via some kind of observation, the researchers then use statistics to determine whether the supervisors whom subordinates report have more participative leadership styles are also those who have better performing subordinates. If so, the researcher might wish to infer that the supervisors' participative leadership styles caused improved subordinates' job performance. This, however, is not a very strong causal inference. It is mostly based on theory. The two variables are related, but whether one caused the other is not certain. There could be reverse causation, for example. That is, supervisors might tend to let people who are already high-performing subordinates participate in making decisions, because they have more trust and confidence in the subordinates who perform well. Indeed some early laboratory experiments indicated that subordinates' behaviors can cause changes in leadership styles (e.g., Barrow, 1976; Farris & Lim, 1969; Fodor, 1976; Lowin & Craig, 1973). The nonexperimental study does not allow the researcher to make a strong causal inference, and that is its weakness, compared to the experiment.

Commonly Used Techniques and Settings in Organizational Psychology Research

As should be apparent now, knowledge about research design is important if we are to understand the implications of and have an appropriate amount of confidence in research results. All research is not equal on all dimensions. In principle, the best research method would seem to be the field experiment, because it is strong on both the causal inference that it allows and the likely ability of researchers to generalize its results to real organizations. It may come as a surprise, therefore, to learn that field experiments are rarely done in organizational psychology. Instead, the most common type of research designs are laboratory experiments and nonexperimental field studies. Furthermore, of these two, nonexperimental field studies are more common than laboratory experiments. Considering the strengths and weaknesses of each method, this implies that many organizational psychologists have chosen to emphasize generalizability over strength of causal inference.

But why don't organizational psychologists use primarily field experiments, since they are the best of both worlds, allowing strong causal inference as well as generalizability? The answer is simple and practical: field experiments are difficult to do. To do a field experiment, first the experimenter must find an organization whose managers are willing to allow a researcher to make changes in the organization (i.e., to manipulate the independent variable). This is only the first step, but it is a very difficult one. Managers usually run organizations the way they do because they believe their way is the most effective. Ordinarily they would not let a researcher make changes in this presumed effective organization just for the sake of finding out what might happen or to test some theory! Simply getting the people who have power in the organization to allow a field experiment is difficult.

Field experiments in organizational psychology, therefore, are usually done only in special situations. One example occurs when the directors of the organization have decided to make a change anyway, expecting that the change will improve organizational effectiveness, and they become aware that they can make change in a systematic way that would make it an experiment. Along these lines, Jackson (1983) reported a field experiment in which management of an organization had decided to change to a more participative leadership style. A second situation concerns field experiments in which there is no change to the organization's current way of functioning. Ganster, Mayes, Sime, and Tharp (1982), for example, conducted a field experiment on the topic of occupational stress in which they provided clinical psychology treatments of employees. They did not, however, change the functioning of the organization in any way. Because of this, however, one could argue that this was actually a clinical psychology study rather than an organizational psychology study.

Even if a researcher can locate an organization in which management is willing to allow a field experiment, the ability of the researcher to control variables is nearly always more limited in the field than it is in the laboratory. In the field, many variables beyond the control of the researcher can potentially affect employees' responses: changes in the demand for the company's product; weather (especially for outdoor jobs); company buyouts and downsizing; work-related accidents and injuries; employees communicating with each other on their own, to customers, or to other outsiders face-to-face or via telephone or mail; and so forth. There are, therefore, many good reasons why field experiments are rare in organizational psychology.

Because of the difficulty of conducting the ideal organizational psychology research project, a field experiment, and because of the trade-off of generalizability versus strength of causal inference in the nonexperimental field study versus the laboratory experiment, researchers sometimes develop hybrid research methods. These can be ways of adapting either the laboratory experiment or the nonexperimental field study to make them take on more of the characteristics of a field experiment. The aim is virtually never to incorporate the characteristics of the nonexperimental laboratory study (see Figure 2.1). I have not described this research method in detail here because it has almost all weaknesses and no strengths. Because of that, researchers do not usually use this method. By now, readers should be able to figure out for themselves why this is so. Two classes of hybrid research designs are depicted in Figure 2.1: simulations and quasi-experimental field studies.

Simulations.   The reader may consider many simulations as attempts to make the laboratory-type experiments more generalizable by incorporating elements of the field experiment. To whatever extent possible, therefore, the simulation attempts to be more generalizable than pure laboratory research, without losing the strength of causal inference inherent in the experiment.

In an example related to leadership research, my colleagues and I once hired college students to code data for us (Gilmore, Beehr, & Richter, 1979). We obtained the student workers by advertising in the university newspaper, had applicants fill out application blanks and go through an employment interview, hired, and paid them. The work lasted about a week, during which time they worked in groups under the direction of a graduate student supervisor. Although we did not tell them until we held a debriefing, we randomly assigned the students to these groups in which they experienced different leadership styles. As far as they were given any reason to believe, the job they were doing was simply a job, not an experiment. In this way, we hoped to bring some of the realism of the field into a setting that could be controlled as well as a laboratory. The independent variable was leadership style, and the dependent variables were job performance and job satisfaction.

Another way of bringing some realism and generalizability into a laboratory-like setting is to study subjects who are similar to those in the real world. College students as subjects of a laboratory experiment are certainly real people, but if the topic is management in the workplace, one must acknowledge that most college students are different from typical managers. On the average, they are usually younger and at a developmentally earlier stage in life, are less experienced in the workplace, and have exercised authority less frequently—to name only a few of the average differences. They, therefore, may not act the same as typical managers do when confronted with an organizational situation. Researchers occasionally, however, study people who are similar to those to whom they wish to generalize research results in what otherwise appears to be a laboratory experiment.

My colleagues and I have done an experiment of this sort also, although it was not on an organizational psychology topic such as leadership. We studied a typical personnel psychology topic, employee selection decisions, and we attempted to make the experiment more realistic or field-like by studying people who actually play a part in such decisions (Gilmore, Beehr, & Love 1986). When campus recruiters came to the university, we asked them to volunteer for an experiment in which they would examine (hypothetical) student applicants' resumes and other qualifications. We randomly assigned recruiters to experimental conditions (in this case, the independent variables were sex of the applicant, attractiveness of the applicant in a photograph, and written descriptions of the type job for which the student was applying).

Quasi Experiments.   While simulations are research methods that combine laboratory experiments with field experiments, quasi experiments combine field experiments with nonexperimental field studies. These occur because researchers working in field settings cannot get enough control to conduct a true experiment, so they bring in some of the characteristics of a true experiment, while maintaining the strength of the field (generalizability). As with simulations, there is more than one type of quasi experiment. The researcher incorporates into the study whatever characteristics of a true experiment lend themselves to a given field research situation. The characteristics this may involve vary widely from study to study.

One common characteristic that usually is present, however, is manipulation of an independent variable. One characteristic that is usually not present in quasi experiments is randomization of subjects to treatments or independent variable groups. Because of this, researchers cannot be sure the groups are truly comparable in the first place. If there are differences after treatments occur, therefore, it is difficult to know if they are due to the treatments or simply to the fact the the groups never were the same. Lack of strong control, which I previously noted as a common characteristic of field research, may also be evident in other ways. For example, the experimenter may not even be the one to manipulate the independent variable. Instead, the organization's managers might have been contemplating changes on their own, and the researcher is studying these naturally occurring changes.

Basically, two general types of quasi-experimental techniques in organizational psychology might be nonequivalent control group techniques and interrupted time-series techniques. The former is probably used more often in organizational psychology. Just as its name implies, a nonequivalent control group is one in which the researcher cannot assume that the no-treatment or control group is similar to the experimental or treatment group in the first place—usually because there was no random assignment of people to the two groups. In interrupted time-series techniques, there is often only one group; everyone in it gets the treatment. The experimenter takes many frequent measurements of the dependent variable both before and after the treatment or intervention occurs. He or she then examines these observations or measurements for patterns of change over time. If the pattern seems to show a marked change at the time of the intervention, then the change might have been due to the intervention or manipulation of the independent variable. By using together these two quasi-experimental techniques, nonequivalent control groups and interrupted time-series measurements, one can obtain more powerful designs.

Using the symbols of Cook, Campbell, and Peracchio (1990) the Figures 2.2 and 2.3 show some quasi-experimental designs. The Os stand for observations or measurements, usually of the dependent variable, and the Xs refer to the manipulation of the independent variable. The X is also often called the treatment, and the group receiving the treatment is often labeled the experimental or treatment group (the other is the control group). In the second example of Figure 2.2, there is a plus sign next to the X for one group

Untreated nonequivalent control group with pretest and posttest

$$\begin{array}{ccc} O_1 & X & O_2 \\ \hdashline O_1 & & O_2 \end{array}$$

Reversed-treatment nonequivalent control group with pretest and posttest

$$\begin{array}{ccc} O_1 & X+ & O_2 \\ \hdashline O_1 & X- & O_2 \end{array}$$

FIGURE 2.2 Examples of Nonequivalent Control Group Research Techniques

and a minus sign next to the other. There is no group without any X, indicating that each group received some sort of treatment—there was, therefore, no typical control group, a group that actually received no treatment. Instead, one group received the treatment (+), and one received a treatment (–) that was opposite from that of the study. The subscript numbers next to the Os simply designate the time of the observation: subscript one refers to the first observation, and two refers to the second observation. There could be more than two observations. The dotted line between the two groups indicates that the groups are separate but unequal, that is, one cannot assume them to be equivalent to each other, primarily because there was no random assignment of people to these groups.

Single interrupted time series

$$O_1\ O_2\ O_3\ O_4\ O_5\ O_6\ O_7\ X\ O_8\ O_9\ O_{10}\ O_{11}\ O_{12}$$

Interrupted time series with nonequivalent control group

$$\begin{array}{c} O_1\ O_2\ O_3\ O_4\ O_5\ X\ O_6\ O_7\ O_8\ O_9\ O_{10} \\ \hdashline O_1\ O_2\ O_3\ O_4\ O_5\ O_6\ O_7\ O_8\ X\ O_9\ O_{10} \end{array}$$

FIGURE 2.3 Examples of Interrupted Time Series Research Techniques

There are many more nonequivalent control group and interrupted time-series techniques than the four in these two figures, but these illustrate the basic ideas. Regarding the nonequivalent control group designs in Figure 2.2, the basic idea is to examine the differences between the groups at the time of the second O, when one group experiences the treatment and the other does not. The researcher can also examine the differences between the first and second observation in the experimental group compared to the differences in the nonequivalent control group, or reversed treatment group, in the second example. A common practice is to use statistical techniques to "equate" the two groups based on their scores on the pretest (the first O). These statistics might include analysis of covariance and partial correlation techniques. Then, considering the initial differences between the groups, the researcher examines the differences at the time of the posttest (the second O) to see whether they are greater than would be expected based on the pretest differences. In the second example in Figure 2.2, the researcher might expect that the changes in the dependent variables for the two groups will be opposite. A "good" leadership style (X+) might improve the score on O (e.g., job satisfaction of subordinates), while the opposite leadership style (X–) might make subordinates less satisfied.

Regarding the interrupted time-series techniques in Figure 2.3, the main feature is that measurements (Os) are taken at *many* times before and after the manipulation of the independent variable, not just one, two or a few times. Random fluctuations of scores, therefore, are less likely to mislead researchers, who can observe and take into account trends when interpreting the results. The top illustration in Figure 2.3 shows the simplest interrupted time-series design. Although there is no control group, trends might help the researcher to understand the effects of the intervention better than if only one pretest and one posttest had been done. If, for example, the scores on the dependent variable (O) had been rising prior to the intervention (X), then one might expect O at time seven might be expected to have a higher score than the O at time six—even without the intervention. Another advantage is that some organizational psychology programs might be effective in the short term but not the longer term or vice-versa. In this case, only one posttest measure would not show the whole picture and could lead to inaccurate conclusions. The time-series design could avoid this problem, also.

The simple interrupted time-series design in the top section of Figure 2.3, however, is a relatively weak time-series design. When the interrupted time-series design gets more complicated, it can get to be quite powerful in providing information about causality. The bottom part of Figure 2.3 shows only one of many possible elaborations of this design, the interrupted time-series with nonequivalent control group design. (For a good summary of others see Cook, Campbell, and Peracchio, 1990.) The addition of the nonequivalent control group obviously gives this research technique all the advantages of the nonequivalent control group design plus the advantages of the time-series design. Because the nonequivalent control group design appeared in this text earlier, the reader should by now be able to discern the advantages of the design at the bottom of Figure 2.3.

One of the four core values of organizational psychology is that theory and research have value (see Chapter 1). For research to be valuable and for the results to be usable, they must first be correct. Rigorous research methods are necessary to have confidence that the results give knowledge about causation and that they generalize to other work settings and times—that they are "correct."

COMMONLY USED STATISTICS IN ORGANIZATIONAL PSYCHOLOGY RESEARCH

In addition to research design or method, organizational psychology research usually uses statistics to analyze the meaning of the data that it gathers. To understand some of the research articles that are published in this field's journals, the reader requires basic knowledge of statistics. I present here some basic descriptions of statistics that are common in organizational psychology research; details, such as how to calculate these statistics and how to critique their nuances, are beyond the scope of this book. My intent is, however, to allow readers to familiarize themselves with the way some statistics are commonly used in organizational psychology. This should make it easier for the beginning reader of the field's scientific journals to make more sense of the statistical results sections of those journals. Some of the major journals publishing articles in organizational psychology are:

Academy of Management Journal
Academy of Management Review
Administrative Science Quarterly
Group and Organization Management
Human Relations
Journal of Applied Behavioral Science
Journal of Applied Psychology
Journal of Management
Journal of Occupational and Organizational Psychology
Journal of Organizational Behavior
Journal of Vocational Behavior
Organizational Behavior and Human Decision Processes
Personnel Psychology

To read the field's primary sources, that is, the original reports of current research and theory, it is usually necessary to read some of these journals.

Measures of Central Tendency and Variability

The simplest statistics are those that characterize the nature of a large set of numbers. Again using leadership or supervision as an example, suppose we asked all employees of a company how satisfied they were with their supervisors and had them answer by choosing a number from one to seven to indicate less or more satisfaction with their supervisors.

One simple thing we might want to do is to come up with one number that best characterizes the whole set of numbers. For this, we would use their mean, median, or mode. The mean is the sum of the numbers divided by the number of numbers (the number of people answering the question in this case). The median is the middle number of a list of numbers arranged from highest to lowest. The mode is the most frequently occurring number (in this case, perhaps more employees rated the satisfaction with their supervisors as a "5" than any other number). The mean, median, and mode are all very basic statistics that you should already know. They are measures of central tendency. We tend to characterize the whole set of numbers as being around a central or middle number such as these. In organizational psychology research, we use the mean more often than the other two measures of central tendency, although we do use the others occasionally.

A second simple thing that would help to characterize the set of numbers representing supervisor satisfaction is the concept of variability. If we use the mean as a measure of central tendency, two departments in the company might have the same mean score, but one might have a wider variety of scores than the other. The degree to which the scores vary or spread around the center can be quite different from one situation to another. Perhaps the simplest measure of variability is the range. The range is sometimes called the "distance" between the highest and lowest score. The highest score minus the lowest score equals the range. If at least one person answered with a seven (the highest possible score) on the supervisor satisfaction questionnaire item and at least one answered with a one (the lowest possible score), the range is six, or we sometimes simply say the range was from one to seven.

Two departments of the same size might have exactly the same range (e.g., from one to seven), and yet the variability in the scores could still seem quite different. As an extreme example, perhaps one department had only one person who marked seven and one who marked one on the supervisor satisfaction survey item, while the other department had many people with scores of one and seven. The second department seems to have more variability in its scores than the first, but the ranges do not show that. It would be nice to have a statistic that would show the average variability of the scores, perhaps the average score's difference from the mean score, for example. The range only indicates the highest and lowest score instead of indicating something about the variability of the average score. The average (or mean) difference of a set of scores from their mean score, however, would not be a useful statistic for comparing variabilities of different sets of scores (e.g., variabilities in two different departments' scores on supervisor satisfaction). The average difference of a set of scores from the mean score in the set is always zero. It is a simple exercise, so I will leave it to you to figure out why.

In most of psychology, including organizational psychology, a measure of variability called the standard deviation has been developed and is frequently used. While the range is something you already knew about, many of you probably do not know what a standard deviation is. If you already know, this will be a quick review. You can think of a standard deviation as something like an average difference from the mean. Obviously, it is not exactly that, however, because this would always be zero. In calculating the standard deviation, one first calculates the difference of each score from the mean. Instead of taking the average of these differences, however, square each of these differences from the mean. If you figured out why their average would have been zero, as suggested above, you will see that this prevents their average from being zero—for one thing, they have all been made positive instead of some being positive and some being negative. Calculate the average of these squared differences by dividing by the number of these squares (which is also the number of questionnaires answered or the number of people who answered them). To get the standard deviation, "unsquare" this average squared deviation, that is, calculate its square root. Although it is not exactly the same, this makes it somewhat like the average deviation of the scores on supervisor satisfaction.

The standard deviation or its square ("variance" of the set of scores) from the next-to-last step in the calculation, is commonly used to describe the variability in a set of scores measuring things (variables) in which organizational psychologists are interested. Furthermore, the standard deviation and variance have some interesting properties that make them even more useful—sometimes in calculating more complicated statistics. Many measures of human-related variables, like the ones in which organizational psychology is interested, have frequency distributions shaped like a normal curve. This is the so-called bell-shaped curve in which there are more scores near the mean score and fewer scores that are very different from the mean. *If* there are a very large number of scores and if these scores have a normal distribution, about two-thirds of the scores will be less than one standard deviation from the mean score, and virtually all scores will be within three (plus or minus) standard deviations from the mean.

If you have followed this all the way through, then you will see that in normally shaped distributions of scores from a very large number of people (e.g., the supervisor satisfaction surveys from a large factory), the standard deviation will be about one-sixth of the range. We can also "normalize" scores, which means taking their differences from their mean score and dividing by the standard deviation. This is the "Z" score, and it is the number of standard deviations that a score is from the mean score.

$$Z = \frac{X - \text{mean of } X}{\text{standard deviation of } x}$$

Inferential Statistics

In addition to the measures of the central tendency and variability of a set of scores, and beyond them really, are a set of very important statistics that can be called inferential statistics. The main thing to know for present purposes is that they, in one way or another, estimate the degree to which two or more organizational psychology variables are related—and this is a separate issue from the research methods used, such as laboratory experiment or nonexperimental field study. When someone conducts an experiment in the laboratory or field, that helps provide us with strong inferences about causation—if the scores on the dependent variable are different for each independent variable group. The inferential statistic describes a relationship between two variables, which are usually the independent and the dependent variables in an experiment. More specifically, inferential statistics estimate the probability that two variables are related.

Table 2.1 on page 45 briefly describes some of the most common statistics found in organizational psychology research journals. The journals are primary sources of information about organizational psychology, because they are the place where the results of research first appear. One of the values of the field is that research and theory have value (see Chapter 1). The journals are where the public reports of such research appear.

Most organizational psychologists require more than one graduate-level course in statistics before they fully catch on to these statistics and are able to use the more complicated ones well. If you have not reached this stage, do not despair. This book will not even try to teach these statistics to you in detail. With the help of Table 2.1 and this chapter, however, you will have a better chance of understanding what the researchers in many journal articles are trying to show with the statistics.

Most of the inferential statistics report a significance level or statistical significance. Probability, or p, might be as less than 0.05, for example. This means that the chances that the relationship between the variables that the

TABLE 2.1   A Quick Guide to Common Uses of Some Inferential Statistics in Organizational Psychology

Typical Purpose of Statistic	Typical Statistic Used
Grouping people according to scores on one variable and examining the group differences between mean scores on another variable.	t-Test or analysis of variance (ANOVA)
Variation when groups' mean scores on more than one other variable are examined.	Multivariate analysis of variance (MANOVA)
Finding relationships between two variables that are measured with continuous scores.	Correlation (usually r) or regression
Variation when relationships between more than one continuous variable and one other continuous variable are found simultaneously.	Multiple correlation (R) and multiple regression
Finding what variables (often variables measured in surveys) seem to be measuring the same thing, so scores on them might be combined to get only one score on each "thing."	Factor analysis
Examining relationships among many variables to see whether the set of relationships is likely to have oc- curred if a model of causation among the variables is correct.	Path analysis, causal modeling, some uses of LISREL

statistic reports is probably not due purely to chance. If the probability is greater than 0.05, it is usually not significant or ns. In this case, the re- searcher does not feel very confident that the variables are related to each other; the relationship in the study might be due to chance and might not occur again in another study.

One major distinction in researchers' choice of what statistic to use to estimate relationships between variables is the nature of the measures of the variables. If there are only two variables and they are measured on contin- uous scales (e.g., a one-to-seven questionnaire item), Table 2.1 notes that correlations are usually used. If you are reading an article in which there are more than one continuous variable being used in relation to (or predicting) one other continuous variable, multiple correlation and multiple regression might be used. In this case, the researchers are trying to show the relation- ship between several variables as a set and one other variable, often called the criterion variable.

Researchers often use correlations in organizational psychology research to show relationships between two variables, and they are relatively simple statistics to understand and even to calculate. There are several forms of the formula for the usual correlation, and one of the forms uses the Z score, which I described earlier. Just as the standard deviation was used in calculating Z, Z can be used in calculating the correlation, r.

$$r = \frac{\text{Sum of } (Z \times Z)}{N}$$

In the numerator, each subject's score on one variable (x) is turned into a Z score and multiplied by the subject's corresponding Z score on the other variable (y). N is the number of pairs of scores in the correlation—in organizational psychology, this usually means the number of people in the study. The correlation has a range from plus one to minus one, and therefore it can be zero. It is usually expressed as a decimal, such as r=0.43.

There are some properties of r that are quite simple and useful. First, if the sign of r is positive, it indicates that as one variable's scores become higher, so do the scores of the other variable. The reverse, therefore, is necessarily also true of positive correlations, that is, as one variable's scores become lower, so do the scores of the other variable. If r is negative, on the other hand, high scores on either variable are associated with low scores on the other variable. If r is zero, there is no relationship at all, either positive or negative, between the two variables. If the correlation is not statistically significant, it is treated as if it were zero, indicating no relationship between the two variables. If r's probability level is not significant (ns), this means it is not significantly different from zero.

As one would expect, higher numbers of r indicate stronger relationships. An r of 0.40 is not twice as strong as an r of 0.20, however. If we want to make this type of judgement, we might use the "coefficient of determination," which is r-squared. This is usually the percentage of variance in one variable accounted for by the variation in scores on the other variable. While r values may not be compared to each other very precisely in a simple, intuitive manner, percentages can be. Using the same example, an r of 0.40 squared is 0.16, while an r of 0.20 squared is 0.04. Sixteen percent is four times greater than 4 percent. An r of 0.40, therefore, might indicate a relationship between two variables that is *four* times stronger than an r of 0.20—which is not precisely what we might have guessed from comparing the r values of 0.20 and 0.40. In reading organizational psychology research results, one will encounter r very frequently.

The formula for r can be transformed in various ways that will allow one to calculate it without first calculating the Z-score for each person on each variable—which is somewhat tedious. If you wish to calculate the r values, it is easier to use one of these. One of these versions of the formula (where Σ means "sum of") is:

$$r = \frac{N\Sigma XY - (\Sigma X)(\Sigma Y)}{\sqrt{[N\Sigma X^2 - (\Sigma X)^2][N\Sigma Y^2 - (\Sigma Y)^2]}}$$

If a study uses either *t*-tests or analyses of variance (ANOVA), it is often because one of the variables is either dichotomous (has only two possible values, such as the sex of employees—male or female) or categorical. If it is categorical, that there might be more than two categories, but the categories do not form a continuous scale from low to high that measures a single concept or variable. For example, a company might have four departments: production, marketing, personnel, and finance. These do not naturally arrange themselves from one to four in some logical way, such as production has the most of the variable "department," marketing has the next most, and so forth. If the researcher measured leadership style within each department and wanted to know whether there were significant differences in leadership style among the four departments, he or she would use analysis of variance to examine the differences between mean scores of leadership style among the four departments.

Table 2.1 shows, if there are more than one variable being examined among the departments, say leadership style, satisfaction with the supervisor, and communications among subordinates, three ANOVAs might be computed (one for each variable). A researcher could examine them all at once, instead, with a multivariate analysis of variance (MANOVA, Table 2.1).

In Table 2.1 there are also several types of factor analyses and several possible uses of them, but the most typical use in organizational psychology is probably to see whether many variables (often many items in a questionnaire) seem to be measuring a smaller number of things or variables. Several questionnaire items might be measuring one leadership style (e.g., consideration). Several other items might measure directive leadership. In this case, a factor analysis of the data from the questionnaire might indicate that there are only two factors or things that the set of items are measuring rather than many. Although I will not try to explain factor analysis computations here, you can think of it this way. If three or four items all ask about the same thing (e.g., considerate leadership style), then some people will answer these items with high scores and other people (who do not have considerate leaders) will provide low scores on these items. This will cause all of these items to have strong correlations with each other. If several other items are all measuring directive leadership style, they will correlate strongly with each other—but not necessarily strongly with the first set of items measuring consideration. If you could identify all the sets of items that correlate more strongly with each other than with other items, all the items within a set are likely to be measuring the same thing as each other. You can think of a factor anlaysis doing this when it identifies factors. This is not exactly what it does, but this provides an intuitive idea about how it obtains its factors. When a factor analysis is completed, organizational psychologists often combine together the scores on the items that form a factor and subsequently use this combination as a score on a single variable in their study. This has several advantages, including making the measures more reliable—and reducing the number of variables that the researcher has to understand and explain!

Finally, as Table 2.1 shows, you might find in journal articles any of a complicated set of statistics using names such as path analysis, causal modeling, structural equations modeling, or LISREL. A common use of these statistics in organizational psychology is to try to get some evidence about the consistency of the observations with causal models, even from a nonexperimental field study. Ideally, to use these statistics, the researcher should first have a strong theory about the causal relationships among the variables, for example, how employees' satisfaction with their supervisors is caused. The researcher usually presents a figure or diagram with the names of all the variables in the theory and arrows between them representing causation. He or she then measures all the variables in this theory. Some variables, according to the theory, should be more strongly related to each other (those next to each other in the diagram) than others are. In addition, some variables might be related to each other positively, but others are supposed to be related negatively according to the theory. Here, you can think of these statistics as determining the degree to which measures of all the important variables in a theory are related to each other in the ways the theory predicts.

If the variables are related to each other in the directions (positively or negatively) and in the strengths that the causal theory had predicted, this is taken as evidence for the theory and causation that it advocates. The reader should note, however, that this evidence for causation is still not as strong as that which true experiments provide. The statistic cannot provide as strong evidence about causation as the experimental research design can.

CONCLUSION

If researchers want to know about causation, they must pay close attention to the research method or design. Specifically, the technique of experimentation, or as close to true experimentation as possible, provides the best evidence for causation. If researchers want to know about generalizability, they must pay attention to method again. This time, however, the setting of the research is important, with field settings usually providing more confidence in generalizability than laboratory settings do. Finally, if researchers want to know about the likelihood that there is a relation between two variables (or more)—in either experimental or nonexperimental studies—they must pay attention to inferential statistics.

Researchers, and we as readers of the research, must pay attention to all of these factors. As I noted in the first chapter, a major value in organizational psychology is that research and theory have value. Research has value, but we cannot interpret or trust it much unless we understand research principles such as technique, setting, and inferential statistics.

REFERENCES

Barrow, J. C. (1976). Worker performance and task complexity as causal determinants of leader behavior style and flexibility. *Journal of Applied Psychology, 61,* 433–440.

Cook, T. D., Campbell, D. T., & Peracchio, L. (1990). Quasi experimentation. In M. D. Dunnette & L. M. Hough (Eds.), *Handbook of industrial and organizational psychology, Vol. 1,* (2nd ed.). (pp. 491–576). Palo Alto, CA: Consulting Psychologists Press.

Farris, G. F., & Lim, F. G., Jr. (1969). Effects of performance on leadership, cohesiveness, satisfaction, and subsequent performance. *Journal of Applied Psychology, 53,* 490–497.

Fodor, E. M. (1976). Group stress, authoritarian style of control, and use of power. *Journal of Applied Psychology, 61,* 313–318.

Ganster, D. C., Mayes, B. T., Sime, W. E., & Tharp, G. D. (1982). Managing organizational stress: A field experiment. *Journal of Applied Psychology, 67,* 533–542.

Gilmore, D. C., Beehr, T. A., & Love, K. G. (1986). Effects of applicant sex, applicant physical attractiveness, type of rater, and type of job on interview decisions. *Journal of Occupational Psychology, 59,* 103–109.

Gilmore, D. C., Beehr, T. A., & Richter, D. (1979). The effects of leader consideration and initiating structure on follower satisfaction and performance. *Journal of Applied Psychology, 64,* 166–172.

Jackson, S. E. (1983). Participation in decision making as a strategy for reducing job-related strain. *Journal of Applied Psychology, 68,* 3–19.

Jenkins, G. D., Jr., Nadler, D. A., Lawler, E. E. III, & Cammann, C. (1975). Standardized observations: An approach to measuring the nature of jobs. *Journal of Applied Psychology, 60,* 171–181.

Lowin, A., & Craig, J. R. (1973). The influence of level of performance on managerial style: An experimental object-lesson in the ambiguity of correlational data. In W. E. Scott & L. L. Cummings (Eds.), *Readings in organizational behavior and human performance* (rev. ed.). Homewood, IL: Irwin.

3

HUMAN NATURE

Organizational psychology is concerned with people in organizations. One of the basic values in the field is we tend to be as concerned with the individual as with the organization. We are interested in the way that organizations affect people and the way that people affect organizations and each other. In addition, however, the members of organizations come to the organization with some characteristics already in place. That is, they have their own natures aside from their organizational lives. The organization might try to use their skills and energies and leave the rest of the person out of these organizational situations, but it often does not work that way. Instead, the person brings desires, temperaments, habits, and extra skills to the organization. These can either lead to problems or be helpful to the organization, but it cannot discard or ignore them without risking some unintended consequences. This is, however, part of what makes organizational psychology so interesting.

Chapter One noted that a basic value in organizational psychology is that the person is as valuable as the organization. In this chapter, I focus on the person to understand what he or she is like and to set the stage for the examination of the way that people interact with the organization and with each other in the organization. Just as the organization has requirements to survive and thrive, so does the person. Although crude, we can divide the characteristics of the person into two broad categories for the purposes of understanding behavior in organizations: capabilities and temperament.

Capabilities consist of things the person can do or is capable of doing on the job, while temperament refers to the person's inclination to do things. Individual differences among people in their capabilities and temperament are a central focus of some areas related to organizational psychology. Personnel psychology is a primary example. Much of the work of personnel psychology is based on finding a fit between individuals and the job. This requires measuring individual differences in capabilities and temperaments to assess a potential fit. If the personnel psychologist has done a good job of this in the hiring process, however, by the time the organizational psychologist begins dealing with people, they have been preselected and their individual differences are reduced. The differences, however, are never really eliminated.

In organizational psychology, one often wants to know what will lead to important outcomes for the individual and the organization (see Chapters 4 and 5), and one of the theoretical answers is usually the nature of the people constituting the organization. In addition, some people in the organization tend to act together in groups (see Chapters 6 and 7), and the nature of these group participants can affect those interactions. For many reasons, therefore, the nature of the human beings constituting the organization is important for understanding principles of organizational psychology.

HUMAN TEMPERAMENTS

By temperament, we mean all the preferences, likes, needs, desires, behavioral tendencies, motives, and personality characteristics a person generally has. They will vary from person to person, and they come in various combinations within some people. In personnel psychology especially, *diversity* has become a key word in recent years meaning diversity in terms of demographics. In addition, people vary much more widely than just by their demographics. All the characteristics discussed here can cut across racial and gender groups and age groups. All older people in organizations do not agree with each other on important issues, and the same can be said about sex and race groups.

One can separately define and discuss the various aspects of temperament. That is, psychologists have sometimes spent great efforts and argued at length about what is a need, a value, a preference, a motive, a personality trait, and so forth. But for our purposes in organizational psychology, such minor distinctions matter very little. Instead of being concerned with whether somebody's preferred situation and behavior are biologically determined (as some needs theorists say needs are), are learned (as some argue that values are), and so forth, it matters to organizational psychology mainly that these preferences (or whatever label we use) do exist and that they affect the outcomes that occur to both organization and to the individuals within them. Organizational psychology theories and research make frequent use of the terms *need, value,* and *interest.* This discussion, therefore, is limited to the way in which organizational psychologists tend to use these three terms.

Needs

The term *needs* often refers to one of the middle-range temperaments. Table 3.1 illustrates that the terms *values, needs,* and *interests* in organizational psychology indicate different levels of specificity of temperaments. Values are the most general. Members of organizations might value equity or fairness, for example. Such a value tends to be so general, however, that it is only generally useful in understanding and predicting people's reactions to organizational situations. Two people who both value equity might still disagree about whether someone should receive a promotion based on seniority. One might see that as fair or equitable and the other not. Interests is the most specific of the three categories of temperament in the table. In organizational psychology, an interest is usually specific to a given job situation, that is, someone might be interested in a job that has opportunities to help people. Needs is between interests and values in the table, because it usually refers to needs for things that are intermediate in nature. A need for affiliation, for example, means a tendency to want relationships with other people. It does not, however, specify the workplace as the setting for or the aid in the relationship—as the term *interest* might. The term *motive,* occurring more rarely in organizational psychology, has a similar use. Relevant motives include, for example, need for achievement, need for affiliation, and need for power (McClelland, 1985). Needs are basic in the sense that they may be biologically based and that they are the building blocks of personality. Various needs may be more basic than others. Maslow (1954) for example, is well-known for having argued that there is a hierarchy of needs that is somewhat stable and perhaps biologically ordained. This hierarchy often consists of five needs in the following order: physiological, safety or security, social, esteem or status, and self-actualization needs. The earlier ones in the order are more basic in Maslow's theory because they must be

TABLE 3.1   Levels of Generality versus Specificity among the Temperaments

Most general, broad and abstract temperaments	Medium-range temperaments	Most specific and concrete temperaments
Values	Needs, motives, personality traits	Preferences, interests
Example: the person is as important as the organization	Example: social needs or need for affiliation	Example: preference for a job that involves assisting people in striving for their own goals

satisfied first for the later ones to become important in people's lives. This well-known theory is important for having led to the development of and popularized the concept of a need hierarchy. There is little actual evidence of the theory in research, but then it is a very difficult theory to test anyway. Self-actualization is a somewhat slippery and value-laden concept as many people use it.

Maslow (1954) said that less than 1 percent of people are likely to be self-actualizating, but the term is used so frequently in management that many people think they are doing it much of the time. There are three main values in Maslow's need-hierarchy theory for present day organizational psychology. First, it is important to know about it because everybody else does. The need hierarchy is well known by many educated people in organizations (e.g., managers). If we did not know what it was, we would sometimes be at a loss to understand what managers are talking about. Second, Maslow's need-hierarchy theory is important for historical reasons. It was a very influential theory in the middle ages of organizational psychology (1960–1980). Other well-known theories were even built, in part, on the Maslowian hierarchy of needs (e.g., Theory X of McGregor, 1960; Existence, Relatedness, and Growth [ERG] theory of Alderfer, 1972). We should at least know what the history of the field has been. Third, the five needs in the hierarchy constitute a handy set of needs to consider when we wonder why people are behaving the way they do in their organizational roles. Temperaments might play a role in people's actions, and here are a set of five characteristics, needs in this case, that might help explain what people are doing. Somebody might be working on overtime projects without pay because of an interest in social needs (gaining social approval), status needs (liking for a promotion), or biological needs (with a large family to feed, believing that extra work now will lead to a higher paying job later).

More recently, in *Existence, Relatedness and Growth* (ERG) Theory, Alderfer (1972) argued that there are needs arranged in a hierarchy, much like Maslow's, but that the hierarchy consists of only three steps instead of five. They are roughly the same set of needs that Maslow noted, but the lower, more basic step consists of both physiological needs and safety or security needs, the second step of social or belongingness needs, and the top step of status or esteem and self actualization needs. As in the Maslow hierarchy, the needs at the lower step must be satisfied before the needs at the next higher step become important in determining people's actions. There are a few differences between this need hierarchy theory and Maslow's. First, of course, there are only three steps instead of five. Second, Aldefer developed his theory with Maslow's theory in mind. Third, he developed and tested the ERG theory using empirical research methods instead basing it semi-philosophically on less formal observation of people. Fourth, Aldefer developed this theory on and for use in organizations specifically. Fifth, and finally, ERG theory more explicitly allows for people to go back down the hierarchy. The frustration-regression hypothesis in this theory argues that if people cannot get fulfillment or satisfaction of their needs at a certain step, they will regress to a lower step. That is, they become interested in the more basic needs again (Alderfer, 1972). To be fair to Maslow, however, his own writings (1954) allowed for much more flexibility in the hierarchy than many subsequent writers have usually acknowledged. He noted many examples of people who seem to skip hierarchical levels and go to the top while letting their other needs go unfilled, of people who seem to switch levels around from the normal order, and who, revert to lower levels in the hierarchy. Maslowian followers in organizations seem to have taken his theory to be very rigid at times—more than he did himself.

In organizational psychology, theories, other than hierarchy theories, have also occasionally explained organizationally relevant activities. Because needs are relevant to motivation, and because any behavior can have a motivation, in principle, needs are relevant to almost any behavior in organizational psychology. Their actual success, however, in predicting human behavior in organizations has been limited. One area in which needs is occasionally a primary explanation for behavior is leadership. At one time, organizational psychologists thought the need for achievement, a tendency to strive for success, was especially important for managers to be successful. More recently, however, the need for using a certain type of power, a power that is derived from organizations rather than from the person, seems to be a better predictor of managerial success. According to McClelland and Boyatzis (1982), this need for power, with need for affiliation and activity inhibition, predicted the organizational success (e.g., promotions) of managers over an eight-to-sixteen-year period. These three needs (achievement, affiliation, power), as well as the set of five needs of Maslow, can be useful in understanding people's organizational behaviors. They are, therefore, a useful set of needs to remember.

Interestingly, some writers (Borgatta, 1964; Peabody & Goldberg, 1989) have assumed that personality traits, or middle-level temperaments (Table 3.1), comprise five types: neuroticism/adaptation, extroversion or sociability, conscientiousness, agreeableness, and culture. Neuroticism/adjustment seems to be the extent to which people are anxious and neurotic versus stable and confident. Extroversion or sociability is the extent to which people are outgoing and energetic versus shy and retiring. Conscientiousness is the degree to which people are neat and dependable versus careless and irresponsible. Agreeableness represents the degree to which people seem to avoid disagreements by tact and consideration of others versus being independent and even rude. Culture, a somewhat misleading term (Hogan, 1991), seems to be the extent to which people are imaginative and original versus unimaginative and literal-minded. It might be a tendency toward creativity and openness to new ways of looking at things. These so-called Big Five personality traits, have somewhat more use in personnel psychology research and theory than in organizational psychology, but they are another set of human temperaments that might help to explain how people think, feel, and act in organizations. As with the five needs from Maslowian theory, these five personality traits might at times seem useful in understanding people in organizations.

Values

A second type of temperament, again one psychologists consider to be relatively stable and to differ across individuals, is a value. Values are usually broader than needs (Table 3.1), and they are usually not biologically based as needs sometimes are. Of the temperaments, values are probably the broadest (Dawis, 1991), in the sense that a value can often be related to several moderately specific needs, preferences, etc., and values tend to be more abstract. The basic value of justice, for example, might include both helping others who are less fortunate and expecting people to pick themselves up by their bootstraps and make it on their own. One expects those who make it on their own to reap the rewards. I have chosen this example because it shows how broad a value can be; it can even comprise beliefs that are somewhat contradictory. In the political arena, we often see evidence of these competing specifications of the same values. Some politicians seem to favor more welfare for the less fortunate, while others argue that incentives are necessary to reward the less fortunate for making the effort to better themselves. The politicians base both of these approaches on the values of justice and fairness. In organizations, companies in previous decades would sometimes quite openly pay some workers more than others for the same work and justify it on the basis of need. Often these differences in pay were related to the sex of the employee, with males getting more money than females. Managers would sometimes even be quite open about doing this in the belief that the male needed more money to support a family while the female did not need to do that. If managers do that today, they certainly would not be very open about it, because it violates laws. In addition, their assumptions were never entirely true even in former decades and certainly are not today. Even at the same time this was occurring on a large scale, the same value of justice also called for equal pay for equal work! Thus, values are broad and abstract enough to encompass even contradictory policies in organizations.

Among the three categories of temperament (needs, values, and interests), values probably have the least use in organizational psychology. Perhaps organizational psychology's applied arm has influenced this. As the temperaments become less specific to jobs and to job-related behaviors, they are less likely to be useful in predicting and understanding human reactions on the job.

Organizational psychology, however, does occasionally use values. For example, the value often labeled the Protestant Work Ethic (PWE), because of its theoretical origin in sociological theory, seems to encompass the general idea that working hard is valuable in itself, and it is hardly limited to American Protestants. Tang (1993), for example, has noted that this belief in the moral correctness of working hard is common among people in eastern Asian cultures. Sometimes organizational psychology invokes PWE to explain why some people seem to enjoy or are satisfied with difficult, challenging work more than others (e.g., Turner & Lawrence, 1965; Hulin & Blood, 1968). In addition, Locke (1976) proposed that job satisfaction might most likely occur in situations in which people satisfied needs that were consistent with their values. Overall, Dawis' (1991) review noted that research has shown that values differ among people in different occupations, much the way that interests seem to.

Interests

Among the temperaments, interests and preferences seem to be at the opposite end of the spectrum from values. That is, they seem much more specific as Table 3.1 illustrates. The choices people make when they are free to choose among alternatives (Dawis, 1991) represent a preference. An employee might choose not to take an offered promotion because it would mean moving to another city where his or her family does not want to relocate. In this case, the employee has chosen to stay in the present job. This is a good example that shows the fuzziness of the free choice concept as preferences represent. If the person would really like to move because the job would be very much better but stays because of pressures from family members, is there really free choice in that situation? In similar situations, people often do not actually want to move, but there is pressure from the organization for the person to make the move. Implicitly or explicitly, there may be the threat that future opportunities for promotions, with or without moving, might be withheld if the person is not a team player enough to take this job and move. There are even psychologists who seem to suggest that there is no such thing as free choice (e.g., some versions of behaviorism, in Skinner, 1971). Organizational psychology has tended to assume that people can make relatively free choices however, even though there are many constraints on those choices.

Another example of preference that is relevant to organizational psychology is the choice to retire. In the United States, most jobs now legally have free choice about retirement. That is, it is now illegal for organizations to require employees to retire at a mandatory retirement age (Beehr, 1986; Talaga & Beehr, 1989). Nevertheless, upon questioning about the extent to which they view their retirement decision as voluntary, retirees give a range of answers (Talaga & Beehr, 1993). Some people perceived the retirement decision to be more voluntary than others. Finances are a major predictor of who will retire, and this is one example of a variable that might make people feel free to retire—the prospect of good financial situations after retirement. Alternatively, some retirees have told my colleagues and me that they felt as if they could not afford to keep working, because their pensions were so good that they actually made as much or more money by retiring—even though sometimes it was by working on another job part-time after retirement! Rather than good finances allowing them a free choice to retire, they felt that finances left them no choice but to retire. We will not try to resolve the argument about whether behavior and choices are free or not, but in organizational psychology, much of the theory seems to assume preferences can be expressed freely within some limits and with some pressures from the environment.

Interest has a long history of research in occupational and vocational psychology, much of which is relevant to organizational psychology. An interest is not very different from a preference, and in fact, Kuder, a major theorist and researcher on interests, defined an interest as a preference for specific activities (Dawis, 1991). Holland's (1985) theory is probably best known in the area of occupational interests, and he argues that there are six major groupings of interests that are relevant to occupations: realistic, investigative, artistic, social, enterprising, and conventional. Realistic interests include pragmatic, problem-solving, action-oriented activities; investigative includes more intellectual and cognitive work with facts and data; artistic interests include creativity and aesthetic pursuits; social interests, of course, include interactions with and helping other people; enterprising interests include power, status, and leadership; and conventional includes systematic, detail work and activities. These six vocational interests are theoretically structured as in Figure 3.1. Holland proposed that interests opposite each other in the figure are opposite or more different from each other than the interests closer to each other in the figure.

Furthermore, Holland's approach assumes that not only interests, but also occupations are also structured along the lines of these dimensions. That is, jobs should have more or less of each of these characteristics. A major implication is that people and jobs should, therefore, match up, which should lead to more satisfaction and presumably better performance in these jobs. The latter assumption, that people who have more interest in a job will perform better in it, has its basis on the idea that interests are likely

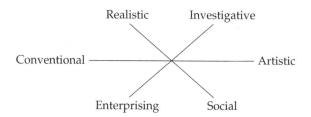

FIGURE 3.1   Holland's (1985) Theory of Occupationally Related Interests: The Structure of Human Interests

to be congruent with abilities and skills. I will turn presently to those personal characteristics (abilities and skills), but the reader should note that there is really little strong evidence that people necessarily have more skill in things they find interesting (Dawis, 1991). This is, however, one of the beliefs that seem to persist even though it does not clearly seem to be true.

Some psychologists have applied Holland's theory to vocational guidance and counseling for a long time. Many studies have shown that people in different occupations vary systematically regarding their interests. That is, there is a reliable relationship between peoples' interests and their occupations (Dawis, 1991). Because of this, vocational counseling often focuses on trying to match peoples' expressed interests with jobs (or more precisely, with occupations) that have the same characteristics. Thus, someone who has realistic interests (according to a test, usually), is likely to be counseled to enter a career with realistic job characteristics. This assumes, as we are assuming here, that interests are relatively stable; therefore, when people enter that career, they will still have the appropriate interests. These types of counseling are prominent in high school and college, before people enter a career. One study that looked at this process over a seven-year period, from the freshman year in college to the person's job seven years later, was not very supportive of the idea that this process works very well (Fricko & Beehr, 1992). People who enter careers based on their expressed interests should be more satisfied with their jobs than people who enter careers that do not match their interests very well. This did not happen in the study by Fricko and Beehr, (1992), however. People whose expressed career interests in college matched their subsequent jobs were no more likely to be satisfied with their jobs than nonmatched people. While this casts doubt on the usefulness of the process for career happiness or satisfaction, it is still true that people, after they are in careers, tend overall to have interests matching their careers. Predicting what future career some young person will be happy in seems to be more difficult, however. Other areas of psychology might provide solutions to this puzzle. For example, college freshmen are still in a rapidly developing stage of their lives. Their interests, even if measured accurately at that time, still have time to change before their careers are through or even begun. This explanation suggests that our assumption that interests are relatively stable must emphasize the word *relatively*. Even once our interests seem set, perhaps they can change to some small degree. Before we are very old, and presumably before our interests are "set," they can probably change to a greater degree. This is an area in which organizational psychology tends to do little research and might be able to borrow from developmental psychology.

Overall, current temperaments have often been related to people's satisfaction with their current jobs, but they have not usually been good predictors of job satisfactoriness in organizational psychology research (Dawis, 1991). That is, research has shown no clear and consistent relationship between temperament and job performance or effectiveness. This means that temperaments are more closely related to individual outcomes than to organizational outcomes. Job satisfaction is probably more important to the person than to the organization, while job performance is necessary for the effectiveness and the very existence of most organizations. Performance is therefore considered an organizational outcome. The distinction between individual and organizational outcomes can be useful for understanding organizational psychology, and I have used it to organize subsequent parts of this book. The attention to both of these types of outcomes is consistent with one of the basic values of organizational psychology (in Chapter 1)—the person is as important as the organization. The field of personnel psychology has a longer history than organizational psychology, and it has usually paid more attention to organizational outcomes than to individual outcomes. One may consider the belief that the individuals and their outcomes are as important as organizations and their outcomes, in part, a reaction to this more one-sided approach of personnel psychology. Nevertheless, because it seems intuitive that there should be some link of temperament with job performance, research on the temperaments and organizational outcomes is likely to continue. It is one of the challenges for future research.

Schneider (1987) argues that the people make the place. In order to understand the nature of a specific organization, its culture, values, structure and processes, we need to understand the nature of the people who constitute it. If this is so, then understanding the temperaments of the people attracted to, selected into, and retained by an organization is probably necessary for full understanding of the organization. In this chapter, we have treated temperament as if it is stable and unchangeable. Of course, that is not completely true. In fact, after people become members of a given organization they might still change some aspects of temperaments. In part, these changes are due to experiences with other members of the organiza-tion—in the form of socialization. Such interpersonal influences, however, are the subject of another chapter.

CAPABILITIES

Skills and abilities of organizational members can fulfill organizational needs, that is they can lead to performance effectiveness or organizational outcomes. Whether organizational members' skills actually do result in good job performance depends on several other things, however. For ex-ample, the people must have adequate tools and equipment, raw materials, and leadership. Furthermore, the people must have the motivation to use their abilities or skills. Subsequent chapters will examine some of these is-sues from an organizational psychology point of view.

As I noted in the first chapter, a common basic value in organizational psychology is the belief the people have high abilities and are trustworthy. Regarding abilities, this tends to mean that people have higher abilities than many organizations or the managers of organizations give them credit for. Also relevant here is the fact that people vary in their skills and abilities, with some people having more of any one ability than other people. In per-sonnel psychology, the process of selection is heavily dependent upon hir-ing people whose skills can be expected to be related to performance in spe-cific jobs. In organizational psychology we have paid less attention to skills and abilities, but this can be a potential failing. Ignoring such a major aspect of human nature seems likely to lead to incomplete understanding of human reactions to organizational life.

We have been using the terms *skills* and *abilities* loosely and inter-changeably. Even though people often confuse skill and ability (Schmitt, 1987), there are some differences in the ways one typically uses these two terms. Just as the different types of temperaments can be classified accord-ing to their degrees of specificity, so can skills and abilities. The term *abili-ties* refers to more general capabilities of organizational members, while the term *skill* is usually reserved for more specific capabilities. Skills are often specific to job behaviors or to even more specific tasks in those jobs (Har-vey, 1991). Thus, while there might be a general interpersonal ability indi-cating that people can get along with others in a number of general ways, there might be a skill of persuasion that would be very useful in jobs re-quiring the task of persuading people—such as a salesperson's job.

Furthermore, in addition to skills being more specific than abilities, skills are usually learned, while abilities are not (Harvey, 1991). This is im-portant for organizational psychology, because it suggests that people can train for job-relevant skills—as long as they have the basic level of required ability in the area. I will discuss more about training later in this book when I examine applications of organizational psychology.

Abilities

Personnel psychology deals with abilities more than organizational psychology does; therefore, it might be useful to consider the way that discipline looks at abilities. One can read some accounts of abilities in personnel psychology and conclude that there are general abilities and more specific abilities, or aptitudes. Table 3.2 illustrates the level of specificity of the three terms: *ability, aptitude,* and *skills.* The reader should remember, however, that there is another important difference among them besides their level of generality—abilities and aptitudes may be relatively stable, at least among adults, while skills are more malleable.

I have suggested previously one reason that organizational psychologists have not dealt very much with ability levels among organizational members. Because the personnel psychology practices often use abilities as a criterion for hiring or selection of employees into specific jobs, the ability levels of organizational members should be relatively high and somewhat uniform among people who are doing similar jobs. Thus, individual differences in abilities and aptitudes are less than they would be in the general population of people.

There may be a single, global ability that is not even as specific as the example of general interpersonal ability in Table 3.1. That is, people might differ in their abilities regarding everything. Personnel psychology usually describes this general ability construct as general *cognitive* ability (Goldstein, 1991; Gottfredson, 1986). It is difficult to believe that all abilities are cognitive, however, considering the myriad of physical or motor behaviors that people can do. The derivation of the idea that general ability is a cognitive factor seems suspiciously to be from the very early work on general intelligence and Spearman's (1927) "g" factor in intelligence—a cognitive

TABLE 3.2   Levels of Generality versus Specificity among Abilities and Skills

Most general, broad and abstract abilities	Medium-range abilities	Most specific skills
Abilities	Aptitudes	Skills
Example: general interpersonal ability	Example: ability to persuade	Example: skill at selling life insurance

construct. One might venture that there is also one or more general ability factors in the physical ability arena—such as gross motor skills in large muscle activities and finer motor skills of coordination and object manipulation. Although this general physical ability might correlate with general cognitive ability, it seems unlikely that it *is* general cognitive ability. Lubinski and Dawis (1991) argue that there are three general ability domains: cognitive, perceptual (e.g., spacial ability), and psychomotor. This seems intuitively reasonable.

As this general ability concept gets broken into three general abilities, it seems that we are moving toward the concept of aptitude. The term *aptitude* usually refers to relatively more specific abilities; therefore, I include them here in the section on abilities. There is apparently a dilemma regarding how finely one can and should break down abilities. How far does one divide general abilities, such as cognitive, perceptual, and psychomotor, before they become the medium-level concept of aptitudes? As in so much of psychology, our categories of ability versus aptitude are probably not so much discrete categories as points on a continuum. As I have already noted, organizational psychologists have assumed that people have relatively high abilities. If personnel systems have done a good job of selection, this is especially likely to be true when we consider the organizational psychologist's usual subjects—people who are already members of an organization.

Skills

Skills are likely to be more interesting to organizational psychologists than abilities are for two reasons. First, skills are more job- and task-relevant than abilities are—that is, they are more directly important to the way that people carry out their roles in organizations. Second, skills may be more malleable and, therefore, more trainable, and some organizational psychologists are interested in various types of training. The term *skill* includes both motor and cognitive skills and, for our purposes, will even include job knowledge. Knowledge about the job is sometimes a separate but related category for personnel psychologists when they analyze jobs for purposes of selection, for example. Skills in doing specific job-related tasks require the necessary knowledge to do the task. Goldstein (1991) argues that such job-specific knowledge is the foundation upon which abilities and skills are built.

If abilities are stable while learning can change and improve skills, this implies that, without learning opportunities, differences between people's performance levels on jobs or tasks might be due to abilities rather than skill. Before the opportunity to learn, therefore, abilities, wherever they come from, might account for performance differences. There are problems with this assumption—for example, some people might have had more opportunity for learning task-relevant skills than others. If so, they will have greater skill, and any performance superiority they have might be as much due to learned skill as to innate ability.

Nevertheless, psychologists interested in selection and training have long wondered whether ability *differences* among people become more extreme, become less extreme, or remain about the same with equivalent learning opportunities. After all, job training is one such learning opportunity, and organizational psychologists are interested in at least some forms of training. Attempts to answer that question have not been perfect, because they usually have relied on general *cognitive* ability as the measure of ability, even though sometimes the tasks were physical. The usual conclusion is that some task performance differences between people that appear due to general ability tend to disappear when people have the opportunity to learn through practice or training (Ackerman & Humphries, 1990; Weiss, 1990). Whatever the cause of individual differences in performance when people first enter a job, the differences in their performances tend to lessen over time on the job. Task-specific skill, which is the skill that one learns in training or in actually doing the job, seems to overcome some of the effects of the general, pre-job abilities. This seems most true, however, when the pre-job general ability is cognitive ability and the actual job or task is psychomotor. The effects of general cognitive abilities on physical task performance tend not to last after people have a chance to develop their (psychomotor) skills for the task.

This seems especially true if the task is repetitive and, therefore, does not require new creative thinking and reasoning very often (Ackerman & Humphries, 1990). There are certainly many tasks in real world jobs of both types—those that require only repetitive work and those that require frequent dealing with novel situations.

One should note also that many organizations have purposely designed jobs in a way that makes them more amenable to specific skills than to general abilities. That is, when possible, organizations have often made jobs simple and repetitive—the kinds of activities that many people can apparently learn to do about equally well regardless of their initial general ability levels, especially their general cognitive ability levels. In fact, it is well known that on many jobs and tasks automaticity occurs. After a while people develop so much skill at their tasks that they can do them with very little conscious effort (Shiffrin & Schneider, 1977). Obviously, in such situations general cognitive abilities hardly even seem relevant. This is similar to driving a car, a specific skill with which many of us are familiar. If we try to tell a novice how to drive, we might miss many small things we do because they have become so automatic over the years that we do not even realize what we do when driving. Highly developed skills regarding specific physical tasks both in and out of organizations seem susceptible to the development of automaticity.

Overall, people in the same specific roles or jobs in an organization probably tend to be rather similar in their skills and abilities for at least two clear reasons. First, organizations select and place people into jobs on the basis of their skill levels. Second, many organizations engage in purposeful training for their members—training aimed at skills development. These two organizational processes, selection and training, help both to increase the skill level of the organization members and to reduce the variations in skill levels between these members.

CONCLUSIONS

The nature of organization implies nonrandomness. Organized sets of behaviors are, by definition, predictable and coordinated with each other. Organizational processes involved in selection and placement, which are in the traditional province of personnel psychology, make people who enter the organization be similar to each other based on temperaments and capabilities. In addition, training makes people further alike in their capabilities (as well as generally increasing skills), and socialization increases their similarity in temperament. Furthermore, according to Schneider's (1987) hypothesis of attraction, selection, and attrition, people who are least similar are less likely to try to become organization members in the first place or to remain in the organization after they become members. Thus, there are many forces leading people in the same organization to be somewhat similar to teach other. In later chapters I will describe the nature of organizations and will show that they can have cultures or climates. In part, these cultures and climates indicate shared values of the organizations members. With so many forces operating toward similarity among members, it is no wonder that they can share some values—or other temperaments and capabilities for that matter.

Compared to personnel psychology, with its emphasis on selection among other things, organizational psychology has placed relatively little emphasis on individual differences as explanations for organizational activities. It is easy enough to find examples of research and theories in organizational psychology that employ some individual difference variable(s), but organizational psychology does not emphasize them the way they are in some other areas of psychology. Furthermore, when individual differences are part of organizational psychology work, they tend to be the temperaments rather than the differences in capabilities.

Perhaps the reason organizational psychologists pay relatively less attention to individual differences in human nature is that they deal with people after they become members of the organizations; personnel psychologists, on the other hand, help select them for organizations. After they become organization members, the tendency toward similarity has already begun, and individual differences become smaller. Nevertheless, some variation in temperaments and capabilities still exist among members of a single organization, and to ignore or to be ignorant of them seems unwise if we wish to understand organizations and the people in them.

Both individual and organizational outcomes are important in organizational psychology, but the two types of individual difference characteristics in human beings relate differently to these outcomes. Temperaments are largely important for understanding some of the individual outcomes such as job satisfaction, while capabilities are likely to be somewhat more relevant for organizational outcomes such as job performance. One way or another, however, both of these general human characteristics are likely to be important to organizational psychologists, who tend to adhere to the value that individuals are as valuable as organizations.

REFERENCES

Ackerman, P. L., & Humphries, L. G. (1990). Individual differences theory in industrial and organizational psychology. In M. D. Dunnette & L. M. Hough (Eds.), *Handbook of industrial and organizational psychology*, Vol. 1 (2nd ed.) (pp. 223–282). Palo Alto, CA: Consulting Psychologists Press.

Alderfer, C. P. (1972). *Existence, relatedness and growth*. New York: Free Press.

Beehr, T. A. (1986). The process of retirement: A review and recommendations for further investigation. *Personnel Psychology 39*, 31–55.

Borgatta, E. G. (1964). The structure of personality characteristics. *Behavioral Science, 9*, 8–17.

Dawis, R. V. (1991). Vocational interests, values, and preferences. In M. D. Dunnette & L. M. Hough (Eds.), *Handbook of industrial and organizational psychology*, Vol. 2 (2nd ed.) (pp. 833–871). Palo Alto, CA: Consulting Psychologists Press.

Fricko, M. A., & Beehr, T. A. (1992). A longitudinal investigation of interest congruence and gender concentration as predictors of job satisfaction. *Personnel Psychology, 45*, 99–117.

Goldstein, I. L. (1991). Training in work organizations. In M. D. Dunnette & L. M. Hough (Eds.), *Handbook of industrial and organizational psychology*, Vol. 2 (2nd ed.) (pp. 507–619). Palo Alto, CA: Consulting Psychologists Press.

Gottfredson, L. S. (Ed.). (1986). The *g* factor in employment. *Journal of Vocational Behavior, 29*(3).

Harvey, R. J. (1991). Job Analysis. In M. D. Dunnett and L. M. Hough (Eds.), *Handbook of industrial and organizational psychology*, Vol. 2 (2nd ed.) (pp. 71–163). Palo Alto, CA: Consulting Psychologists Press.

Hogan, R. T. (1991). Personality and personality measurement. In M. D. Dunnette & L. M. Hough (Eds.), *Handbook of industrial and organizational psychology*, Vol. 2 (2nd ed.) (pp. 873–919). Palo Alto, CA: Consulting Psychologists Press.

Holland, J. L. (1985). *Making vocational choices* (2nd ed.). Englewood Cliffs, NJ: Prentice-Hall.

Hulin, C. L., & Blood, M. R. (1968). Job enlargement, individual differences, and worker responses. *Psychological Bulletin, 69,* 41–55.

Locke, E. A. (1976). The nature and causes of job satisfaction. In M. D. Dunnette (Ed.), *Handbook of industrial and organizational psychology* (pp. 1297–1349). Chicago: Rand-McNally.

Lubinski, D., & Dawis, R. V. (1991). Aptitudes, skills, and proficiencies. In M. C. Dunnette & L. M. Hough (Eds.), *Handbook of industrial and organizational psychology,* Vol. 3 (2nd ed.) (pp. 1–59). Palo Alto, CA: Consulting Psychologists Press.

Maslow, A. H. (1954). *Motivation and personality.* New York: Harper & Row.

McClelland, D. C. (1985). *Human motivation.* Glenview, IL: Scott, Foresman.

McClelland, D. C., & Boyatzis, R. E. (1982). Leadership motive pattern and long-term success in management. *Journal of Applied Psychology, 67,* 737–742.

McGregor, D. (1960). *The human side of enterprise.* New York: McGraw-Hill.

Peabody, D., & Goldberg, L. R. (1989). Some determinants of factor structure from personality trait descriptors. *Journal of Personality and Social Psychology, 57,* 552–567.

Schmitt, N. (1987). *Principles III: Research issues.* Paper presented at the annual meeting of the Society for Industrial and Organizational Psychology, Atlanta.

Schneider, B. (1987). The people make the place. *Personnel Psychology 40,* 437–453.

Shiffrin, R. M., & Schneider, W. (1977). Controlled and automatic human information processing: II. Perceptual learning, automatic attending, and a general theory. *Psychological Review, 84,* 127–190.

Skinner, B. F. (1971). *Beyond freedom and dignity.* New York: Bantam Books.

Spearman, C. (1927). *Abilities of man.* New York: Macmillan.

Talaga, J., & Beehr, T. A. (1989). Retirement: A psychological perspective. In C. L. Cooper & I. T. Robertson (Eds.), *International review of industrial and organizational psychology 1989* (pp. 186–211). Chichester: John Wiley & Sons.

Talaga, J., & Beehr, T. A. (1993). *Retirement types differ in predicting retirement adjustment.* Paper presented at the annual meeting of the American Psychological Society, Chicago.

Tang, T. L. (1993). The meaning of money: Extension and exploration of the money ethic scale in a sample of university students in Taiwan. *Journal of Organizatonal Behavior, 14,* 93–99.

Turner, A. N., & Lawrence, P. R. (1965). *Industrial jobs and the worker.* Boston: Harvard Graduate School of Business Administration.

Weiss, H. M. (1990). Learning theory and industrial and organizational psychology. In M. D. Dunnett and L. M. Hough (Eds.), *Handbook of industrial and organizational psychology,* Vol. 1 (2nd ed.) (pp. 171–221). Palo Alto, CA: Consulting Psychologists Press.

4

INDIVIDUAL OUTCOMES

If one of the values of organizational psychology is that the individual is as important as the organization, then outcomes or criteria that are important in the lives of the individual members of organizations are important to organizational psychology theory, research, and practice. Outcomes that the person may value are not necessarily irrelevant to organizations or their representatives (in the form of higher-level management). Managers often do care about their lower-level employees and their welfare, but they surely do not care as much about the employee as that employee does. The point is that the designation of some outcomes as being primarily relevant to the individual while others are primarily relevant to the organization's welfare is a relative matter. Here I discuss three types of outcomes that are more directly important to the individual employee than to the employing organization: job satisfaction, tangible outcomes such as pay and fringe benefits, and psychological and physical strains due to stressful work. Each of these has been studied so often that they almost have their own separate research histories and literatures.

JOB SATISFACTION

Job satisfaction is probably the grandaddy of all the individual outcomes in organizational psychology in the sense that it has a long history of study and is still a commonly studied variable in the field. It is so old that Landy (1989) suggested that in the seventeenth century Rammizzini may have measured it by observing the looks of disgust on cesspool workers' faces in Modeno, Italy. More recently, organizational psychology's early history showed great concern with variables that consisted partly of affect toward the job—morale in the Hawthorne studies, for example. Job satisfaction can be an attitude toward one's job. Organizational psychology has characterized job satisfaction primarily as affect, or emotional reactions, toward the job (Locke, 1976). Measurements are usually via self-reports (asking people directly to report about their own levels of satisfaction). Organizational psychologists then frequently test their hypotheses to see whether these reports of affect are related statistically to behaviors and cognitions (perceptions and thoughts). The behaviors and cognitions, in most organizational psychology research, are not part of the job satisfaction variable. Instead, they are separate variables that may or may not be related to it.

Theories of Job Satisfaction

There have been several theories of job satisfaction in organizational psychology, but nearly all of the prominent ones fall into one of three broad categories: discrepancy, dispositional, and social influence theories.

Discrepancy Theories of Job Satisfaction

Discrepancy theories of job satisfaction argue that job satisfaction is caused by, or perhaps actually is, the inverse of one or more discrepancies between the perceived nature of the job and some other state. The less the discrepancy, the more satisfied the organization members are. Exactly what the other state is that compares with the present job varies, however. *Needs, wants or desires, interests, values, expectations,* and/or *beliefs* about what would be *fair* could determine the other state. These states are basically individual differences in human nature as I discussed in Chapter 3, and the discrepancy theories of job satisfaction show the importance of understanding human characteristics such as these in organizational members.

Discrepancy theories of job satisfaction are the most common types that organizational psychologists use to explain job satisfaction (Locke 1976; Weiss, 1990). If we consider, in a common sense way, the various types of discrepancies, it becomes obvious that discrepancies between the current job situation and the various other states can be more or less similar or different from each other. Taking pay levels as an example situation, consider the following. An employee might *need* very little pay because of few financial responsibilities; he or she might nevertheless *want* or desire a great deal of pay to buy many "unnecessary" luxury items; the same employee might simply be *interested* in money; he or she might, alternatively, simply place a high *value* on money on the grounds that its possession is a sign of self-worth; the employee might have *expected* very low pay before even taking on the present job; or the employee might think it would be *fair* and equitable to receive the same amount of pay as anyone else doing similar work, neither more nor less.

There could be similar comparisons for any type of situation on the job, not just pay levels. People can experience such discrepancies between what they have on their jobs and what they need, want, are interested in, etc.; regarding the amount of autonomy and variety on their jobs, the nature of the supervision and coworkers, the types of skills they use on their jobs; and so forth.

There could be research to see whether differences between what one has on the job and these other states were correlated with direction questions to employees about their job satisfaction. There have been some nonexperimental field studies of this nature. Dawis (1991) review of the studies on *interests* and *values* and their roles in job satisfaction concluded that they have not been studied as much as the theoretical importance would seem to warrant. Nevertheless, there is some modest evidence. The field of vocational psychology, with its interest in careers and individual outcomes, has generally found that people who are in career situations in which they are interested generally report being more satisfied than people with less of this interest-career "congruence." If such interests are relatively stable characteristics of people, then their interests at one time should also match or be congruent with the characteristics of their occupation at a later time for the person to be satisfied. A study by Fricko and Beehr (1992), however, measured college freshmens' career interests with a standard interest test, and measured their satisfaction with their jobs approximately seven years later. The congruence between their expressed interests and their later job situations was not significantly correlated with job satisfaction. One can take this congruence as a measure of low discrepancy. In general the few studies that have tested in this way interests–job situations as predictors of job satisfaction over a period of time have not found as strong a relationship between these discrepancies and (dis)satisfaction as have studies measuring discrepancies and satisfaction both at the same time.

Among the versions of discrepancies leading to job satisfaction, organizational psychologists have discussed and studied most the discrepancy involving *needs*. In fact, it once was very popular to measure the discrepancy between needs and actual job situations by subtracting scores on the questions asking about needs (asking people directly what they need from the workplace) and about actual situations (asking people what they are actually getting out of the workplace) (e.g., Porter Need Satisfaction Questionnaire; Porter, 1961). One often simply assumed this difference score, instead of being a variable that was then tested for its correlation with a measure of job satisfaction, to *be* a measure of peoples' job satisfaction levels. Organizational psychologists assumed, therefore, the discrepancy theory of job satisfaction to be correct instead of testing it to see whether, or the degree to which, it is correct. Such measures of job satisfaction are no longer in favor, although organizational psychologists today still widely believe the general idea of discrepancies and of job satisfaction as some sort of need satisfaction.

The discrepancy between what one has on the job and what one *expects* (or perhaps what one had expected prior to taking the job) has a strong background in social psychology. Hulin (1991), although not focusing entirely on expectations, discrepancies, and job satisfaction, has done a nice job of reviewing Thibaut and Kelley's (1959) explanation of attitude formation. Briefly, in forming an attitude toward an object (satisfaction with a job in this case), the person tends to compare the object (job) with previous experience and with the alternatives (other jobs) as he or she knows them. We can make the leap from there to see that these comparisons with past job experiences or with present perceived alternative jobs could create expectations. The discrepancy between these expectations and the experiences on the present job then determine the degree of job satisfaction.

Finally, another popular version of discrepancy theory of job satisfaction focuses on the discrepancies between what one has on the job and what one thinks is *fair* or equitable—what one should have. Again organizational psychology has borrowed a theory from social psychology for this explanation: equity theory. While previous experience and current alternatives can help to explain how people develop expectations, comparisons with other people are important for understanding one of the sources of people's judgments about fairness or equity (Greenberg, 1987). In the work organization, everybody has inputs and outcomes. Inputs are the valuable things that people bring to the workplace and use in the service of the organization, including skills, efforts, and actual performance on the job. Outcomes are the individual outcomes that are the subject of this chapter. They could include almost anything of value to the person that the organization gives, including pay and fringe benefits, promotions, the quality or working conditions, and so forth. Most of the organizational psychology research on equity theory, however, has focused on pay.

Theoretically, one can calculate a ratio between any person's inputs and outcomes: inputs ÷ outcomes. We assume that people implicitly make such calculations for themselves and for one or more relevant persons of their choosing. One then compares the ratios, and if they are similar they are seen as fair or equitable. In discrepancy theory, we might assume, for example, that the amount of outcome another person with similar input receives is likely to be seen as fair. This, therefore, is the amount of outcome the person believes he or she *should* receive. The discrepancy between this level of "fair" outcomes and one's actual outcome determines the degree of job satisfaction.

Equity theory is one of the better-known theories that can help explain where people get the idea that they should receive a certain level of outcome. While research on equity theory in organizational psychology has slowed over the last decade or so, this may be due more to the difficulty of conducting research on the topic than on its lack of validity. In recent years there has been a renewed interest in similar topics, often under the label "justice." Justice and fairness or equity are, of course, very simlilar concepts. Two common types of organizational justice are taken from theories about verdicts in the judicial system—process and content dimensions of justice (Greenberg, 1987). In organizations, we may have procedural justice in which people consider the fairness or justice of the processes organizations use to allocate outcomes (e.g., promotions), and we also have distributive justice in which people are concerned with the content or actual distribution of the outcomes. That is, organizational members can independently consider just or unjust the process that allocates rewards or punishments and the actual distribution (or who gets them). It stands to reason that either type of justice can be related to satisfaction of organizational members. We are generally more satisfied with situations that are just than with unjust situations.

In addition to the complexity of equity theory, there are other obvious and sometimes simpler sources of opinions about fairness. For example, someone might tell people what level of pay would be fair—that someone might be a supervisor, coworker, politician, union leader, or trade magazine. Any source that people find credible can influence their estimate of the kind of situations and outcomes they should receive in the name of fairness. Cesar Chavez, a famous farm labor organizer once passed small cards to workers with a one-item survey on them (Mathiessen, 1969). The item asked how much they should be paid. There was an implicit comparison with the actual average wage of these workers, ninety cents per hour. As a practitioner, Chavez was using the discrepancy theory of satisfaction to judge the degree of dissatisfaction.

Social Information Processing and Job Satisfaction

Although discrepancy theories are the most popular explanations for job satisfaction in organizational psychology, two alternatives are prominent. Weiss (1990) maintains that social information processing systems are currently the most notable alternative explanation. The basic principle is that the workers' perceptions and feelings about the workplace are influenced by other people with whom the workers interact (Salancik & Pfeffer, 1978). At work, these other people are often thought to be coworkers or peers, but in principle they are anyone with whom the employee interacts and by whom the employee's perceptions are influenced. Why do employees in one workgroup or one company doing a specific kind of task describe it as having a lot of variety, while another workgroup or employees in another organization performing objectively the same task see it as very repetitive? According to the social information processing approach, people develop norms about how they perceive the situation. They communicate with each other, and they influence each other. To the extent that this does occur, changing the objective nature of the task will only change perceptions of it if the group's perceptual norms also change.

Social information processing affects job satisfaction in one or both of two ways. First, discrepancy theory could explain it, just as a combination of it with equity theory could explain job satisfaction. While equity theory can address questions regarding the source of people's beliefs about what they *should* be receiving from the workplace, social information processing can describe the source of people's perceptions about what they *actually* experience and perceive in work situations. Using the example of variety again, people might need, want, value, have interest in, or expect a certain level of variety in their work, and they might believe that is fair for them to have a certain level of variety. Discrepancy theories then compare those levels to the level of variety that people perceive they actually have on their jobs, and the discrepancy between the two determines satisfaction. The objective reality of the nature of the task does not entirely determine the perception of the level of variety that people believe they have on their jobs. Instead, there are the social influences of other people in the workplace that help to determine the employees' beliefs about their levels of task variety. Research suggests that both people and the nature of the task itself probably influence our perceptions (Glick, Jenkins, & Gupta, 1986). Thus, there is probably some truth to the position of social information processing, although it does not seem to explain everything about perceptions of the job.

The second way that social information processing can affect job satisfaction is more direct than affecting the perceptions that go into the subtraction process of discrepancy theory. In addition to influencing perceptions about the job, it is a short step to see that people can also influence each other's emotions or affect them more directly. There can be a group norm regarding the appropriate way to feel about the job. If most people express dissatisfaction with a job, others in the job might also come to feel dissatisfied with it. The social information processing principles are especially consistent with one of the major values in organizational psychology—interpersonal activities are important. People influence each other's levels of job satisfaction through interpersonal interactions. One could use social information processing theories to argue that, in an extreme form, job satisfaction is probably a group-level phenomenon rather than individual-level. Most organizational psychologists do not see it that way, however, and therefore we have included it under individual outcomes.

Gupta, Jenkins, and Beehr (1992) studied employees of five different organizations over a period of one and one half years, including people who remained in the same job in the same organization, people who moved to a similar job in another organization, people who changed to a different job in the same organization, and people who changed to a different job in a different organization. The job satisfaction of people who made each of the job changes did not change very much. One would expect that the people making the biggest changes (to a different job in a different organization) would have had the biggest changes in their job satisfaction, and those who kept the same job in the same organization would have had the least change in their job satisfaction changed the least. Instead, none of them seemed to change their levels of job satisfaction very much. This is consistent with the dispositional approach to job satisfaction (Staw, Bell, & Clausen, 1986). At the extreme, this approach sees job satisfaction as a stable individual difference variable, much like a personality variable—relatively stable and unalterable in the short run by changes in the job environment. This is counter to nearly all traditional thinking in organizational psychology about job satisfaction. One usually assumes that if someone is dissatisfied with the job, the solution is to change the job.

A related variable that has been the topic of study in recent years in organizational psychology is negative affectivity (Brief, Burke, George, Robinson, & Webster, 1988; Williams, Cote, & Buckley, 1989). This is treated as a stable personality variable that affects the way people relate emotionally to the world. People who are strong in this trait of negative affectivity have negative affect or feelings in most situations (Watson & Clark, 1984). People we think of as pessimists and people who seem constantly in a depressed mood might be exhibiting negative affectivity. Because negative affectivity is stable, and because it affects people's levels of satisfaction and dissatisfaction, then job satisfaction should also be stable. It would then act just like a trait of the person rather than like something that varies by the way the person is treated on the job. Negative affectivity is a relatively controversial concept in organizational psychology at present. To whatever extent it exists, however, it may cause problems for nonexperimental field studies of job satisfaction (the most typical research method in this area) that use all self-report survey measures (questionnaires and interviews). For example, if there is a theory that supervisory styles predict job satisfaction, and if self reports measure both supervisory styles and job satisfaction, then the negative affectivity trait might influence the persons' answers on both the questions about the supervisor and about job satisfaction. It might cause people with high levels of negative affectivity to answer both types of questions in a negative manner and people with low levels of negative affectivity to answer such questions in a manner that is consistently more positive. Then a strong correlation between supervisor's styles and job satisfaction will result, but it might not have anything to do with the "true" or objective nature of the supervisory styles that are present in workplace. For our present purposes, however, the main point is that a personality trait may affect job satisfaction and, therefore, job satisfaction would not necessarily vary much according to the nature of the job.

Aside from personality traits as an explanation for the stability of job satisfaction, there is the possibility of a biological explanation for why people feel satisfied to the extent that they do. One such theory is opponent process theory (Landy, 1978), although it has not been the subject of much research. According to this theory, job satisfaction might be stable over the long run, because any changes in it due to changes in the job environment are only temporary. When something in the workplace might make the person unusually happy or sad (i.e., increase or decrease his or her levels of satisfaction), then an opposing process, biologically based and supposedly influenced or controlled by parts of the autonomic nervous system, react to oppose this feeling of elation or depression and bring the person back to his or her normal emotional state. This restores the person to his or her usual level of job satisfaction. Opponent process theory presumes job satisfaction to have a steady state for the person, and any deviation from that state is only temporary. This would make job satisfaction a rather stable part of a person's permanent disposition.

A third approach to understanding how job satisfaction could be a stable disposition of the person is also biological, but it is more explicit about how the biological effects occur. This is a heredity approach, and primarily one relatively recent and well-known study supports it. In a study of identical twins raised apart, whether people were identical twins determined a significant portion of job satisfaction (Arvey, Bouchard, Segal, & Abraham, 1989). This is taken as an indication that biology—specifically genetics—can influence job satisfaction. One assumes, of course, that the hereditary characteristics of people are determined at conception and stable thereafter. The hereditary approach to job satisfaction can, therefore, be seen as a dispositional approach or an explanation for why people seem to have stable dispositions to have a certain level of satisfaction regardless of the nature of their job environments.

There are occasionally very strong arguments in favor of the dispositional approach, and some managers seem to prefer it as an explanation for the dissatisfaction of their employees (after all, it implies that they have no responsibility for their subordinates' unhappiness). Research has generally shown that only a portion of job satisfaction might be dispositional. That is, even *if* there is a stable, dispositional effect of the person on job satisfaction, it is probably only a moderate effect. Other factors apparently also influence job satisfaction. Most organizations psychologists would argue that many of those other factors are in the environment of the workplace. We will now examine some of them briefly.

Facets of Job Satisfaction

Facet satisfaction refers to satisfaction with a facet or part of the job rather than with the job as a whole. One often assumes that the satisfactions with all of the facets of a job combine in some way to determine overall job satisfaction. This combination might be, for example, a weighted average or mean (Locke, 1976). The weight of each facet might be related to some of the human characteristics I described in the previous chapter (e.g., needs, values, interests). Thus, for people who have especially strong needs for power, for example, their high degree of satisfaction with the facet of job power would mean that this facet is weighted heavily in determining their overall job satisfaction.

Weighting is often simply multiplying a score by a number (a weight) before adding it to other numbers and dividing to obtain a mean. In a simple example, suppose that a questionnaire having possible scores ranging from one to five measures all satisfaction facets. If the facet of power in the job is twice as important as any other facet for a person (due to a strong need for power), then this employee's one-through-five satisfaction score on power is multiplied by two before the mean of all the facet satisfaction scores is computed to estimate overall job satisfaction. For another employee, some other facet satisfaction would be weighted heavily because needs would be different (e.g., a strong need for affiliation might require a higher weighting for the facet of satisfaction with people in the workplace). In general, this type of weighting has not been very successful in the empirical research on job satisfaction. That is, weighting the measures of facet satisfaction in this way rarely strengthens their correlations with a measure of satisfaction with the overall job. Reasons for this might include either the use of poor measures or lack of complete understanding of what is being measured with job satisfaction facet measures. We could speculate, for example, that people have already done an intuitive weighting when they answer the facet satisfaction questions. They might report a more extreme score on the facet satisfaction measure itself (i.e., more extreme satisfaction or dissatisfaction) for facets that are more important to them. Regardless of the empirical evidence, it seems very likely that in some way, individual differences in preferences, needs, and so forth play some role in job satisfaction. The discrepancy theories of job satisfaction I discussed earlier are the most popular types of theories about job satisfaction and they assume this in one form or another.

What Are the Facets of Job Satisfaction?

One basic issue regards the listing of the facets of job satisfaction. A complete, exhaustive list is impossible, because there is not total agreement that a certain set of job characteristics and no others exist. The facets of job satisfaction correspond to the facets of jobs. In principle, people can be satisfied with anything about a job. In addition, the concept of facet satisfaction implies that the discrepancy or perhaps the social information processing theories are correct. A wholly dispositional approach would imply that any one person would be equally satisfied or dissatisfied with every facet, because the person's own disposition causes each facet of satisfaction. One usually assumes that satisfaction with a job facet has in some significant way a cause due to the nature of that facet or part of the job in combination with the person's needs, values, etc. regarding that facet. Some facets of jobs include tangible rewards, the people in the workplace, the nature of the work itself, the workplace's physical environment, the power inherent in the job, the job's prestige, and the degree of job security.

Tangible Job Facets.   One of the aspects of the workplace with which people can be satisfied or dissatisfied consists of the tangible rewards. Pay, fringe benefits, and even promotions (partly because they are usually related to pay) can be tangible rewards. Although organizational psychologists have probably not shown as much interest in satisfaction with the tangible facets as with some others, notably satisfaction with the supervisor and with the work itself, the tangible parts of jobs are surely important to job incumbents. Satisfaction with tangible rewards tends to be positively correlated with the actual level of rewards in nonexperimental field studies (Lawler & Jenkins, 1992), as one would expect. The strength of the relationship leaves room, however, for speculating that other factors also might lead to pay satisfaction—equity theory, for example would suggest perceived fairness of the pay system.

Satisfaction with benefits might be a separate facet from pay satisfaction (Heneman & Schwab, 1985; Scarpello, Huber, & Vandenberg, 1988). Our current knowledge about benefits satisfaction is extremely weak, however, because there has not been much research (Gerhart & Milkovich, 1992).

Social Facets.   Consistent with the basic organizational psychology value on people and interpersonal activities, there has been a good deal of research on satisfaction with some of the people in the workplace. Within the social facet, there has probably been more research on satisfaction with the supervisor than with other people. The second largest amount of social facet research has been on satisfaction with coworkers or peers. On the average, people tend to be satisfied with supervisors to the extent that the supervisors treat them considerately and, to a lesser extent, are helpful in accomplishing their jobs (Bass, 1981). While satisfaction with peers, coworkers, or workgroup members has not been the topic of study nearly as much as satisfaction with the supervisor, it is likely to follow some basic principles. Hackman (1992) has noted that peer members of workgroups are likely to have favorable attitudes toward belonging to the group to the extent that the workgroup is a prestigious set of people or that there are pleasant surroundings or rewards associated with belonging to the group. Furthermore, as the reader will see in the following discussion of satisfaction with subordinates, people often like each other to the extent that they are similar in a number of dimensions.

Besides supervisors and coworkers, however, there are still other people present in many workplaces. Two that come to mind are subordinates and customers. Not everybody has subordinates, of course—only supervisors and managers. Furthermore, not everybody deals with customers. For those who do, however, the reactions to these other people in the workplace could easily have some influence on satisfaction. One of the very few studies of satisfaction with subordinates found that two classes of relationship variables seem to be related to it, and they could theoretically cause it: entity relationships and functional relationships (Beehr, Weisbrodt, & Zagumny, 1995). Entity relationships mean that the supervisor might be satisfied with subordinates based on who they are, while functional relationships indicate that supervisors are satisfied with subordinates based upon what they do. Similarity might explain entity relationships, such that supervisors tend to be satisfied with subordinates to the extent that they are similar to the supervisor in terms of their demographics, background characteristics, current interests and activities, and basic values. Functional relationships probably have effects on satisfaction with subordinates in addition to the effects of the entity relationships. Supervisors tend to be satisfied with subordinates to the extent that they are functional to the supervisor in accomplishing the supervisor's own goals. While these two types of relationships were the topic of study as correlates of satisfaction with subordinates in a nonexperimental field study (Beehr, Weisbrodt, & Zagumny, 1995), they are likely causes of satisfaction with *anybody* in the workplace including supervisors, coworkers, subordinates, and customers (Locke 1976).

The Work Itself Facets. In addition to the social satisfaction facets and especially satisfaction with the supervisor, satisfaction with the work itself has been a favorite target of research by organizational psychologists. The phrase, *the work itself,* usually refers to the nature of the activities involved in carrying out the actual tasks of the job. The job characteristics that constitute the nature of the work itself are autonomy, variety, task identity, task significance, and task feedback (Hackman & Oldham 1980). Most of these labels are self-explanatory but not task identity. It is the extent to which an employee completes a whole, identifiable task, as opposed to only doing a small part of the whole project. This can probably be quite subjective, however. The person on the assembly line who adds a few bolts to a car seems to have little task identity, but perhaps the person who builds a whole carburetor feels as much task identity as one who builds an entire car. Each seems to have completed a whole, easily identifiable task.

A couple of other comments might also help explain two of the other task characteristics. Task significance specifically refers to the significance of the job to other people, even to the world at large. An example would be to compare working in two jobs with the same amount of autonomy, variety, task identity, and feedback, but one involves building artificial hearts while the other involves building toys. The person might feel that working on the hearts is more significant. Finally, task feedback is not feedback from other people in the workplace, such as from supervisors, coworkers, or customers. Instead, it is feedback that comes simply from doing the task itself. On some jobs, employees can tell exactly how well they are doing as they do it, with no need for someone else to give them feedback. On other jobs, however, employees might have a more difficult time knowing how well they are doing just from doing the task itself.

Hackman and Oldman (1980) introduced this set of five characteristics of the job itself to organizational psychology as factors leading to intrinsic job motivation rather than to satisfaction. I, therefore, discuss them further in the next chapter for their theoretical ability to motivate organizationally valued behavior. For our present purposes, however, they are often related to job satisfaction. Fried and Ferris (1987) in a meta-analysis concluded that, on the average, the reported correlation found between the combined job characteristics and overall job satisfaction in the research literature is about 0.45. In general, correlations of this size tend to be regarded seriously in organizational psychology. It seems likely that there can be facets of satisfaction that correspond to these job characteristics as well, for example, satisfaction with autonomy. Researchers have also developed questionnaire measures of these facet satisfactions (Hackman & Oldham, 1980).

Other Facet Satisfactions: Work Itself, Power, Prestige, and Security. Other facet satisfactions have not seen as much research activity in organizational psychology as the ones I discussed previously. Physical working conditions, power, prestige, and security seem obviously to be facets of work that could be important to people's satisfaction, however.

People can be more or less satisfied with their physical working conditions and settings. Engineering psychologists more so than organizational psychologists have studied these. People can prefer outdoor work versus inside jobs, for example. They might be satisfied or dissatisfied with the temperature, noise, cleanliness, newness of furnishings, and so forth. In some office work, it is even common for people to complain about not having enough windows.

People also can probably be more or less satisfied with the degree of power in their jobs. *Power* or *authority, control,* and *responsibility* are terms that sometimes organizational psychologists define separately to study their differences, but we can lump them together here and suggest that the employee can have varying degrees of satisfaction with the power over other people that the job allows.

It also seems likely that the prestige of a job might influence people's satisfaction with it; therefore, there might be a satisfaction with prestige facet. Public image of a job surely can make at least some people attempt to enter or stay away from an occupation, influence the way that people respond to those who are in the occupation, and therefore influence the satisfaction of job holders in that occupation. Consider the differences between the status and esteem afforded to physicians versus used car salespeople, for example. The public adulation versus the wisecracks offered to people in these occupations could easily influence their satisfaction.

Finally, job security is a characteristic of work that people could be more or less satisfied with. Jobs in which people are very unlikely to be laid off or fired seem to attract some people more than others—even if the job might pay less money. This suggests that there might be varying degrees of satisfaction with this facet of work.

Overall, the facets of job satisfaction may indicate major parts of the job that can, in part, cause job satisfaction. This fits with some theories of job satisfaction quite well (e.g., discrepancy theories) but not so well with others (e.g., dispositional theories).

What Does Job Satisfaction Cause?

While facets of the job imply causation of job satisfaction, another important issue is what job satisfaction causes. One has nearly always assumed that job satisfaction, while important in it own right if we care about employees, is also important because it leads to or causes employees to behave in ways that are important to organizations. In other words, one has usually assumed that job satisfaction, an individual outcome, is important because it also leads to organizational outcomes. In the formative stages of organizational psychology's history, during the Hawthorne studies some of the workers were both happy and productive. This observation led to the supposition that "A happy worker is a productive worker." This even became a slogan during an early version of the human relations movement in the workplace. In organizational psychology theory and research, that slogan translates into the idea that job satisfaction causes job performance. If we can just make the workers satisfied, then they will perform well. This is a simple idea that does not seem to go away, at least among the general public, but it is not true. Job satisfaction does not cause job performance.

It was never clear why anyone would expect job satisfaction to cause performance; the theoretical basis for it was never spelled out very clearly.

Perhaps one assumed an exchange theory or gratitude theory. One is so grateful for having satisfying work that, in exchange, he or she works hard for the organization. This might even happen on occasion, but the research has shown that job satisfaction tends to be practically uncorrelated with job performance overall. It is not that research is lacking on this point. A great deal of research has been done, and reviews have quite consistently concluded that there is little or no correlation between job satisfaction and job performance (Iaffaldano & Muchinsky, 1985). While the studies are nearly always nonexperimental field studies, we can still infer lack of causality—because if there is no relationship at all, then there can be no causal relationship.

Apparently the idea that job satisfaction causes job performance is comfortable, because as I noted earlier, it is an idea that does not go away easily. If job satisfaction, however, does not cause job performance, what might it cause that is relevant to somebody? There are some likely answers to this. Two other organizational outcomes do tend to be related to job satisfaction in research, and theories argue that these are causal relationships. Again, the research has been largely nonexperimental field studies, and therefore, the research method itself does not lend strong inference to the idea that there is a causal relationship for these outcomes either. The outcomes are absenteeism and turnover. I will discuss these further in the chapter on organizational outcomes, but for now we will note they might be related to job satisfaction—negatively. If people are dissatisfied with their jobs, it would be quite rational for them to try to avoid their jobs, either through staying away temporarily as in absenteeism or permanently as in turnover. This process could be something so simple as avoiding an unpleasant situation. Of course, other things besides job satisfaction might also influence absenteeism and turnover, but we will save that for a later chapter.

More recently, research has shown that job satisfaction is negatively correlated with employees' voting in favor of unionizing their workplace—especially satisfaction with pay and with the company's administration (Premack & Hunter, 1988). Again, this points to the aversive consequences to organizations for having dissatisfied employees. Most organizations or their managers prefer not to have unionized employees. Unions are another party that can put pressure on managers when they are making decisions about how to manage their section of the organization.

In short, the question about what job satisfaction causes has probably been asked in part because some people want to know why it is important, and they do not agree that it is very important just for employees to be happy. Those valuing the organizational outcomes seem especially likely to ask this question, because the answers they usually seek and get are that job satisfaction causes one or more organizationally valued outcomes. While job satisfaction probably does not cause job performance, its lack might very well be one of the causes of absenteeism, turnover, and unionization, three employee behaviors organizations value negatively.

TANGIBLE INDIVIDUAL OUTCOMES

In addition to the attitudinal outcome of job satisfaction, an obviously important set of individual outcomes of jobs are the tangible ones. These directly parallel the tangible facet satisfactions I discussed previously: pay, fringe benefits, and promotions. Organizational psychologists have not studied them as individual outcomes nearly as much as they have studied job satisfaction, although they have examined these outcomes as potential motivators of various job behaviors. Here, I briefly describe the ways that people seem to obtain these individual outcomes. Lawler and Jenkins (1992) have characterized the research on tangible outcomes in general, and pay in particular, as examining its effects on employee recruitment and turnover, motivation to perform the job or to develop skills for job performance, the organization's culture and structure, and the organization's costs. In other words, the focus of the research has been on the effects of pay systems on organizations.

Here we are more interested in the effects of pay systems (or other tangible rewards) on the individual and on the degree to which the individual has control over obtaining these valued rewards. One effect of tangible rewards on the individuals are their effects on satisfaction. I have addressed this facet satisfaction previously. The effects of tangible rewards on the person is in some ways obvious. More rewards make life easier and more pleasant outside the work place in a few specific ways. Higher standards of living result, entailing better housing, food, transportation, access to more and different (although not clearly "better") forms of entertainment. Examination of the effects of tangible rewards on these would largely entail the examination of whether money can buy material goods. It is self-evident that it can in most normal circumstances; therefore, let's go on to the other issue: the degree to which people can control their own receipt of tangible rewards in work organizations.

Pay in different organizations and in different jobs within the same organization is based on different criteria. People are paid according to the judged value of the jobs they perform, the degree of skill they have, the amount of seniority they have, the amount or quality of their job performance, the financial success of the organization for which they work, and the amount of time they work (e.g., hourly pay). In each of these pay systems, there can be arguments regarding whether pay is fair (i.e., *should* pay be based on these criteria and how different should pay be, based on differences in these criteria) and whether the pay system actually does base pay on its criteria (i.e., has the criterion been measured accurately).

If people are paid according to the value of the job they perform, they have little short-run control over their own pay. They can only obtain more pay by changing jobs, which might require changing skills; obtaining a promotion, because higher-level jobs tend to pay more; or changing organizations, because some organizations pay more than others. The principle is to find a way to move to a job that the current or some other employer values more highly. To do this, the person must find out what these jobs are, wait until there is an opening in them, and get the decision makers in the organization to choose him or her for the job. These things are only somewhat within the control of the person, and even if they are, it may still take some time (e.g., time to develop new skills and time for a higher-paying job to become available). An alternative is to get the organization to value the person's current job more highly. While this does happen through periodic job reevaluations, the amount of control the job incumbent has over whether and when this is done and on the job reevaluation's outcome is often small.

An interesting and unique situation is the value the organization places on top executives' jobs, which, in corporations, a board of directors determines. Executive pay is typically higher than the pay of people at lower hierarchical levels in the same organization, but the degree of difference might be due to the influence these high-level job incumbents have on the evaluation of their own jobs. No formal job evaluation usually occurs in the same manner as with lower-level jobs. In many cases, the top executive is a member of the board that determines the pay level for his or her own job, and in some cases executives from corporations are members of each others' boards (Lawler & Jenkins, 1992). The amount of personal influence over one's own pay levels can thus be high because the executive can probably influence the board of which he or she is a member and because some executives help determine each other's pay (i.e., to give low pay to another might influence the other to give low pay in return). Furthermore, aside from corporations, in many privately owned firms the top executive is the owner. This one has the greatest influence of any person in setting one's own pay levels.

A second type of pay system, skill-based pay, is also under the control of the person to only a moderate extent. The employee can develop skills by taking training courses or workshops, going back to school for more formal education, practicing, and simply learning from experience on the job. The company can offer training, but it may restrict who is eligible for it, taking the control of skill-based pay away from the employee. The employee generally can increase skills if he or she wants to do it badly enough, but in some cases extremely different new skills might take a long time to develop. If the person wishes to increase pay on a skill-based pay system, it is possible, but not easy.

Employers also can pay people based on seniority. The longer the person stays, the higher pay he or she can expect to receive. This tends to be relatively within the employee's control aside from constraining circumstances such as family needs to move, health needs that require changing jobs, the company downsizing and laying the employee off, and a myriad of other possible reasons why the employee must leave the organization. Nevertheless, gaining seniority is largely within the control of the person, but again it takes time. Obviously, the essence of seniority is time.

If pay is based on the quality and quantity of job performance, it can be somewhat under the control of the employee. The employee can work harder to produce more and better or easier to produce less and worse. There is, therefore, some variation in performance that is attributable to the employees' own efforts. There may be jobs in which the employees' efforts have less effect or more effect on performance, but they usually have some effect. Individual performance-based pay systems usually have some potential for allowing the employee to control some of the tangible rewards in the form of pay.

If the pay of an organization or a job is based on the financial success of the organization, the employee's ability to influence pay under this system is probably less than it is under individual performance-based pay systems. This is because the persons' efforts as an individual usually can just influence the organizations' financial success in combination with everyone else's efforts and with environmental effects such as the nation's economic cycle, the level of competition in the industry, and so forth. As an example, profit sharing is a form of pay based on the success of the organization. It seems likely to leave pay under control of the person only to a small extent. Perhaps in very small organizations, one person might be able to influence the organization's success more significantly than in larger organizations, but this form of payment generally does not leave pay very much under the control of the person.

The organization can also pay based on time spent at work. Hourly pay is not exactly based only upon time at work; it also requires some minimal amount of effort and performance while at work. Nevertheless, the amount of time the person is at work during a given pay period is a major factor in determining pay levels. This type of pay system does not typically leave much control over pay level to the individual. Often, the amount of hours employees work are not totally under their control. The managers might tell them when to come to work and when to leave—even when to work overtime. In many organizations, managers will allow as much flexibility as possible in scheduling so that employees can have some say, but overall this type of pay system only allows very limited control to the employee over how much pay he or she will be able to obtain.

Overall, this discussion suggests that most pay systems do not allow much influence for the person on the amount of pay they receive. Perhaps pay-for-performance systems allow the most control.

Regarding another tangible outcome, fringe benefits, the types of fringe benefit systems most employers use do not allow the employee to have much control over the receipt of these tangible individual outcomes either. Usually fringe benefits are fairly standard, at least within a job class, with only very minor choices. A frequently recommended fringe benefit system is the so-called menu plan (Lawler & Jenkins, 1992). With these plans, there is some choice clearly involved. While the person might not have choice over how much (in dollar value) fringe benefits he or she will get, the specific nature of the benefits could vary greatly according to the individual's choice. If the person is awarded a certain amount of money that can go toward fringe benefits, the employee can allot all or part of it to a number of alternative benefits—as if choosing from a menu. Clearly, menu-style fringe benefits programs allow the employee some control over which benefits are received.

The other tangible reward that people can receive as an individual outcome in the workplace is a promotion. In a series of studies, my colleagues and I (Beehr, & Juntunen, 1990; Beehr & Taber, 1993; Beehr, Taber, & Walsh, 1980) found that there seem to be a few systematic ways that people think they can get promotions or obtain better jobs in their current organizations. These "perceived mobility channels" within organizations include two performance factors (exceptional performance and routine or reliable performance) and two nonperformance factors (demographics and personal favoritism). As with pay systems, we can surmise that promotions based on performance might be somewhat under the influence of the individual. Regarding the two nonperformance factors in promotions, however, one might be more amenable to control by the individual than the other. If promotions are based on demographics, that is people of one gender or one race are more likely to get promotions than another, there is little that the employee can do about obtaining this tangible individual outcome. While it is technically possible to change one's sex through operations, this is not a procedure that many people are willing to undertake for the sake of a promotion. Regarding personal favoritism, however, there might be more that the person can try to do to obtain a valued promotion. The employee can go out of the way to impress or to praise the boss or to associate with the boss off as well as on the job. These "political" types of behaviors might make the boss more likely to recommend a promotion for the employee when the time comes. Certainly some employees seem to try to use these techniques.

Overall, regarding the person's ability to obtain tangible individual outcomes, there seems to be only a modest amount of control that many people will be likely to have if they are already employed in an organization. Some reward systems, however, allow the individual more control than others. One of the biggest choice points, at which time the individual has a great amount of control over the tangible individual outcomes he or she will be able to obtain over a lifetime, is at the early stages of choosing a career. Some occupations or careers are likely to reward the individual with more tangible rewards than others. This choice point is the time when an individual can choose a career with the most ease. Theoretically, this could be done at any time, but it is more typically at fairly early stages of one's adult life. Choices made at this time probably overwhelm any decision opportunities that arise later in terms of the amount of tangible individual outcomes the person will receive over his or her lifetime.

EMPLOYEE STRAINS

In relatively recent years, a third type of individual outcome, a health-related one, has emerged in the organizational psychology research. The study of occupational stress has shown that the nature of the social psychological work situation can sometimes lead to aversive effects on employees' physical or mental health or well-being. These outcomes are called strains.

There are differing definitions of the word *stress.* There are so many meanings of the word that we probably cannot simply ask people whether they have much "stress" and assume that they can really answer it in a manner that would be satisfactory to an organizational psychologist. One study showed that the word *stress* probably has multiple and inconsistent meanings to the general public (Jex, Beehr, & Roberts, 1992). Even in the scientific research, the word *stress* refers both to the nature of the occupation that causes the illness and to the illness itself. There is so much confusion about the precise meaning of the term that we mainly can use the word *stress* in organizational psychology just to refer to a general area of study and practice and not as a label for any single, specific variable (Jex & Beehr, 1991).

Instead, organizational psychologists use two other terms in describing and studying this general topic of occupational stress. *Stressors* refer to the characteristics of the work environment that cause the stress problem (Beehr, forthcoming; Kahn & Byosiere, 1992). It could be a characteristic of the workplace (e.g., crowding of people in small spaces), a characteristic of relationships with other people (e.g., interpersonal conflict), a characteristic of the organization as a whole (e.g., size), or the nature of the expectations and demands that the organization places on the person (e.g., expectations that are ambiguous, conflicting, or overloading). *Strains* refer to the psychological or physical problems of the person that the stressors cause (Beehr, 1995; Jex & Beehr, 1991). Because of individual differences, some people seem more susceptible to the aversive effects of stress than others are. The same stressors, therefore, will not always have the same impact on strains for every person. This presents a problem for the definitions, because stressors and strains are defined in relationship to each other. That is, stressors are characteristics of the workplace that are, in part, defined by the fact that they cause strains. Because strains do not result equally for everyone from the same workplace characteristics, it is common to define workplace characteristics as stressors if they lead to strains *for most people.*

Recent reports (e.g., Beehr, 1995; Kahn & Byosiere, 1992) show frequent classification of strains as psychological, physical or physiological, and behavioral. Common psychological strains include depression, anxiety, tension, and burnout. Even though it is a somewhat newer topic, burnout has its own research literature. One of the most common definitions of burnout is that it includes emotional exhaustion, depersonalization, and (lowered) personal accomplishment (Maslach, 1976).

As a strain that is due to job stressors, emotional exhaustion is probably the most important of these three subtypes of burnout, for three reasons. First, it is aversive to the person, as strains are supposed to be by definition. Second, it is very similar to the other potential psychological strains that people experience in the workplace—especially depression with its accompanying loss of energy and activity. Third, emotional exhaustion is applicable to all occupations. This is particularly *not* true of depersonalization. Depersonalization is the tendency to depersonalize or dehumanize the way the person thinks about his or her clients. That is, clients are not thought of in a personal and caring way when they are depersonalized. Instead, the person considers them almost as objects upon which to work. Obviously, only occupations in which one deals with clients can really develop this aspect of burnout. The theory and research on burnout began with such occupations, and this aspect of burnout is probably an outgrowth of studies with these occupations. Because of this, some research on occupational stress has used emotional exhaustion as a measure of strain without using the other two burnout indices (e.g., Gaines & Jermier, 1983).

Physical and physiological responses to job stress that have been classified as strains include a wide variety of aches and pains, cardiovascular disease or its risk factors (e.g., hypertension, serum cholesterol, and catecholamines), and perhaps ulcers (Jex & Beehr, 1991; Fried, Rowland, & Ferris, 1984). Although there is widespread belief that a great many diseases are related to occupational stress, the evidence for this, other than for cardiovascular disease, has been very sparse so far (Jex & Beehr, 1991). The pace of such research has been rapid, however, and we may know more clearly about other potential physical strains in the near future.

Consistent with the definition of strain, behavioral strains that might be due to occupational stress would be actions the person takes that are self-detrimental. Therefore, changes in job performance, for example, would not be included. Discussion of such organizational outcomes is reserved for a later chapter. Instead, strain behaviors might include alcohol abuse, marital problems, smoking, and self-destructive behaviors such as suicide. Except for smoking, there is little strong evidence that occupational stress likely causes these strain behaviors or makes them more severe (Jex & Beehr, 1991). These potential behavioral strains need more study before we can do anything more than speculate about them.

The Organizational Psychology Approach to Stress

One reason for the confusion regarding occupational stress definitions and terminology is that several different disciplines have studied it. Table 4.1 (Beehr & Franz, 1986) lists four of the major approaches to occupational stress, so that we can see how the organizational psychology approach compares with others. The medical and physiological approaches to occupational stress pay the most attention to physical stressors such as noise, heat, and toxic substances. They look for physical strains or physical injuries and illnesses, and they typically treat the individual rather than the

TABLE 4.1   Four Approaches to Occupational Stress in the Workplace

Approach	Typical Stressor	Typical Outcome	Typical Primary Target of Treatment
Medical	Physical	Physical Strain	Individual
Clinical/ Counseling Psychology	Psychological	Psychological Strain	Individual
Engineering Psychology	Physical	Job Performance	Organization
Organizational Psychology	Psychological	Psychological Strain	Organization

Reprinted from Beehr, T. A., & Franz, T. M. (1986). The current debate about the meaning of job stress. *Journal of Organizational Behavior Management, 8,* 5–18.

organization. That is, they are likely to try to treat the strain directly by the use of medicine, surgery, and so forth—administered directly to the person.

The clinical psychology approach is similar to the medical approach, except that it focuses on psychological rather than physical stressors and strains or outcomes. The treatment again typically consists of treating the individual strains, although with psychotherapy rather than with medicine. Thus, if the person is anxious (a possible strain), then counseling or psychotherapy is undertaken. The two approaches below the dotted line in the table are different from those above it by focusing more on the organization in some ways. Engineering psychology looks at the physical characteristics of the workplace as potential stressors (e.g., heat, noise, and light). It tends to be different from all the other approaches to occupational stress by its emphasis on job performance as an outcome (rather than strains, as we have defined them). If there are problems, the usual recommendation is to change some aspect of the working environment in the organization. For example, either reduce noise levels or give the employee protective hearing equipment—change the job equipment and requirements.

By contrast to these, the organizational psychology approach to occupational stress looks for psychological characteristics that could be stressors, and it has tended to focus on psychological strains. When problems arise, organizational psychology usually recommends changes in the organization. The changes often aim at reducing the stressors. While there has been quite a bit of study of occupational stress from the organizational psychology point of view, there have been relatively few attempts to implement this approach's recommended changes (Beehr & Franz, 1986). It is difficult, therefore, to say whether the recommendations work very well.

Many types of stressors that organizational psychologists study have a common theme of uncertainty (e.g., Beehr & Bhagat, 1985). When people are in jobs in which they are not certain what they need to do to perform well or to receive valued rewards, they are more likely to experience strains. Furthermore, the longer they are in such situations, the worse the strains are likely to be. Thus, Beehr and Bhagat (1985) suggest the formula, $S = U \times I \times D$ to describe this type of occupational stress, in which S = the amount of strain experienced, U = the uncertainty, I = the importance of potential outcomes (both rewards and punishments), and D = the duration or time over which the uncertainty persists.

Figure 4.1 (Beehr, 1995) illustrates the likely process through which stress variables are linked in organizational psychology. The core relationship between stressors and strains defines the existence of stress, but other variables may have important effects as well. If there are stressors causing strains in the workplace, this is likely to lead to adaptive responses in which the person (or perhaps someone else) tries to alleviate the stress. Such adaptations might be labeled coping, stress treatments, self-help seminars, and

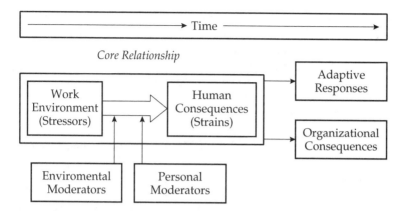

FIGURE 4.1 Model of Occupational Stress
Reprinted from Beehr, T.A. (1995). *Psychological stress in the workplace.* London: Routeledge.

so forth. There are large numbers of ways to try to deal with the problems due to occupational stressors and strains (Beehr, 1995; Beehr, Jex, & Ghosh, forthcoming). Two logical types of adaptations are to try to change the organizational stressors or to try to directly affect the individual's strains.

Furthermore, as Figure 4.1 shows, organizational consequences, such as changes in absenteeism, turnover, or job performance may occur. It is not clear that job stress consistently affects an individual's job performance in one direction or another. A popular theory holds that, up to a point, increasing job stressors will lead to better performance; after some point, however, further increases in stressors will lead to declining performance. The research evidence for that theory, however, is not strong. If we consider all the possible types of job stressors (e.g., role ambiguity, role overload, role conflict, underutilization of skills, interpersonal conflict, shiftwork, pressure for production) and all the types of performance (e.g., quality, quantity, speed, reliability, creativity), it would be surprising if all occupational stressors affected all forms of job performance in exactly the same way.

One often thinks that absenteeism and turnover are, in part, forms of withdrawing from the organization. It makes sense that people who are experiencing any unpleasantness in the organization, including stress, might try to get away and stay away from the unpleasantness. There is some evidence that this is correct (e.g., Gupta & Beehr, 1979). More discussion of organizational outcomes, however, is saved for another chapter.

Figure 4.1 shows that some aspects of the work environment or of the person might help to moderate the effects of stressors on strains. Social support is often thought to moderate the relationship between stressors and strains, although the research results are not entirely consistent (Beehr, 1995; Beehr & McGrath, 1992). People can support each other either by helping to solve the problems and accomplish the work (instrumental support) or by listening to the problems and offering sympathy for their emotions (emotional support). If social support is a moderator of the stressor-strain relationship, then one would expect stressors to be related (e.g., correlated statistically) less strongly with strains among people who have received such support than among people who have not. The research results are not consistent on this point, however, and therefore the idea that social support is a moderator of the stressor-strain relationship may not correctly explain how social support affects stress—in spite of this popular theory.

Well-known personal characteristics that have been proposed as moderators are Type A and Type B. People who are Type A tend to be competetive, aggressive, time-oriented, and hostile (Ganster, 1987). Type-B people, on the other hand, lack these characteristics. Type As appear to be hypersensitive to stress; that is, the relationship between stressors and strains is stronger and more certain than it is for Type Bs (Ganster, 1987). The apparent lesson is, if you are a Type-A person, you should especially avoid stressors in the workplace, because you are more likely than other people to become ill (i.e., get strains).

Finally, time is part of the occupational-stress process in Figure 4.1. In the formula $S = U \times I \times D$ for explaining stress (Beehr & Bhagat, 1985), the duration of time during which people experience the stressors is likely to have an effect on the severity of the strains the individual experiences.

CONCLUSIONS

Organizational psychology's growth brought with it a renewed interest in the person, as the basic value notes that the person is just as important as the organization. Therefore, one considers outcomes that are most directly important to the individual organizational member worthy of study and application regardless of whether they lead to organizationally valued outcomes such as job performance.

The individual outcome that has received the most attention in organizational psychology is job satisfaction. In fact, it is the topic of study so often that it almost seems that studies of many other organizational psychology topics routinely "toss in" job-satisfaction measures even though it is not the main thing in which the researchers are interested—as if implying that it is understood that job satisfaction is worth considering in relation to any other variable.

Two other categories of individual outcomes have received far less attention than job satisfaction. One, tangible outcomes, has been the subject of remarkably little attention. Surely people in work organizations consider their pay and benefits to be important, and yet we have often studiously ignored such outcomes. Perhaps they do not seem "psychological" enough for organizational psychologists. Whatever the reason, we are probably missing important factors in the individual's work reactions when we ignore such tangible outcomes.

Finally, individual strains due to stressors in the workplace have received the attention of a large number organizational psychologists in the last ten years. It is now a major interest in the field and rightly so. How could we claim to be interested in the person without paying attention to the effects of occupational stress on that person? Yes, the individual is just as important and worthwhile as the organization.

REFERENCES

Arvey, R. D., Bouchard, T. J., Segal, N. L., & Abraham, L. M. (1989). Job satisfaction: Environmental and genetic components. *Journal of Applied Psychology, 74,* 187–192.

Bass, B. M. (1981). *Stogdill's handbook of leadership: A survey of theory and research.* New York: The Free Press.

Beehr, T. A. (1995). *Psychological stress in the workplace.* London: Routledge.

Beehr, T. A., & Bhagat, R. S. (1985). *Stress and cognition in organizations.* New York: Wiley.

Beehr, T. A., Jex, S. M., & Ghosh, P. (Forthcoming). The management of occupational stress. In C. M. Johnson, W. Redmon, & T. Mawhinney (Eds.), *Handbook of organizational performance: Behavior analysis and management.* New York: Pergamon Press.

Beehr, T. A., & Franz, T. M. (1986). The current debate about the meaning of job stress. *Journal of Organizational Behavior Management, 8,* 5–18.

Beehr, T. A., & Juntunen, D. L. (1990). Promotions and employees' perceived mobility channels: The effects of employee sex, employee group, and initial placement. *Human Relations, 43,* 455–472.

Beehr, T. A., & McGrath, J. E. (1992). Social support, occupational stess and anxieety. *Anxiety, Stress, and Coping, 5,* 7–19.

Beehr, T. A., & Taber, T. D. (1993). Perceived intraorganizational mobility: Reliable versus exceptional performance as means to getting ahead. *Journal of Organizational Behavior, 14,* 579–594.

Beehr, T. A., Taber, T. D., & Walsh, J. T. (1980). Perceived mobility channels: Criteria for intraorganizational job mobility. *Organizational Behavior and Human Performance, 26,* 250–264.

Beehr, T. A., Weisbrodt, D. M., & Zagumny, M. J. (1995). Satisfacation with subordinates: A neglected research issue concerning supervisors. *Journal of Applied Social Psychology, 24,* 1665–1684.

Brief, A. P., Burke, M. J., George, J. M., Robinson, B., & Webster, J. (1988). Should negative affectivity remain an unmeasured variable in the study of stress? *Journal of Applied Psychology, 73,* 193–198.

Dawis, R. (1991). Vocational interests, values, and preferences. In M. D. Dunnette & L. M. Hough (Eds.), *Handbook of industrial and organizational psychology*, Vol.2 (2nd ed.) (pp. 833–871). Palo Alto, CA: Consulting Psychologists Press.

Fricko, M. A. M., & Beehr, T. A. (1992). A longitudinal investigation of interest congruence and gender concentration as predictors of job satisfaction. *Personnel Psychology, 45*, 99–117.

Fried, Y., & Ferris G. R. (1987). The validity of the job characteristics model: A review and meta-analysis. *Personnel Psychology, 40*, 287–322.

Fried, Y., Rowland, K. R., & Ferris, G. R. (1984). The physiological measurement of work stress: A critique. *Personnel Psychology, 37*, 583–615.

Gaines, J., & Jermier, J. M. (1983). Emotional exhaustion in a high stress organization. *Academy of Management Journal, 26*, 567–586.

Ganster, D. C. (1987). Type A behavior and occupational stress. In J. M. Ivancevich & D. C. Ganster (Eds.), *Job stress: From theory to suggestion* (pp. 61–84). New York: Haworth Press.

Gerhart, B., & Milkovich, G. (1992). Employee compensation: Research and practice. In M. D. Dunnette & L. M. Hough (Eds.), *Handbook of industrial and organizational psychology*, Vol. 3 (2nd ed.) (pp. 481–569). Palo Alto, CA: Consulting Psychologists Press.

Glick, W. H., Jenkins, G. D. Jr., & Gupta, N. (1986). Method versus substance: How strong are underlying relationships between job characteristics and attitudinal outcomes? *Academy of Management Journal, 29*, 441–464.

Greenberg, J. (1987). A taxonomy of organizational justice theories. *Academy of Management Review, 12*, 9–22.

Gupta, N., & Beehr, T. A. (1979). Job stress and employee behaviors. *Organizational Behavior and Human Performance, 23*, 373–387.

Gupta, N., Jenkins, G. D. Jr., & Beehr, T. A. (1992). The effects of turnover on perceived job quality: Does the grass look greener? *Group and Organization Management, 17*, 431–445.

Hackman, J. R. (1992). Group influences on individuals in organizations. In M. D. Dunnette & L. M. Hough (Eds.), *Handbook of industrial and organizational psychology*, Vol.3 (2nd ed.) (pp. 199–267). Palo Alto, CA: Consulting Psychologists Press.

Hackman, J. R., & Oldham, G. R. (1980). *Work redesign*. Reading, MA: Addison-Wesley.

Heneman, H. G., III, & Schwab, D. P. (1985). Pay satisfaction: Its multidimensional nature and measurement. *International Journal of Psychology, 20*, 129–141.

Hulin, C. (1991). Adaptation, persistence, and commitment in organizations. In M. D. Dunnette & L. M. Hough (Eds.), *Handbook of industrial and organizational psychology*, Vol. 2 (2nd ed.) (pp. 445–505). Palo Alto, CA: Consulting Psychologists Press.

Iaffaldano, M. T., & Muchinsky, P. M. (1985). Job satisfaction and job performance: A meta-analysis. *Psychological Bulletin, 97*, 251–273.

Jex, S. M., & Beehr, T. A. (1991). Emerging theoretical and methodological issues in the study of work-related stress. *Research in Personnel and Human Resources Management, 9*, 311–365.

Jex, S. M., Beehr, T. A., & Roberts, C. K. (1992). The meaning of cocupational "stress" items to survey respondents. *Journal of Applied Psychology, 77*, 623–628.

Kahn, R. L., & Byosiere, P. (1992). Stress in organizations. In M. D. Dunnette & L. M. Hough (Eds.) *Handbook of industrial and organizational psychology,* Vol. 3 (2nd ed.) (pp. 571–650). Palo Alto, CA: Consulting Psychologists Press.

Landy, F. J. (1978). An opponent process theory of job satisfaction. *Journal of Applied Psychology, 63,* 533–547.

Landy, F. J. (1989). The early years of I/O: J. D. Houser and J. D. I. *The Industrial-organizational psychologist, 26,* 63–64.

Lawler, E. E. III, & Jenkins, G. D., Jr. (1992). Strategic reward systems. In M. D. Dunnette & L. M. Hough (Eds.), *Handbook of industrial and organizational psychology,* Vol. 3 (2nd ed.) (pp. 1009–1055). Palo Alto, CA: Consulting Psychologists Press.

Locke, E. A. (1976). The nature and causes of job satisfaction. In M. D. Dunnette (Ed.), *Handbook of industrial and organizational psychology* (pp. 1297–1349). Chicago: Rand McNally.

Maslach, C. (1976). Burned-out. *Human Behavior,* 16–22.

Matthiessen, P. (1969). *Sal si puedes.* New York: Delta.

Porter, L. W. (1961). A study of perceived need satisfaction in bottom and middle management jobs. *Journal of Applied Psychology, 45,* 1–10.

Premack, S. L., & Hunter, J. E. (1988). Individual unionizationa decisions. *Psychological Bulletin, 103,* 223–234.

Salancik, G. R., & Pfeffer, J. (1978). A social information processing approach to job attitudes and task design. *Administrative Science Quarterly, 23,* 224–251.

Scarpello, V., Huber, V., & Vandenberg, R. J. (1988). Compensation satisfaction: Its measurment and dimensionality. *Journal of Applied Psychology, 73,* 163–171.

Staw, B. M., Bell, N. E., & Clausen, J. A. (1986). The dispositional approach to job attitudes: A lifetime longitudinal test. *Administrative Science Quarterly, 31,* 56–77.

Thibaut, J. W., & Kelley, H. H. (1959). *The social psychology of groups.* New York: Wiley.

Watson, D., & Clark, L. A. (1984). Negative affectivity: The dispositon to experience negative emotional states. *Psychological Bulletin, 96,* 465–490.

Weiss, H. M. (1990). Learning theory and industrial and organizational psychology. In M. D. Dunnette & L. M. Hough (Eds.), *Handbook of industrial and organizational psychology,* Vol. 1 (2nd ed.) (pp. 171–221). Palo Alto, CA: Consulting Psychologists Press.

Williams, L. J., Cote, J. A., & Buckley, M. R. (1989). Lack of method variance in self-reported affect and perceptions at work: Reality or significant problem? *Journal of Applied Psychology, 74,* 462–468.

5

ORGANIZATIONAL OUTCOMES

One of the basic values of organizational psychology, as I have previously noted, is that the person or individual is as important as the organization. Chapter 4 examined typical individual outcomes with which organizational psychologists study and work, and this chapter looks at the other half of the field's valued outcomes. While individual outcomes are criteria that most directly affect the individual, organizational outcomes refer to criteria that most directly affect the welfare of the organization.

Although organizational outcomes are criteria that are primarily important to the organization, they may still be considered as variables at the individual *level* of organizational psychology. That is, they are variables that vary among different individuals. The most obvious organizational outcome variables are individuals' behaviors rather than internal psychological states. The employees' behaviors seem more likely to affect the organization than their feelings, beliefs, and perceptions do. The exceptions include instances in which an internal psychological state leads directly to an organizationally relevant behavior, as in the case of motivation to work hard, which usually leads to the behavior of better job performance (an organizationally valued outcome).

Personnel psychology, a field I discussed in Chapter 1 as being closely related to organizational psychology, has traditionally focused on organizational outcomes. In that field, the phrase *criterion development* frequently describes the choice of and measurement of criteria or outcomes that are important. While the measurement of outcomes tends be a technical, science-driven task, the initial choice of relevant criteria is heavily dependent on values. Personnel psychology has tended to focus on outcomes that the organization values heavily, and among the most traditional personnel psychology outcomes are job performance, attendance, and membership. These three individual behaviors are necessary for organizations to survive and thrive. People must become and remain members (employees) of the organization, they must attend or show up regularly for work, and they must perform at least at some minimally acceptable level while they are there. Research on two of these, membership and attendance, has usually been problem-oriented, focusing on their lack. Consistent with this trend, we will refer to turnover and absenteeism in discussing these organizational outcomes.

Each of these three behaviors, job performance, turnover, and absenteeism, is more complex than a single label indicates. There are subdivisions of each. There is more than one type of or indicator of performance, for example. A simple breakdown would include quantity and quality of performance. In many jobs, one can achieve quantity without necessarily achieving a good quality product. Both of these, however, are usually important types of performance regarding the success of an organization. In addition to normal role performance, or meeting a job's minimum required performance standards, an employee can also go beyond the required performance for the job and perform some extra-role behavior, that is perform in some helpful ways that the job does not actually require. An example would be helping a fellow employee get a job done, staying later than is expected to satisfy a customer's request, making useful suggestions on how to improve a product or service, and so forth. Although such behaviors might not be part of or a requirement of the employee's job or role, they can help the organization to be more effective and are, therefore, important elements of performance.

Similarly, absenteeism has types subdivisions. Employees with equal total amounts of absenteeism can be absent for a few long durations or for frequent short periods of time. They also can be absent at important times when a great deal of important work needs to be done or they can be absent during lulls in the organization's activities. In addition to the probability that the total amount of absenteeism will adversely affect the organization's effectiveness, some patterns of absenteeism seem likely to be more detrimental than others.

Turnover, or leaving the organization permanantly, also can take more than one form. A common breakdown is whether the individual who leaves the organization does so is voluntarily or involuntarily. People can voluntarily leave for many reasons, and the organization can force the employee to leave for more than one reason as well (Colarelli & Beehr, 1993). Employees might find better paying jobs elsewhere, jobs with better working hours or conditions, jobs in geographical locations they prefer, and so forth. In addition, they might not only leave the organization but also their occupations or professions (e.g., Lane, Mathews, & Presholdt, 1988) or even leave the workforce entirely. That is, they might be abandoning the occupation to take up another line of work, or they might simply opt out of paid employment entirely, for example, by retiring.

Until recent decades, turnover had almost always been considered harmful to the welfare of the organization. The organization incurs costs during the recruiting, selection, and training processes in hiring some new employees. To recover those costs, the newly hired employee needs to work effectively for the organization for some period of time. If the employee leaves very soon, then the organization must incur those replacement costs again. While all these factors are important, it is also true that some employees do not contribute much to the organization, and the organization might benefit by replacing them with more productive persons. In addition, employees' pay often increases at least partly as a function of time. More senior employees, therefore, cost the employer more (per time spent on the job), and yet they may not be contributing proportionately more than less senior employees. If this happens, the temptation is obvious for organizations to replace the more costly employees with equally productive but less costly new employees. In such sitatuations, it can even become financially advantageous for the organization to offer the person a large amount of money to retire voluntarily. This can be considered as a form of selection— selection *out* of the organization (Colarelli & Beehr, 1993). The whole idea that turnover may not be bad for the organization's fortunes, and that it may even be good, has been the topic of discussions of functional versus dysfunctional turnover in recent years (Dalton, Todor, & Krackhardt, 1982). Functional turnover would help the organization in some way, while dysfunctional turnover would harm it.

THE MOTIVATION OF
WORK-RELATED BEHAVIORS

Although one could argue that our behavior might be randomly determined in part, it is usually also motivated in some way. Any behavior can be motivated, which in everyday terms simply means it has a cause. Knowing the causes of work-related behaviors would be valuable to organizations, because these behaviors are valuable to the organization's survival. If causes of behavior are known, then it is easier both to predict and to control the behavior. Control of employees' work-related behavior is one of management's important functions.

The basic organizational psychology value about theory and research is evident regarding motivation. Both psychologists and even "normal" people tend to believe in and use theories. Every person tends to have a theory (or perhaps more than one) of motivation. We tend to attribute causes to the behaviors that we see and hear about, and when we believe that we know the causes of behavior, we have an implicit motivation theory—implicit because we don't usually sit down, think it through in detail, and write it down for others to see. Perhaps only psychologists do that! A major dichotomy of causes of behavior is whether we believe the causes are in the nature of the person or in the person's environment. Most psychologists would readily say the causes are in both places, but even we sometimes focus more on one than on the other. It was long ago noted that when we see other people's behaviors we are likely to attribute the cause to them as people (an internal attribution of causality) more than we should, whereas we have a greater tendency to attribute causality of our own behavior to our environment (Ross, 1977). This tendency is called the fundamental attribution error. It probably operates more clearly when we are attributing causes of poor behavior such as poor job performance than when we are judging more successful behavior (Colarelli & Beehr, 1993). We can infer that our implicit theories of motivation tend to have some built-in bias. The value organizational psychology places on systematic, less biased, formal research is well-placed. If we want to know the causes of employees' organizationally relevant behaviors, we need to study it carefully rather than assuming that our off-the-cuff hunches, inferences, and attributions are correct. Motivation has actually been the topic of a great deal of study in organizational psychology, although usually in regard to one specific behavior—job performance.

PRODUCTIVITY OR JOB PERFORMANCE

Aside from personal theories of motivation, researchers have developed and tested a large number of more formal theories. Three that have some of the best evidence regarding their validity and usefulness in organizational psychology are expectancy theory, organizational behavior management, and goal setting theory (Table 5.1). There are many other motivation theories that I do not discuss here. One notable one is equity theory, a well-known theory in organizational psychology. I discussed equity theory in the previous chapter rather than here, because (1) the experience of equity is a pleasurable individual state in itself (and, therefore, is an individual outcome) and (2) the evidence for it as a simple, direct, and clear motivator of behaviors as organizational outcomes is spotty.

There has been a long-term fascination in organizational psychology with the dichotomy of intrinsic and extrinsic motivation, and Table 5.1 describes the manner in which each of these three theories deal with this concept. Both intrinsic and extrinsic stimuli can help to motivate people, that is

TABLE 5.1   Three Motivational Approaches to Understanding
Behavior in Organizations

Sources of Instigating Stimuli	Motivational Approaches		
	Expectancy Theory	Organizational Behavior Management	Goal-Setting
Internal	Subjective (internal) expectancy that behavior will result in external or internal rewards	Internal reinforcement not usually addressed, although some theorists think some unseen reinforcements can occur	Behavior is stronger when working toward a specific, high, self-accepted (internalized) goal
External	External stimuli not a direct cause of behavior, although they might affect expectancies	Reinforcing (external) stimuli (e.g., rewards) following a behavior results in continuation of or increased strength of behavior	(External) feedback helps increase goal-directed behavior

both factors that are within people, and which others do not see, and factors that come from outside the person.

Expectancy Theory

Expectancy theory of motivation argues that what people expect to happen influences or motivates their behavior. These expectations are internal to the person and, therefore, the stimuli that are most directly motivating are intrinsic factors. A common version of the theory can be expressed mathematically: $M = E \times sum(I \times V)$. That is, motivation equals expectancy times the sum of instrumentalities times valences. Both expectancy and instrumentality refer to some expectations that people have. Expectations are largely characteristics that are internal to the person; therefore, Table 5.1 notes that external stimuli are not a direct cause of motivation in this theory. Expectancy is the employee's subjective or perceived probability that his or her efforts will lead to good performance (sometimes expressed as

E→P); instrumentality is the employee's subjective probability that his or her performance will lead to attaining some outcomes (P→O). These outcomes can be things that the employee values positively, negatively, or not at all. The value that the employee places on the outcomes is called valence (V in the equation).

Outcomes might include promotions, pay raises, praise from the supervisor or coworkers, or something less observable such as a feeling of achievement (an outcome that is internal to the person). While the variables in the theory (E, I, and V) are all internal to the person, external stimuli may affect these internal beliefs. If, for example, there is a contract that says that employees who perform well will receive more money, the employee may come to have a high subjective instrumentality that his or her good performance will result in more money (an outcome). Stronger expectancies, stronger instrumentalities, and stronger valences on the outcomes combine multiplicatively to lead to stronger motivation, and the employee will work harder. Each possible outcome has its own instrumentality, that is, the person might believe there is a strong likelihood that performance will lead to a pat on the back from the supervisor but does not believe at all that performance will lead to a promotion. Likewise, each possible outcome has its own valence for the person. That is, the person might value a pay raise very much but not value the praise from the coworkers as much. There are actually, therefore, a whole set of instrumentalities and accompanying valences. That is why the motivation formula above indicates that instrumentalities, multiplied by valences, would be summed before they are multiplied by expectancy. Because the variables are multiplied together, this means that if any one of them is zero, then there will be no motivation at all to exert effort toward performing well. There must be at least some level of E→P, P→O, and some valence (positive or negative) of the outcome for the person before there will be any effect on motivation.

Compared to instrumentality, expectancy is usually conceived more simply as having only one value. That is, there is only one subjective probability that one's effort will lead to good performance. This is because one assumes that performance is a single thing and not a set of things like an instrumentality. Because I have already noted that performance is actually many things, one could question this; but, we will leave that for the researchers and theorists to worry about.

Core Characteristics of Intrinsically Motivating Jobs

One of the most traditional ways of thinking of intrinsic motivation is as a type of motivation for which there is no obvious, observable external reward, punishment, or other outcome that other agents provide or are expected to provide. Such agents are usually supervisors or other people, who could provide pay raises, promotions, praise, smiles, pats on the back, and so forth. In principle, agents administering such outcomes could even be impersonal—such as a slot machine motivating people to gamble. Why, then, do people engage in behaviors such as job performance when no agent administers any observable outcome? In expectancy theory terms, for what outcome do they expect their performance to be instrumental? Common answers argue that a sense of achievement, accomplishment, or pride are the outcomes that might motivate such behavior.

Rather than factors intrinsic to the person being the only important element explaining intrinsic motivation, the nature of the job also is part of the theory of intrinsic motivation. A job that is challenging seems necessary for people to receive a sense of accomplishment from performing it well. The best-known theory of job design argues that there are five core characteristics of intrinsically motivating jobs. In other words, there are five job characteristics that make it likely that people will receive a feeling of accomplishment based on doing the job well.

Hackman and Oldham (1976, 1980) developed the model of intrinsic work motivation depicted in Figure 5.1 on page 104 based on other people's research and theory and on research of their own. This is the same job characteristics theory I described in Chapter 4 on individual outcomes. While research shows that the five job characteristics of autonomy, skill variety, task identity, task significance, and feedback lead to individual outcomes such as job satisfaction, they were actually developed as important elements of a theory of intrinsic motivation that would lead to organizational outcomes— because intrinsic motivation should lead to good performance.

Although the arrows in the model note that causation flows from left to right, it might be easiest to consider the meaning of the model by examining it from right to left. Internal or intrinsic work motivation means motivation that comes from just doing a good job. A questionnaire called the Job Diagnostic Survey (JDS) (Hackman & Oldham, 1980), developed along with some of the original studies of the theory, has measures of each of the variables. A sample item from the internal work motivation scale on the questionnaire is "I feel a great sense of personal satisfaction when I do this job well." A close look at this item shows that, because the word "when" means "if," this is an internal work motivation item that is written to be consistent with the expectancy theory definition of instrumentality. It asks the extent to which the person believes (expects) that an pleasant internal feeling follows good job performance. Instrumentality is the subjective belief that job performance will lead to an outcome. In this case, the outcome (a great sense of personal satisfaction) is intrinsic, and there is no indication in the item that an outside agent provides anything.

It should be apparent now that the job characteristics theory of intrinsic motivation is based on expectancy theory of motivation. It identifies the characteristics of jobs that make it likely that people will feel a sense of

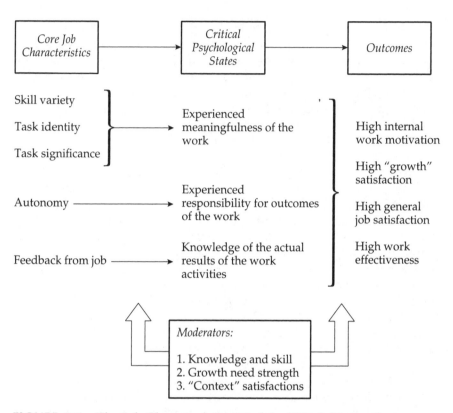

FIGURE 5.1   The Job Characteristics Model of Work Motivation
Reprinted from Hackman, J. R., & Oldham, G. R. (1980), *Work redesign.* Reading, MA: Addison-Wesley.

accomplishment *if* they perform well. The expectation that they will feel good *if* they do well is an instrumentality belief that motivates them.

Working backward in Figure 5.1 from internal work motivation, there are three psychological states that are critically important for people to receive this good feeling or sense of accomplishment from doing their work well: (1) the person must experience the work as meaningful, (2) the person must feel responsible for the work performance, and (3) the person must have reason to believe that he or she did perform successfully (knowledge of results). If the person's work has no importance or meaning at all, or if the person has no reason to believe that his or her own efforts were responsible for the successful performance, or if the person does not even know whether he or she has performed the job well, there is no reason for feeling satisfied or proud of the performance. Because lacking any one of these critical psychological states would mean there could be no internal motivation, this can be expressed algebraically as internal motivation = experienced meaningfulness × experienced responsibility × knowledge of results. An important effect of multiplying them together is that if any one of them equals zero, then the amount of internal work motivation would also be zero.

Working back all the way to the left side of Figure 5.1, Hackman and Oldham (1976, 1980), based on their own and a few previous studies, identified five core job characteristics that would lead to these three critical psychological states. Work is likely to be meaningful if the job uses a variety of the person's skills, if the task is to complete a whole, identifiable piece of work, and if the task has a significant impact on people's lives. The person is likely to feel responsible for the good performance if he or she has a job with a substantial amount of autonomy in carrying out the work. If the job provides feedback, the person is likely to have knowledge about how well he or she has done the job. Of course feedback from other people might substitute for a lack of feedback from the task or job itself and still allow the person to have knowledge about the results of his or her work. Internal work motivation implies, however, that someone can be motivated just by doing the task itself apart from interactions with other people who might be agents delivering outcomes.

If we want to estimate the potential for a job to motivate people intrinsically, therefore, we could take the algebraic formula regarding the three critical psychological states, above, and substitute the appropriate job characteristics. The first three job characteristics all contribute to the same psychological state, and so their average is taken as the first part of the equation:

$$MPS = ((SV + TI + TS)/3) \times A \times FB$$

The motivating potential score (MPS) of a job can, therefore, be calculated if the five core characteristics are measured quantitatively. This is done with the questionnaire (JDS) that tests the theory.

The development of the original version of this theory was in conjunction with a nonexperimental field study of employees in a variety of jobs in seven different companies (Hackman & Oldham, 1976). The study is a classic in organizational psychology and is one of the most frequently cited articles in the field. The authors collected most of the data with the JDS; therefore, the data were the subjective reports of the employees themselves. Because expectancy theory argues that the variables that most directly affect motivation are internal to the person, this method was consistent with the theory. We should keep in mind, however, that the nonexperimental nature of the study means that there was not strong evidence for the causality implied in the theory.

Figure 5.1 illustrates moderator variables in a typical way. It shows arrows from the moderator variable pointing to another arrow. That is, an arrow from employee growth need strength points to the arrow from the core job dimensions to the critical psychological states. This means that the moderator variable, growth need strength, affects the relationship between the two other variables. People with strong growth needs desire a chance to use and expand their skills and responsibilities and thereby to increase their skill levels and "grow" as a person. When such people are exposed to the job characteristics in the model, they react very well, that is, they work very hard. When people who are weak in such needs experience these types of jobs, however, they are not as motivated. The employees' growth needs, therefore, moderate the relationship between job characteristics and motivation for job performance. Such needs are related to the concept of valence in expectancy theory, because people with strong growth needs value growth as an outcome.

Similarly, the model proposes that two other individual differences moderate the job characteristics–employee motivation relationship: contextual satisfaction; and knowledge, skills, and ability. The employee must be satisfied with the elements of the job context before the core job characteristics can have their full impact on their motivation. Context refers to elements of the job surroundings that are not part of the act of doing the job itself, including satisfaction with people (e.g., supervisor and coworkers), pay, and job security. Without being at least minimally satisfied with these, the employee will not be as motivated by the job characteristics as he or she would otherwise be. In addition, the employee must have sufficient abilities in the task at hand to perform well. This last item seems clearly related to the outcome of job performance if not necessarily to motivation. We might surmise that even if motivation were just as high without as much ability, the lack of ability will keep performance low.

In spite of its acclaim, research on this job characteristics theory of intrinsic motivation has surfaced some problems. In an earlier chapter, I noted that a study by Glick, Jenkins and Gupta (1986) suggested that the social milieu probably affects in part the questionnaire reports upon which most of the studies rely. That is, as social information processing theory predicts, the answers that employees provide on the questionnaire are only partially "objective" descriptions of the job; they are also due in part to opinions that other people communicate to us about the job. The meta analysis by Fried and Ferris (1987) suggested that there were fairly strong correlations between job incumbents' reports of their jobs' characteristics and their supervisors' descriptions of the characteristics of the same jobs. Correlations over 0.50 were fairly common. Such agreement is often taken as confirmation that the incumbents' reports have some accuracy, but it could also mean that the perceptions of both supervisor and subordinate are susceptible to the same social influences. Also, that meta analysis indicated that the average correlation reported between the job characteristics and internal work motivation was in the high 0.30s. By itself, this sounds good, but I noted in Chapter 4 (on job satisfaction) that their correlation with job satisfaction was higher than this. Theoretically, the job characteristics model was developed to be an explanation of internal motivation; therefore, it might be seen as disappointing that this correlation is not stronger.

We can also see some of the typical values of organizational psychology in this theory. Chapter 1 noted that one value of organizational psychology is that people have high ability and are trustworthy. In the job characteristics theory, to motivate people intrinsically, the organization must trust employees enough to give them some autonomy in their jobs, but this will only be successful to the degree that they have high ability.

Expectancy theory of motivation, through both intrinsic and extrinsic expected outcomes, is the oldest of the three dominant motivation theories in organizational psychology. It is a cognitive theory of motivation, because it emphasizes the importance of cognitions or thinking in motivation. The theory I discuss in the next section comes from almost the opposite point of view in one way: it deemphasizes cognitive factors and even discounts them entirely in some of its extreme forms.

Organizational Behavior Management

Organizational behavior management (OBM) refers to the systematic application of behavior modification (behavior analysis) principles to the behaviors of people in organizations. Table 5.1 indicates that OBM focuses on external sources of stimuli that motivate people. In fact, this focus is so strong that the use of the term *motivation* to refer to OBM principles might meet objection from some of OBM's proponents. Motivation, after all, seems to refer to some type of internal state of the person. I am using it here, however, simply to refer to causes of behavior, and that is precisely the domain of OBM. In some ways OBM and expectancy theory provide a good contrast in motivational approaches. Expectancy theory tends to explain behavior primarily by proposing variables internal to the person, while OBM tends to explain behavior by emphasizing variables external to the person.

There is also a major similarity between OBM and expectancy theory— both include the concept of contingency. In expectancy theory, both the expectancy and the instrumentalities are subjective contingencies. That is, they are beliefs or estimates about the extent to which one event is contingent on another. In expectancy theory either good performance is contingent on effort or outcomes are contingent upon good performance. In OBM, the focus is on contingencies about actual events rather than people's beliefs about those events. The OBM approach focuses primarily on one of the two contingencies in expectancy theory—the performance-to-outcome contingency. The language used is different, however.

OBM emphasizes operant conditioning principles in which some external stimulus acts as a reinforcer for an employee's immediately preceding behavior. Reinforcing stimuli, by definition, result in the employee being more likely to repeat the behavior that it followed and on which it was contingent. In everyday terms, many reinforcers are considered to be rewards. For example, high performance by an employee might be followed by a pay raise or bonus. Most employees would consider the increase in money to be a reward. Reinforcement, however, is not limited to tangible stimuli such as money. It can include supervisor praise, coworker praise, awards, recognition, and a variety of other observable stimuli in the environment. Reinforcement is defined by its effect rather than by its innate nature. If a stimulus has the effect of increasing the strength, probability, or frequency of the behavior, then it is a reinforcer.

In conjunction with reinforcing stimuli, other stimuli can help to control behavior. Antecedent conditions or discriminative stimuli can act as cues to the employee to perform the behavior. If the cues are not present, the behavior may not be followed by the reinforcer. When the boss is seen in the vicinity, for example, the employee might be more likely to work hard. This might happen because the employee has received the boss' praise for hard work in the past—but only when the boss was seen to be present. In this discussion of motivation, we are concerned with the causes or control of behavior, and, therefore, both the discriminative stimuli and the reinforcing stimuli are important for understanding employee motivation from an OBM standpoint (O'Hara, Johnson, & Beehr, 1985).

In laboratory experiments, including and perhaps especially with animals as subjects, some reliable principles have been developed regarding the nature of the "schedules" by which reinforcement is given. One dimension of reinforcement schedules is ratio versus interval. With a ratio schedule, people would be reinforced as a function of a number of responses. A simple ratio would be 1 : 1, the so-called continuous reinforcement schedule, meaning that an employee might receive reinforcement every single time he or she performed the required behavior. An employee might be paid a certain amount of money, perhaps two dollars, every time he or she produced a small product (e.g., assembled a windshield wiper) or performed a service (e.g., served a customer at a restaurant). Alternatively, the ratio might be anything other than 1 : 1. In a 3 : 1 ratio (labeled Fixed Ratio 3), for example, the employee might receive the two dollars only after assembling three windshield wipers; after three more are assembled, two more dollars would be received. With an interval schedule, on the other hand, time plays a role. In this case, the person might receive the reinforcement only when the behavior occurs after a certain time interval. The reinforcement might only be received for serving customers after half a day goes by.

In addition to ratio versus interval reinforcement schedules, reinforcement can also be presented on a fixed versus a variable basis. Fixed schedules are those in which the ratio or the time interval is fixed or constant. The description of reinforcement schedules above implies that these are fixed ratio and fixed interval schedules. Alternatively, they could be variable schedules. For example, the employee doing the assembly job could be reinforced with two dollars at a 3 : 1 ratio on the average, but not necesarily for every three assemblies. The employee might receive the reinforcer for every three assemblies averaged over a month's time, but sometimes the reinforcement might come after only one or two assemblies while at other times it would come only after four or five assemblies. That would be a variable ratio schedule. A variable interval schedule would work in a parallel manner. The employee might receive reinforcement after assembling pieces for an hour, for a whole day, or some other time period but on the average receive reinforcement after performance each one-half day. Piece-rate pay systems in industry seem to be good examples of fixed ratio reinforcement systems (assuming that the pay is reinforcing). One often assumes that hourly or yearly salary pay is similar to an interval reinforcement system, but this assumption is questionable, at least if job performance is the behavior being reinforced. In many of these pay systems, it is not clear that pay is very contingent on the individual's performance. Instead, it often appears to be based on a combination of membership, minimal attendance behaviors, and minimal performance measures or sometimes on the whole organization's performance or other variables that are largely outside the control of the individual worker.

OBM studies seem to show that ratio schedules lead to greater job performance than interval schedules, but that it might not matter whether the schedule is fixed or variable. This was found, for example, in an experiment of the performance of mountain beaver trappers (Saari & Latham, 1982). One must note that much of the research on OBM has been conducted using field experiments, which give one reason to believe that the results might both provide strong evidence about causality and be generalizable to real-world jobs. By contrast, most of the research on expectancy theory has used either laboratory experiments or nonexperimental field studies, which have one or the other weakness (see Chapter 2).

It is easy to see that the practical programs based on expectancy theory and on OBM would have a great deal of overlap. The most obvious example is that both would argue for making outcomes or reinforcement contingent on performance. In the case of expectancy theory, one would then argue that this works only because it is likely to increase the subjective instrumentality of the employee, while OBM might not consider it wise or important to make any further explanation at all.

Goal-Setting Theory

Goal-setting theory is a cognitive approach to employee motivation, like expectancy theory, and, therefore, some of its important concepts are internal to the person (see Table 5.1). It assumes that people rationally and consciously try to do what they intend to do. That is a pretty straight-forward and even common-sense description of how many of us think we behave. Much of the early evidence for the theory came from laboratory experiments, which meant that causal principles were relatively certain, but that the extent to which they generalized to a variety of real-world situations was less clear. Since then, however, enough research has been conducted in the field, usually field experiments or quasi experiments, to increase confidence that the same principles apply in real work settings. Various goal-oriented principles and programs have been used in business for a long time, even before much of the formal experimentation that led to the current goal-setting theory was undertaken. The research has, however, given insight into specific details regarding the best way to use goal setting for employee motivation.

Research has shown that two of the most important features of goal setting, if it is to improve the employee's performance, are that the goal be high or difficult and that it be specific (Kanfer, 1990). It seems obvious that people with higher performance goals tend to perform better than people with lower goals. Goal specificity, however, is also important. When people are given a goal to simply do their best, they are less likely to perform as well as when they have a goal such as producing a specific, high number of the products.

Besides goal difficulty and specificity, the goal setting approach to motivation has usually argued that some other goal-related variables are important as well. The most prominent of these is probably goal commitment, which means the person's determination to reach the goal (Locke, Latham, & Erez, 1988). As with goal difficulty, this almost sounds obvious; if people are not committed to reaching the goal, they are probably less likely to produce up to the level of the goal.

In addition to goal difficulty, goal specificity, and goal commitment, one other variable has received special attention in relation to goal setting in recent years. As Table 5.1 shows, feedback seems to be important in conjunction with goal setting. That is, it helps if people know how they are doing in meeting their goals. Usually the feedback is external in the research on goal setting, that is, it comes from agents or other people. In principle, it could also be intrinsic to the task itself, however, as in the job characteristics theory of Hackman and Oldham (1980) (see Expectancy Theory). The importance of feedback in motivating performance is clear, because it is present in some parts of all three major theories I discuss here. Organizational behavior management often considers feedback to work as a reinforcer. In fact, there is some controversy between goal setting and OBM theories regarding the role of feedback. If it is a reinforcer, then OBM would consider it to have a prime role in determining (motivating) behavior; goal setting theory usually relegates feedback to a lesser role, however, as a variable that enhances the effects of goals but has little effect on its own without goals.

Goal setting theory of motivation appears to be very useful in explaining work performance, but expectancy theory and OBM also have some ability to explain it. The roles of contingency, cognitions, and especially feedback all cut across more than one of the theories suggesting that they might usually be good features of attempts at motivating performance.

Job Satisfaction and Job Performance

One of the organizational psychology values is that empirical research and theory are valuable (see Chapter 1). The potential association between job satisfaction and job performance is a good example of the need for empirical research. As I noted in Chapter 4, job satisfaction is an individual outcome, that is, it is valued primarily by the individual. In this chapter, I examine job satisfaction not as an organizational outcome but as a potential cause of an organizationally valued outcome, job performance. I examine also other ways in which these two types of outcomes might be related.

After the Hawthorne studies, people often advocated and widely believed that there was a simple causal relationship, with job satisfaction causing job performance. To some extent this seems to be a belief that exists in the mind of the public to this day, and it probably is due in part to confusing the concept of satisfaction with motivation. There has been a great deal of empirical research, however, showing that there is little or no simple relationship between these two variables. Based on expectancy theory, it seems likely that there could be an indirect relationship in which job performance causes job satisfaction, however, and this relationship is explained well with the important concept of contingency.

If job performance leads to valued outcomes, the obtaining of valued outcomes should satisfy people. If an organization, therefore, bases its extrinsic rewards (including praise, money, promotions, and any other positively valued extrinsic outcomes) on performance, then performance will be related to satisfaction because of this contingency between performance and extrinsic outcomes. Similarly, if the employee's good performance results in a sense of pride or personal satisfaction (internal rewards), then performance will lead to satisfaction because of the contingency of personal satisfaction on performance.

Of course, all extrinsic rewards are not based on performance. Organizations paying employees an hourly wage or awarding promotions primarily on seniority clearly do not base these rewards on performance. People often give praise or other social rewards even if people are not performing well; therefore, external rewards frequently are not clearly linked to performance, and the strength of relationship between performance and satisfaction due to contingent external rewards is often very weak. Similarly, "intrinsic" personal satisfaction in the form of feelings of achievement or accomplishment are not likely to follow good job performance if the job lacks the five core characteristics of autonomy, skill variety, task identity, task significance, and feedback. In jobs without these characteristics, therefore, there will be little or no relationship between performance and satisfaction. It is easy to see why the relationship between performance and satisfaction is so tenuous. Even if job performance causes job satisfaction, it only does so under certain conditions—conditions that often are not present.

Expectancy theory, while considering performance-to-outcome linkages, actually considers their perception rather than the real linkages to be important in motivation. If performance causes satisfaction as described, however, it is because there is a real link between performance and outcomes, not a perceived one. The motivational approach that focuses on this real link is OBM. This theory, therefore, would explain performance-satisfaction links, except for one thing—it generally is uncomfortable even admitting that internal states such as satisfaction exist!

MOTIVATING ATTENDANCE

In addition to job performance, a second employee behavior that one can consider an organizationally relevant outcome is attendance. Because attending work (or not being absent, to phrase it more negatively) is a behavior, it should also be subject to motivation principles. Compared with performance, fewer studies have explicitly taken a motivation theory and applied it to employees' attendance behaviors, but we can examine the implications of the three motivation theories for understanding, predicting, and controlling attendance.

Expectancy theory would argue that the subjective expectancies that effort will lead to successful attendance and that attendance will lead to valued outcomes should motivate attendance. Furthermore, the alternative behavior is absence, which consists of a wide variety of activities. The main question for expectancy theory should be the value of the expected outcomes if the employee goes to work versus the value of the expected outcomes if he or she does something other than going to work.

In many jobs, absenteeism is punished in one way or another, and so it is primarily when absenteeism is excused that people will stay away from work. Smith (1977) had been doing a satisfaction study among over 3,000 managers in the New York and Chicago offices of a retail company when a severe snow storm hit Chicago. Chicago of course had more absenteeism on that day than New York did, but something else happened that was very interesting. The correlation between attendance and satisfaction among the Chicago managers (r over 0.40) was much stronger than among the New York managers (r under 0.10). We often find small correlations between satisfaction and attendance (or absenteeism), but this particular pattern of correlations can be interpreted using expectancy theory. The correlation in Chicago tells us that managers who had reason to expect that they would not feel good about attending work (low P→O expectancy where the performance, or P, is attendance) were less likely to attend than managers with a reason to have a higher P→O expectancy. This did not happen in New York, because the managers there had no "excuse" for not attending. That is, those with low satisfaction might have wanted to stay home, but because there was no valid excuse, they did not. In fact, without a valid excuse, both satisfied and dissatisfied managers in New York might have expected to receive negatively valued outcomes if they stayed home! There was almost no correlation, therefore, between satisfaction and absenteeism in New York on that day.

As with motivation to perform the job, the perceived contingency (a cognitive state) of a valued outcome on the behavior is the explanation for the behavior. In short, if the person expects more positively valued outcomes and less negatively valued outcomes from going to work than from doing something else, he or she is motivated more to go to work than to do those other things, and attendance is the most likely behavior.

One can also use OBM to understand motivation to attend, however, and a number of studies have actually shown that it indeed can help understand and even control employee attendance. By the 1970s several field experiments had been conducted showing that tangible rewards (reinforcers) for attendance could reduce absenteeism over periods of months and even years (Kempen, 1982). In a recent example, hourly paid counselors of a residential treatment facility for emotionally impaired adolescents became eligible for a small lottery within their workgroup if their group's absences were low (Brown & Redmon, 1989). Two members of the work-group were winners in this lottery if the group's absences were between one and six hours for a two-week period, and one member was chosen if the group's absences were between seven and sixteen hours. Winners received their choice of four hours paid leave, twenty dollars, four movie passes, or paid lunch with the supervisor. As a result, absenteeism was reduced for these employees for the duration of the study (several weeks).

The basic principle is that attendance should improve if good atten-dance behaviors are followed by more reinforcing stimuli than if poor at-tendance behaviors are. The specifics might vary, such as the exact rein-forcement schedule or the precise definitions of adequate and inadequate behavior.

Goal setting studies of attendance are rarely undertaken, unlike OBM efforts at improving attendance. It is clear, however, how the goal-setting theory would predict attendance. Goal setting theory would argue that peo-ple could set specific goals regarding how frequently they want to show up for work during a given period, say one month. It seems intuitively unlikely that the people do this on a routine basis. We might speculate that people are typically working on a nonspecific goal regarding attendance, such as trying to get to work as much as possible (similar to "do your best"). Perhaps when there are specific attendance programs (such as an OBM program re-inforcing good attendance), goal-setting theory would then argue that the program works best when people are adopting the study's criteria as their own specific, high goals.

Job Satisfaction and Attendance

Job satisfaction, an individually valued outcome, has long been suspected as a factor in motivating attendance (e.g., model by Steers & Rhodes, 1978), although the relationship between satisfaction and attendance is not overly strong. Although OBM has shown a clear ability to predict and control at-tendance, job satisfaction is the kind of internal cognitive and affective state that OBM has often tried to avoid in explaining causes of behavior. Between the two more cognitive theories, expectancy theory probably has the more ready explanation of this relationship between satisfaction and attendance. If the expectancy (instrumentality) that going to work will result in valued outcomes is less than the expected value of some other activity (e.g., sleep-ing in, going on a date, going to a baseball game), then the person will en-gage in the other behavior. If job satisfaction is currently low, employees probably have not received valued outcomes from the workplace. In this case, we might expect that valued outcomes will continue to be missing when we go to work. This lowers the expected value of going to work; by comparison, some other behavior has a better chance of having a higher expected value than attendance. The interpretation thus offered for the results of the snowstorm study (Smith, 1977) is an example.

MOTIVATING MEMBERSHIP

An analysis can also be made of the three motivation theories' explanations of employee membership as a behavior.

Expectancy theory would argue that people will maintain their membership in the organization when they believe that membership will lead to more valued outcomes than leaving or "turning over" would. This fits with a labor economics approach, which usually finds that, at the macro or national level, people will be more likely to quit their jobs during times of low unemployment than during times of high unemployment (Hulin, 1991). In times of high unemployment, employees might logically expect that they would have a difficult time getting another job; therefore, the expected value of quitting their current job would be very low.

Other factors should enter into turnover decisions at the individual level, such as individual's preferences for living in a given geographic area, attachments to people in the organization, accumulation of privileges due to seniority, and so forth. Nevertheless, during times of high unemployment, there should be less expectation that a better job could be found—that is, less expectation that quitting will be followed by obtaining a job that provides more valued outcomes than the present job does.

One of the best known models for explaining turnover at the level of the individual explicitly acknowledges that people search for other alternatives and evaluate them in comparison with their current jobs before deciding whether to "turnover" (Mobley, 1977). Expectancy theory models of motivation specifically argue that employees base their choices between alternative behaviors on the expected value of each behavior (e.g., Naylor, Pritchard, & Ilgen, 1980), and this seems to fit quite well with expectancy theory explanations of turnover.

OBM, while explaining absenteeism and performance quite well, has not dealt with membership or its opposite, turnover. Membership or turnover does not seem to be the type of behavior that OBM works with most easily, that is, it is not a brief, time-limited behavior that is repeated in the one setting, identifiable as having been done at a particular time, and having been reinforced afterward. One could argue that people who turnover often have been reinforced (perhaps by a new job with more reinforcing characteristics) for it and, therefore, are likely to do it again soon. This is an unsatisfying description, however, and does not seem likely to apply to many people. The trouble with using OBM to explain turnover is that, if the person takes another job, one can not assume that he or she did it because of experiencing the other job and its reinforcement before taking it.

Alternatively, we could look for reinforcers for keeping one's membership in the organization. Pay increases, promotions, and better job choices in the organization, if these are reinforcing stimuli and if they are based on seniority, would help to explain why people stay in the same organization. Yearly pay raises could be seen as reinforcing remaining for a year, and this seems more consistent with other OBM examples of reinforced work behavior. The behavior is more time-limited and identifiable as having a beginning and especially an end (when the reinforcement occurs).

Researchers have not often used in theory or research goal setting approaches for explaining either absenteeism or turnover, but if they are truly accurate explanations of behavior, they should apply. Although not studied under the goal-setting paradigm, people often talk about goals such as "becoming the head of a major corporation by the time I am 50 years old," or "becoming a senior officer in my company in the next 10 years." Both of these might be related to membership behaviors. If someone is committed to becoming the president of a major corporation by age fifty but is not currently in a major corporation, there seems to be a goal of leaving or terminating membership in the current organization. On the other hand, the second example suggests a goal of keeping membership in the present organization. Do high, specific goals to which people are committed make a difference in membership behavior? It seems that it could, although in these examples a long time might have to pass before we would know.

Job Satisfaction and Membership

Job satisfaction has often been a predictor of turnover or membership (Muchinsky & Tuttle, 1979). It makes intuitive sense that if people are not satisfied with their employment they will try to quit. Of the three theories of motivated behavior I described in this chapter, expectancy theory might have the simplest explanation of this phenomenon, because of its emphasis on cognitive choices of alternative behaviors. If one is dissatisfied with one's current organization, he or she might expect that choosing the behavior of remaining in the organization will result in more dissatisfaction. If there is an alternative that is expected to result in more satisfying outcomes, the employee might quit and take that alternative. Just because one is dissatisfied in the present is not a guarantee that one expects to be dissatisfied in the future. One might expect that there is a career progression to better jobs in the organization in the future. In addition the alternative jobs that are believed to be available if one should quit might not be very good ones; therefore, the relationship between (present) satisfaction and turnover is far from perfect.

CONCLUSIONS

Organizationally valued outcomes include those employee behaviors that organizations and their representatives have usually considered to be important for the effectiveness of the organization. The three most traditional of these are job performance, attendance, and membership. In principle, behaviors can be motivated, and there are three especially prominent motivation theories in organizational psychology: expectancy theory, organizational behavior management or OBM, and goal-setting theory.

Expectancy theory and goal setting both are basically cognitive theories of motivation, because the primary variables that directly cause behaviors are internal cognitive states such as expectations and goals. In contrast, OBM focuses on observable, noncognitive events to explain behavior. All three of these motivation approaches can be used to explain all three organizationally valued behaviors, but organizational psychology theory and research has probably used them more often in conjunction with performance than to explain the absenteeism and turnover. Nevertheless, they also have some utility in explaining these behaviors.

REFERENCES

Brown, N., & Redmon, W. K. (1989). The effects of a group reinforcement contingency on staff use of unscheduled sick leave. *Journal of Organizational Behavior Management, 10,* 3–17.

Colarelli, S. M., & Beehr, T. A. (1993). Selection out: Firings, layoffs, and retirement. In N. Schmitt & W. C. Borman (Eds.), *Personnel selection in organizations.* San Francisco: Jossey-Bass.

Dalton, D. R., Todor, W. D., & Krackhardt, D. M. (1982). Turnover overstated: The functional taxonomy. *Academy of Management Review, 7,* 117–123.

Hackman, J. R., & Oldham, G. R. (1976). Motivation through the design of work: Test of a theory. *Organizational Behavior and Human Performance, 16,* 250–279.

Hackman, J. R., & Oldham, G. R. (1980). *Work redesign.* Reading, MA: Addison-Wesley.

Hulin, C. L. (1991). Adaptation, persistence, and commitment in organizations. In M. D. Dunnette & L. M. Hough (Eds.), *Handbook of industrial and organizational psychology,* Vol. 2 (2nd ed.). (pp. 445–505). Palo Alto, CA: Consulting Psychologists Press.

Kanfer, R. (1990). Motivation theory and industrial and organizational psychology. In M. D. Dunnette and L. M. Hough (Eds.), *Handbook of industrial and organiza-*

tional psychology, Vol. 1 (2nd ed.). (pp. 75–170). Palo Alto, CA: Consulting Psychologists Press.

Kempen, R. W. (1982). Absenteeism and tardiness. In L. W. Frederiksen (Ed.), *Handbook of organizational behavior management* (pp. 365–391). New York: John Wiley & Sons.

Lane, I. M., Mathews, R. C., & Presholdt, P. H. (1988). Determinants of nurses' intentions to leave their profession. *Journal of Organizational Behavior, 9,* 367–372.

Locke, E. A., Latham, G. P., & Erez, M. (1988). The determinants of goal commitment. *Academy of Management Review, 13,* 23–39.

Mobley, W. H. (1977). Intermediate linkages in the relationship between job satisfaction and turnover. *Journal of Applied Psychology, 62,* 237–240.

Muchinsky, P. M., & Tuttle, M. L. (1979). Employee turnover: An empirical and methdological assessment. *Journal of Vocational Behavior, 14,* 43–77.

Naylor, J. C., Pritchard, R. D., & Ilgen, D. R. (1980). *A theory of behavior in organizations.* New York: Academic Press.

O'Hara, K., Johnson, C. M., & Beehr, T. A. (1985). Organizational behavior management in the private sector: A review of empirical research and recommendations for further investigation. *Academy of Management Review, 10,* 848–864.

Ross, L. (1977). The intuitive psychologist and his shortcomings: Distortions in the attribution process. *Advances in Experimental Social Psychology, 10,* 173–220.

Saari, L. M., & Latham, G. P. (1982). Employee reactions to continuous and variable ratio reinforcement schedules involving a monetary incentive. *Journal of Applied Psychology, 67,* 506–508.

Smith, F. J. (1977). Work attitudes as predictors of attendance on a specific day. *Journal of Applied Psychology, 62,* 16–19.

Steers, R. M., & Rhodes, S. R. (1978). Major influences on employee attendance: A process model. *Journal of Applied Psychology, 63,* 391–407.

6

THE NATURE OF
ORGANIZATIONAL GROUPS

In a earlier chapter, I discussed the nature of individuals. Groups also have their own characteristics. It is risky to assume, however, that the nature or characteristics of a group are equivalent to the sums of the characteristics of the individuals making up the group. Sometimes groups will choose to do things (group behavior) that are not what all or even most of the individuals would do if deciding individually.

Groups in organizations have always interested organizational psychologists. One can interpret much of the well-known work in the Hawthorne studies as research on and inferences about groups. One theory of organizations (System Four; Likert, 1961, 1967) argues that effective organizations consist not of individuals or individual positions but function more as groups that are connected through overlapping memberships. If organizational psychology is the social psychology of organizations, groups can encompass nearly all the interesting topics in the field. One of the basic values in organizational psychology is that interpersonal activities are important, and interpersonal activities are certainly basic elements of group life. Furthermore, one might even consider groups to be small organizations themselves—if they have the characteristics of formal organizations (see Chapter 9).

Considering the importance of groups in organizations, it is somewhat distressing that groups cannot be defined precisely and in a manner that all organizational psychologists consider perfectly accurate. The most basic definition of a group is probably that it consists of two or more people who have some relationship with each other. This is a minimal definition to which nearly everyone would like to add something. For our purposes, because we are interested in groups in organizations, we can add that an organizational group is imbedded in a formal organization. That is, it is part of the organization. Not only is an organizational group at least two or more people (who have some relationship to each other), but it also is less than the number of people in the whole organization.

Admittedly, the definition of groups is a bit hazy, and it has been that way for quite some time, judging from well-known definitions of groups over the last few decades (e.g., Cartwright & Zander; 1968; Guzzo & Shea, 1992; McGrath, 1984). Beyond these simple criteria for identifying an organizational group, the definitions of such groups might include the following: Group members interact or potentially will interact; they are aware of each other and of their mutual membership in the group; nonmembers also recognize it and treat it as a group; there is a specialization or differentiation of roles among the members of the group; the members have a common goal; they share some common thinking, such as what behaviors, beliefs, and values are appropriate; and they have a common formal or informal leader. Although the minimum definition of an organizational group is that there be more than one member, that there be less than all members of the organization of which the group is a part, and that the members have some relationship to each other, this is a pretty inclusive definition and might seem too broad at times. Regarding the other possible elements of the definition, there is surely a continuum of being a group—the more of these characteristics a set of people have, the more likely they are a group. It is also easy, however, to identify sets of people within an organization who do *not* seem to have one or more of these "extra" characteristics of groups. Many times when writers define a group more narrowly, I would assert that they are actually studying one *type* of a group. I turn now to types of groups in organizations.

TYPES OF GROUPS

Groups come in many styles, sizes, and shapes, although some are more likely to be in organizations than others are. Some of the most commonly recognized and studied types of groups are described in Table 6.1 on pages 122–123. It presents each set of types as a dichotomy, and this is quite consistent with most of the history of investigating group types. In some cases (obviously group size is one), the apparent dichotomization of a continuous variable does not seem to make much sense, but this is the way that organizational psychologists have often considered groups.

Formality is the essence of organizations, but the distinction between *formal* and *informal* groups is well-known and important for understanding organizations. Organizations often have organization charts. They represent formal positions of individuals in the organization, but by inference one can identify some of the formal groups. A board of directors, for example, is a formal group. If a "staff" is on the chart, that is another formal group; similarly, a department or division is a formal group. Furthermore, because reporting relationships are on organization charts, a supervisor or manager and all immediate subordinates might be on a chart, and they constitute a group. The charts represent the official structure of the organization (see Chapter 9 on "macro" organizational psychology).

The formal groups on an organization chart are supposed to be permanent, but, of course, the chart changes occasionally. A formal group, however, can be temporary. A task force can form to accomplish a certain goal, such as to provide advice to an executive about a certain issue that the organization must resolve in thirty days. In that case, the group is usually formal, because it will have a formal leader and official rules and procedures; but, its life is short, and it will not appear on the organization chart. Such "task forces" can be very useful in organizations.

Informal groups have no official leader, although they often do have a leader or someone who has more influence than others on the group members. They are likely to have rules and procedures, although they are not usually official, public, or even discussed. Although these groups have no official standing in the organization, one should not assume that their activities are either irrelevant or harmful to the organization. Such groups can act in ways that are either organizationally relevant or irrelevant. They can work to help the organization to be successful, their activities can be harmful to the organization's goals, or they may have no impact one way or the other on the organization. In an organization of significant size, however, they are bound to exist.

The existence of formal task forces shows that not all groups last forever, even if they are formal. Informal groups can also be relatively long-lasting or more temporary. The length of a group's life is obviously on a continuum rather than the dichotomy of *permanent versus temporary*. Even the formal, "permanent" groups on an organization's chart may only exist until the chart is changed, and some temporary groups might last for many years. A temporary group can also be quite powerful, for example, when its task is to determine how to downsize the company.

The dichotomy of *small versus large* groups is another example of using a dichotomy when the concept is obviously a continuum. Very small groups have more opportunity for the members to get to know each person more closely; therefore, they should be able to form stronger bonds and cohesiveness. Larger groups seem more likely to splinter into subgroups that might compete against each other for dominance and control of the groups' activities. Most research on groups has focused on small groups, usually with no more than a dozen members and often substantially less than that. We have tended to assume that what we know about these small groups

TABLE 6.1 Common Types of Groups in Organizations

Categorizing Variable	Labels for Groups	Description of Group Types	Comment
Formality	Formal	Formal, explicit (often written) rules about interrelationship among members	Formal groups usually found in structure represented in organizational charts; but widely recognized that informal groups affect behavior in organizations
	Informal	Rules not written and may not often be spoken	
Time	Temporary	Group does not exist over long period of time; the time of its ending is often known	Many formal organizational groups of both types exist; task forces common type of temporary group
	Permanent	Group exists relatively permanently with no known or expected end	
Size	Small	Few group members	Obviously a continuum; a largely neglected dimension of organizational group research, yet seems likely to be important in many ways
	Large	Many group members	
Proximity	Face-to-Face	Members frequently interact face-to-face	Large organizations more likely to have some dispersed groups; greater trust and influence likely to develop in face-to-face groups
	Dispersed	Members rarely or never interact face-to-face	

Composition	Homogeneous	Members all alike on some important dimension, usually biological, demographic, or historical	With increasing diversity apparent in many organizations, heterogeneous groups seem likely to increase in future. Heterogeneity commonly thought to have both advantages and disadvantages for group performance.
	Heterogeneous	Members different from each other	
Belonging/Desiring	Membership	Focal person belongs to the group	Individual's preference is to be influenced by reference group; membership group nevertheless also has effects
	Referent	Focal person identifies with and likes or would like to belong to the group	
Intimacy	Primary	Members are intimate and interact at many levels including close, personal, and emotional	Organizations known as collectivities of secondary groups; primary groups develop there, too, even if they are considered virtually taboo
	Secondary	Members interact at somewhat superficial level and may not care about each other as people	
Organizational Basis	Identity	Membership based on biological, demographic, or historical individual differences	Organizationally harmful conflicts can arise when people's identity groups influence treatment of and behaviors by people more than their organizational groups do
	Organizational	Membership based solely on occupying a specific position in organization	

applies to all groups. Group size, however, seems likely to be an important variable for understanding the functioning of groups; therefore, we are probably ignorant of some of the ways that groups in organizations actually operate.

Groups can also be categorized according to whether they operate on a *face-to-face* or *dispersed* level spatially and geographically. This proximity might be a continuum, because groups can meet more or less often face-to-face and work on group activities and influence each other from a distance when they are not immediately present. Most studies of groups have focused on groups that function in each other's presence, but some organizations must rely on both types of groups—especially larger and geographically dispersed organizations. As Table 6.1 indicates, social psychological principles of interpersonal influence would suggest that the face-to-face groups are likely to have greater influence over their members.

There has been speculation about the wisdom of an organization comprising groups that are either *homogeneous or heterogeneous*. The question has usually been, should members of a group be alike in terms of skills and abilities or in terms of personalities, but one could easily address the homogeneity question on other dimensions as well. Guzzo and Shea (1992) come to three conclusions regarding this issue. First, having all group members be high in ability, a specific form of homogeneity, appears to result in highly effective group performance—not too surprising, except that the performance might even be higher than one would expect from the average ability of the group members. This specific type of homogeneity, therefore, appears to be beneficial for group performance. Second, heterogeneous groups, especially in regard to personality and demography might be related to turnover; people tend to leave groups that are heterogeneous. Third, the types of members in the group probably affect the patterns and nature of interactions among group members. On the whole, people seem to like being in homogeneous groups better.

Although there have been theories arguing for heterogeneity over homogeneity, there is little consistent evidence that heterogeneity has a clear advantage. Still, if an organization were to form certain types of groups, say a project team to work on developing a new product, and if such development required expert knowledge about manufacturing principles, accounting and finance and scientific research and development, such skills might only be available in the form of several different people in combination in the organization. Thus, skill heterogeneity would seem necessary. By chance, the set of employees with these necessary skills might also happen to vary demographically or in personality. Compared to some other types of social collectivities, the workplace organization tends to focus heavily on task accomplishment, and heterogeneity would, therefore, seem necessary at times.

There are also groups to which people *belong* and others to which they *desire* to belong. Groups to which people belong are their membership groups, while groups to which they refer for their standards of thinking, feeling, and behavior are reference groups. People look up to reference groups and like belonging to them. They may or may not actually belong to their reference groups. If they do not belong to them they would probably like to belong to them. I worked for a while in a factory in which one hourly employee came to work in a dress shirt and tie every day (and night when on the night shift). He stated that he intended to become a member of the supervisory and management ranks some day. Basically, although his membership group was the rank-and-file production workers, his reference group was management. He used their norms for his own standards of dress (and probably for standards of some less obvious behaviors, feelings, and opinions). He did eventually get promoted into his reference group, by the way!

Of importance here, however, is the fact that we do not necessarily draw our own standards from our membership groups; we draw them from our reference groups. When people are not acting like the others in the organizational groups to which they belong, it is sometimes informative to consider the possible effects of groups to which they might like to belong. Of course, someone's membership and reference groups might be the same, that is, people might draw their standards from, look up to, and desire to be in the group in which they actually are members.

Groups can also be classified according to their degree of intimacy—as *primary versus secondary* groups. Members of primary groups are very close or intimate with each other, and care about each other as people (Table 6.1). Members of secondary groups, on the other hand, deal with each other more impersonally. They often care about each other less personally and more as means to reach goals. They have to get information from someone to do their jobs, or they need to get a commitment that someone will attend a meeting at a certain time. In these instances, other people in the group are instrumental in getting one's job done or in reaching one's own goals. Formal organizations are characterized by such instrumental relationships. In fact, primary relationships are almost taboo—consider, for example, the taboo some organizations have regarding office romances (clearly primary relationships). While secondary groups are considered the normal state of affairs in organizations, we would be missing important influences on behavior if we did not acknowledge that groups of people at work can become closer over time. When this happens, they are moving toward becoming a primary group. Regarding some of the other distinctions in Table 6.1, group intimacy is also probably a continuum rather than a true dichotomy.

The final entry in Table 6.1 is the classification of groups regarding their organizational basis. They can be either *organizational or identity* groups. I have been using the term *organizational group* to mean any group existing within an organization, but groups can exist in organizations without being organizational groups in this special use of the term. Alderfer and Smith (1982) refer to any groups that exist only because of people's membership in an organization as organizational groups. People belong to identity groups, on the other hand, before and after they are members of an organization. They are members of identity groups independently of any membership in an organization. Identity groups are often based on variables that psychologists generally think of as individual differences. For example, people can be classified on the basis of their age, sex, race, religion, and ethnicity, and one can consider these groups in some senses. People in organizations, as well as elsewhere, often treat others based on the perceptions that the others are in such categorical groups. Sometimes they see themselves that way as well. In addition to these individual difference variables, sometimes the members of an identity group have in common only some experiences in their personal history. They might all be veterans of the Vietnam War, for example, or have attended Woodstock.

Such "groups" can be influential in the way people treat each other, just as organizational group membership can be. In most formal organizations, the identity groups are not officially supposed to influence organization members as much as their organization groups are, but they sometimes do. Again, we might not understand the functioning or malfunctioning of organizations if we did not recognize both of these types of groups.

Overall, there are clearly many types of groups existing within formal organizations, and we rarely notice all of them in a large organization. Specific group theories, research, and practices often focus only on a very small number of these types of groups; more is unknown about their effects on their members and organizations as a whole than is known about other types of groups. Groups have proved very difficult to study rigorously, but we do know some things about how they seem to operate. The types of groups I have outlined here can be reconceptualized as "variables" that vary among groups. It might prove more useful to examine *the extent to which* groups are formal, large, intimate, and heterogeneous, for example, than to consider all groups alike or even to classify a group as belonging entirely on one end of any of the dichotomies in Table 6.1. In studying groups in a laboratory experiment, therefore, researchers would want to create groups with certain levels of these characteristics, and in nonexperimental field studies they should measure the extent to which the groups they find in organizations have these characteristics. By doing this, organizational psychologists can learn about the extent to which these group characteristic variables are important in group functioning. It might turn out that some of them are very important while others have little impact; or, we might find that some of these variables matter for the performance of certain types of group tasks and not for others. It seems likely, however, that at least some of these are important group characteristics for some purposes.

A final note about types of groups concerns the label "team." As with Guzzo and Shea (1992), I use the words *group* and *team* here interchangeably. The word *team* has become popular in recent years, perhaps from notions about successes of Japanese management, but it is not clear yet that there is a concrete distinction between the two types of collectivities. Instead, it often seems as if a well-functioning group, one that is achieving goals, is called a team. The label is probably not the important thing, however. Instead it is the nature of the people, their situation, and their interactions that make them successful. When the word *team* is commonly used, it is often applied to relatively cohesive, motivated, goal-oriented, successful groups. Here these characteristics are group-related variables, any of which can range from strong to weak for any group. I will not provide a special label for groups that are strong on these variables, because to do so would imply that they are something different from groups and would take away from the more important focus on these variables themselves.

TWO MAJOR QUESTIONS ABOUT GROUPS IN ORGANIZATIONS

Two of the major questions that have interested organizational psychologists are (1) how do groups influence their members, and (2) are groups more effective or less effective than individuals. There are some clear and reliable answers to the first question. In fact, we know so much about it that the whole next chapter is devoted to some of the specific ways that organizational groups influence their members. I discuss this generally here first, however. The second question, regarding the effectiveness of groups versus individuals seems to generate about as much disagreement today as it ever did. It is a crucial question for organizations, because their groups are always involved in working on some task, and task effectiveness is important for the organization. But first things first—how do groups affect people at all?

The Influence of Groups on Their Members

It is part of the essence of groups that they influence their members' thoughts, emotions, and behaviors. The main and most obvious influence is to make these actions and reactions more uniform than they would be otherwise. Both formal and informal groups in organizations probably have members who resemble each other for two major reasons: selection and socialization. Some formal organizational groups, such as departments, are relatively homogeneous on some dimensions because the organization's selection processes intentionally insured it. An accounting department as a formal organizational group, for example, is likely to have a lot of members who have college degrees in accounting and who are skilled with numbers. A selection system that hires accountants without these characteristics would probably not be very effective for the organization.

Aside from these intentional selection criteria, people are also often hired based in part on performance-irrelevant criteria. People in charge of hiring, for example, might recruit harder and be biased in favor of graduates from their own alma mater. It is common to find organizations in which many of the professionals "just happen" to come from the same university. In addition, there are well-known and illegal hiring biases regarding race, sex, age, and so forth against which most organizations try to guard (but surely with only partial success). There are, therefore, both intentional and unintentional forces in the organization's selection process that tend to make their formal groups somewhat homogeneous. In addition, people probably select themselves into groups of people whom they resemble, if they are given a choice. People who apply for jobs only in New York City, for example, will end up together. Whatever personal characteristics made them follow this strategy also tended to bring them into a formal organizational group with some other people who possess this characteristic. Thus, both organizational selection processes and self-selection processes can make group members somewhat alike in their emotions (a love of New York) and probably in their thinking and behavior as well.

If selection into formal groups can result in formal members who tend to be alike, then the same is even more likely to occur in informal groups. People are even more likely to self-select themselves into informal groups than into formal groups, and self-selection is especially likely to result in homogeneity among group members. Almost by definition, members of informal groups affiliate with each other because they have something in common, for example an interest in music or in sports.

Because of selection processes, therefore, organizational groups are likely to be somewhat homogeneous to start with, but socialization forces within the group influence members to become even more alike. Hackman (1992) has analyzed these forces at the interpersonal level and notes that there are two kinds of stimuli that people experience in groups that can affect their feelings, thinking, and behaviors: ambient stimuli and discretionary stimuli. One of the most important effects of these types of stimuli is to reduce the variability of group members' actions and reactions, that is, to increase their conformity.

Ambient stimuli are parts of the environment that everyone experiences just because they are members of the group. The potential types of ambient stimuli are endless but might include, for example, the number of people present (and their dress and manners), the arrangement of furniture, elements that are intrinsic to the group's task (including materials and equipment), and so forth. Everyone in the group is exposed about equally to these stimuli or characteristics of the group's situation. Based on the individual's past experience and learning, he or she may interpret these stimuli as signifying that certain behaviors are likely to be appropriate or inappropriate. Graffiti on the walls versus posters taped to the walls versus original framed art work on the walls, for example, might be taken as a sign about the degree to which formality is expected in group members' behaviors. These are ambient stimuli, because everyone in the group is exposed to them. In a meeting room, if all chairs are placed facing a stage and lectern, people usually take this as a cue that those sitting in the chairs are supposed to listen more and the person at the lectern is expected to talk more. Thus, ambient stimuli from within the group can affect the behavior of group members.

In spite of the influence of ambient stimuli on the behaviors of group members, most of us immediately think of discretionary stimuli when searching for effects of group membership on members' behaviors, thoughts, and feelings. Other members, at their own discretion, provide to or withhold from individual group members these stimuli. In the motivation theory, organizational behavior management, (see Chapter 5) discretionary stimuli seem to act as reinforcers or punishers, because they often affect the behavior of the member toward whom they are directed. Thus, organizational group members might provide praise, warnings, or information to selected members at selected times. They might even provide more tangible stimuli, such as job or task assignments, assistance when a group member is overloaded on the job, or letters of recommendation for a new job.

Discretionary stimuli, however, are provided at the discretion of the provider. That is, group members are likely to give "desirable" discretionary stimuli to a group member who is doing something they like and to withhold desirable stimuli or even provide undesirable (punishing) stimuli to a group member doing something they do not like. Group norms are standards of behavior that the group members expect of each other, and the administration of discretionary stimuli is one of the most obvious ways in which norms are enforced. When group members adhere to the group norms, we observe conformity in the group.

In addition to behavior, discretionary and to some extent ambient, stimuli may affect members' thoughts and feelings (Hackman, 1992). These reactions are less observable than behaviors, however, and members might maintain their nonconforming thoughts and feelings more easily than they can keep up their observable nonconforming behaviors. They might succeed more easily, for example, in retaining their beliefs (thoughts) that there is a good opportunity for promotion even though the group does not believe it; and they might keep their feelings or attitudes, such as dissatisfaction with the supervisor, even though the rest of the group argues that the supervisor is very good. Some examples of behaviors in organizations that group membership can influence include the quantity and quality of job performance, volunteering for "extra" assignments, the way people dress, the way they talk (e.g., standard English versus slang or profanity), the degree of intimacy shown, and support versus conflict. Some of these are more important to the individual than others, that is, a group member might not mind dressing to conform to the group but might find it objectionable to alter his or her performance levels by working harder or easier. One can also see that some of these behaviors might be more important to the organization than others are. For example, job performance levels and volunteering for extra work is almost certainly important to the organization's functioning, but the style in which group members talk to each other might not matter to the organization, at least on some jobs. This concept of importance of group conformity to the individual or the organization corresponds to the individual and organizationally valued outcomes that I discussed in previous chapters.

Are Groups More Effective Than Individuals?

The second major question about organizational groups that has interested organizational psychologists is whether groups or individuals are more effective in accomplishing tasks. In the subhead above, I have phrased the question positively for groups, that is, asking specifically whether they are better than individuals. This was done to emphasize some of the underlying inclinations that one can find among many people in organizational psychology. One of the values of the field, that interpersonal interaction is valuable, is consistent with an underlying belief in the value of groups. One can also observe that when research does *not* find that groups are superior to individuals in some ways, we do not always give up the question. Instead, organizational psychologists often begin wondering about moderators or contingencies. That is, the next question of study would be something like, under what conditions are groups superior to individuals? Groups in organizations have been of interest in organizational psychology for a long time, but it is probably safe to say there is no simple answer to the question about which is more effective, groups or individuals. It probably does depend on other things.

Knowledge about the comparison of group and individual effectiveness is important for organizations, because it could inform them about the best ways to organize. They could assign tasks either to individuals or to groups, depending upon which would be more effective. They could have five individuals work separately on a task, or they could have them work to-gether as a group or team. People often have strong opinions about which is better, but the research results do not provide a simple, clear, and consis-tent answer.

In some situations, it seems the answer must be that groups are indeed more effective than individuals. Some tasks require group efforts and can-not be done alone. In a baseball game, the rules require a team or group of nine people. In order for the pitcher to pitch the ball, there must be a catcher who is cooperating with the pitcher. For many tasks in modern work orga-nizations, however, there is a choice. Even if the sheer quantity of work in-volved requires more than one employee to work on it, in many cases they do not really have to work together. Instead, jobs could be designed in which the employees could each work separately, in parallel, each doing a little piece of the work without necessarily seeing, hearing, or interacting with any of the others. In fact, in manufacturing, this has been the tradi-tional way of designing jobs (consider the typical assembly line, for exam-ple). Alternatively, assignments could be given to teams that would do the same work interactively.

If we want to know how group effectiveness compares with individual effectiveness, there are two questions that we must consider first: What do we mean by effectiveness, and what individual(s) should we compare to the group?

Effectiveness is an elusive concept, as one could infer from the two pre-vious, "individual-level" chapters on outcomes to the individual and the organization. Value judgments very much affect effectiveness. The effec-tiveness of a group, to some people, might mean that the group provides emotional support and a pleasant social environment in which to work. For others, it might mean the degree of task accomplishment, the speed of task accomplishment, or the amount or quality of task accomplishment. If tasks are involved in the definition of effectiveness, we might consider that groups in organizations often have multiple tasks to accomplish; therefore, we must wonder which task(s) provide the measure of effectiveness or, if all tasks, then whether all tasks are equally important. In organizations, someone outside the group (a higher-level manager or group) assigns some tasks, and the group itself adopts some tasks. Whose tasks should one con-sider in evaluating the task accomplishment of groups? These issues arise at any level in addressing effectiveness, whether one examines individuals' behaviors, groups' behaviors, or the behaviors of the whole organization. Organizational psychology maintains a value that the individual is as im-portant as the organization. At the group level, this translates to meaning that we are concerned with both task accomplishment and the well-being of the members of the group. When the word *effectiveness* is used, we more often think of task accomplishment (sometimes using the word *productivity*) than of group well-being, but group liking or satisfaction are also often used as indicators of effectiveness.

Aside from the meaning of the word *effectiveness* for groups, the other basic question involves the comparison of the group's effectiveness with some measure of individual effectiveness. Who is the appropriate individual for comparison? In experimental research, we would usually want a comparison or control condition that is as comparable as possible to the experimental condition except for the independent variable of interest. Here we are concerned with the variable group (versus individual). It seems that the people working under group conditions and those working as individuals should be alike in temperament, ability, and so forth.

In a traditional research design, we could randomly assign people to work on tasks either in groups or as individuals, and, therefore, all the characteristics of the people in the two conditions should be the same, on the average. Traditionally, then, we could compare the performance, effectiveness, or productivity of the group with the average of the people working as individuals. This would have the effect of comparing group performance with the performance of the group's average member. Many such experiments have been done in the laboratory, and the researchers usually find that the group does as well or better than the average individual.

Many times in organizations, however, we are concerned with costs and benefits. We would not want to pay five people, working as a group, to do a task, if we could pay one person a fifth of that amount of money who would do the task just as well. In fact, the group needs to perform five times as well just to break even with the individual on a cost-benefit basis. This shows how we must refine our research questions about groups to make sure that they are the exact ones appropriate to organizational psychology.

Guzzo and Shea (1992) have identified three historical schools of thought regarding the effectiveness of groups versus individuals: Bion's group-as-a whole perspective, Homans' subsystem approach to groups, and the Tavistock sociotechnical theory. These three approaches to groups focus on different aspects of the group situation, and each of them suggests reasons why individuals and groups might perform tasks differently.

Bion's perspective is psychoanalytically oriented, using some Freudian concepts, especially the idea of the unconscious. While the unconscious was originally conceived as an individual level variable, Bion argued that groups also have an unconscious. In this view, the group should be treated as a whole; it is not a set of individuals whose interactions need to be understood separately. Many group theorists now agree with this, although the idea of a group unconscious is not generally accepted. In explaining why people seem to act differently, in part conforming, Bion proposed the group unconscious to control the members. Three notable group unconscious motives or forces were supposed to be flight-fight, dependency, and pairing. Fighting with others, often with other groups, or fleeing from them (literally or figuratively) is a motive aimed at preserving the group. It is protective. The same analysis applies to subgroups. Fighting within a group might be an effort to save the subgroup from other subgroups. In the kinds of organizational groups we think of today, fighting need not mean physical fighting but any form of conflict with people outside the group. Vying against other groups in the organization for higher budgets or other scarce resources would represent this type of activity.

Dependency occurs when people in a group act helpless or dependent, usually upon the group's leader (Guzzo & Shea, 1992). Rather than take actions on their own, the group waits for instructions from elsewhere. This often means the group waits for the leader to tell them what to do. In modern organizations, temporary groups like task forces or committees often form on the basis that the people in the group have some skills, knowledge, and efforts to contribute to the group's task. Too much dependency in such groups would seem to be unnecessary and would prevent the group from being as effective as it could be. In a traditional, bureaucratic, rigidly and hierarchically structured organization, power is greater at higher levels of the hierarchy. In a permanent part (group) of such organizations, such as a department, there can be a tendency for people not to take initiative unless they are formally at the top of the group (the manager or supervisor), and the hierarchical organizational structure probably encourages this dependent behavior in its subgroups.

Pairing refers to attraction among group members (Guzzo & Shea, 1992). While the word *pairing* implies two people, the ultimate reflection of the pairing phenomenon in modern organizational groups is probably embodied in the concept of group cohesiveness. In cohesive groups, the members of the group like being in the group, help each other, and stick up for each other to outsiders. Anyone who has been in very many organizational groups can see that they vary on group cohesiveness. Some have more of it than others.

While Bion's concepts of flight-fight, dependency, and pairing seem to be relevant to organizational groups, there seems to be little reason to assume that a group unconscious directs these tendencies, or that a group unconscious even exists, for that matter. Many people are quite aware of these activities in their groups, understand when they are occurring, and at times even try to make them happen. Considering them to be the forces of a group unconscious is consistent with the old idea of a group "mind," that groups have a mind much as individuals do—a largely discredited idea today. One can argue that a group that fights or flees appropriately and, therefore, survives, a group that avoids excessive dependency, and a group in which

pairing leads to cooperative work will be successful, perhaps more successful than individuals working alone might be. If these conditions are not met,
however, the group is less likely to be successful.

Homans' approach focuses on group boundaries and the forces on each
side of such boundaries. There is an invisible boundary between the group
and everything in the group's environment. Indeed, one can observe that
there does seem to be such a boundary. Not everyone is allowed into the
group, as if there is some kind of screening boundary; information and
physical things such as equipment also may or may not be taken into the
group from the outside world, almost as if there is a boundary that it takes
some effort to cross. When things are taken into the group, sometimes they
are changed. For example, information is often interpreted in ways that are
consistent with the group's orientation or previous beliefs. If the leadership
tells a department that it must change its ways, (e.g., increase efforts, take
on new customers or tasks, or change to a more participative management
style), the members of this formal organizational group might interpret this
as meaning that they need to pretend they will do these things for a while
until things blow over and the top management will have a new faddish directive for them to follow.

Homans argued that groups have two important subsystems, one related to external conditions and one to internal group conditions. External
conditions such as the physical aspects of the environment, the technology
available in the environment that might be relevant to the group's tasks, and
the nature of the social milieu in which the group is embedded, affects what
happens in the group (Guzzo & Shea, 1992). One expects these external conditions especially to affect the group's work on its tasks. Homans' concern
with the internal environment, on the other hand, focused on the socioemotional aspects of the group—how well they like, get along with, and
work with each other. There is some relationship between the external influences and the internal processes occurring in the groups; they do not
exist independently of each other. There is a hint in Homan's theory of the
old and well-known categories of task and socioemotional group processes
(e.g., Benne & Sheats, 1948), because the external environment is primarily
related to the group's task performance, while the internal environment
refers to the socioemotional relations within the group (Guzzo & Shea,
1992). The task and socioemotional (or instrumental and expressive) group
processes are prominent in many theories and applications of organizational groups. Obviously, if the external and internal environments orient
toward productivity, the group might be successful, perhaps more successful at the task than the individuals would have been alone; if not, individuals might have done better.

Of the three schools of thought regarding groups that Guzzo and Shea
(1992) cite, the sociotechnical approach has had the most clear and direct

association specifically with organizational psychology and organizational groups. Primarily, the Tavistock Institute in England developed and promoted the sociotechnical approach. Homans had noted the technical aspects of the group's environment, but technology is one of the two major concerns of the Tavistock researchers. The other, which the name of the approach indicates, is the social system or the socioemotional processes that occur within the group. In a classic case study in British coal mines, teams of coal miners were generally cohesive; the study concluded that they needed cohesiveness to feel that they would receive the help and support they needed in this dangerous work. New coal mining technology, however required workers to be physically more separate from each other as they worked, and this worked against the socioemotional processes that had been important to the workers.

Because new technology has the potential to improve task effectiveness, it is usually desirable to use it. Breaking groups apart, however, can adversely affect satisfaction, morale, and criteria important to the organization such as absenteeism and turnover—if not task performance or productivity, as well. The key, in the sociotechnical approach, is to find ways to optimize both the technology and social systems simultaneously. The most frequent approach to doing this seems to be the creation and use of autonomous work groups (Guzzo & Shea, 1992). Autonomous work groups are given a task, usually a complex one, and are allowed some degree of autonomy about how they organize themselves, the degree to which they interact with each other, and so forth in getting the task(s) accomplished. The details of how they go about the work are left up to them.

One can infer that the sociotechnical approach to groups assumes that groups will usually be superior to individuals, because (1) it emphasizes the necessity of considering the social system in making any change in technology, and (2) it recommends autonomous groups as a means for solving the sociotechnical interface problems. Because the groups are autonomous, however, in principle they actually can restructure the work in any way they want—and this would include structuring it so that the group members work individually! The flavor of the approach, however, seems to favor groups over individuals.

Overall, the simple research on the effectiveness of groups versus individuals indicates that groups are often more effective than their average individual, but that groups are usually less effective than the best individual in the group. This is very important, because if an organization wants the job done best, it might simply have the best person do it (assuming it knows who that person is). If we think about this, it seems obvious that it must depend on the kind of task being done. Some tasks cannot be done by one person. Most of the studies have been laboratory experiments, and the tasks have usually been very cognitive oriented, such as brainstorming or problem solving of some sort. It makes sense in these situations that a single individual could rival the group's performance. If, however, it were a physical task requiring heavy lifting or using multiple hands at once, more than one person might be quite useful. McGrath (1991) noted that the groups we usually study (in the laboratory) are not very much like groups we actually encounter in real life. Organizational groups in real life are loosely coupled with other groups in the environment, not isolated like laboratory groups usually are; they are purposive, not artificial situations in which people have no serious, common, long-term goals; they often have multiple tasks instead of only one; and they have to deal with temporal problems because they usually exist over a longer period of time than laboratory groups do.

If groups, at least on certain tasks in the laboratory, tend not to perform as well as the best individual could do, why is this? All the group would have to do is have its best individual solve the problem or perform the task, and then let the group take credit for it. The means of doing as well as the best individual member is readily available to the group, because the best individual is one of the group's members! Guzzo and Shea (1992) call this loss of effectiveness by groups "process loss." This implies that energy of the group was siphoned off the task and onto the internal group processes, such as interpersonal politeness inherent in taking turns talking; making people comfortable; resolving, avoiding, or confronting conflicts; and some members not working hard because they are offended or simply feel that the others should be able to do the task without their help. Process loss means that the group members' knowledge, skills, and efforts combined in less than the optimal way.

Process gain, however, is also theoretically possible. That is, a group might be able to solve problems or complete tasks better than the best member if they are able in some way to work harder or smarter, or if their creativity is enhanced by hearing each other's ideas. When this happens, a group "synergy" has developed (Hackman, 1992).

A possible example of such process gain (or "assembly bonus effect") can be seen in a study of students working in groups in which their grades are partially dependent upon the success of the group (Michaelsen, Watson, & Black, 1989). In many classes over a five-year period, 222 groups of three to eight students each took courses in organizational behavior. The tasks were taking the normal tests for the course, and most of the learning and some of the testing occurred in the groups. The courses were heavily experiential, with the groups spending a large portion of class time (and out-of-class time as well) learning and practicing group problem-solving. There was some reason, therefore, to believe that these groups might be quite good at group processes involved in problem solving. Instead of having a control group of people acting as individuals, the researchers used a "within subjects" design in which people served as their own controls. First, they took the test as individuals, then they immediately took it as groups. Each group had to come up with exam answers by concensus. Every group outperformed its average member on the course exam, and 97 percent of them outperformed their best member, thus showing a process gain. There were some potential problems with the study (e.g., taking the test first as individuals gave the students a chance to think and practice the task before doing it as a group). There were some strengths also, compared with many of the past laboratory experiments on group versus individual effectiveness. Strengths especially include the facts that the task was meaningful, with grades being dependent upon it, and the groups existed for a longer duration (a semester) than most laboratory groups. It does suggest, though, that groups that have good group process skills might show a process gain in being more effective than their best member would be alone at cognitive work. This is a rare finding in favor of groups, but it shows the way that organizational psychologists can study the issue of group effectiveness.

WHAT MAKES GROUPS EFFECTIVE?

If groups are not always or even not usually more effective than individuals, it is still important to know about them, for two reasons. First, some work almost necessarily needs to be done in groups, as I noted earlier, and, therefore, the more we know about groups the better organizations can manage their work. Second, in the large number of task situations for which organizations have a choice in assigning work either to groups or to individuals, it would help to know whether there are situations, defined by type of tasks or other variables, in which groups might be more effective than individuals. Thus, knowledge about what makes groups effective would help organizations use groups in the most effective manner. Fortunately, research on groups and organizations has provided some insight into factors making them more effective: the design of the group's jobs or tasks, the interdependence of the group's members on each other, the composition of the group, the context in which the group is embedded in the organization, and the group's process. One must consider all of these to understand the effectiveness of groups and to avoid narrow approaches that will miss something important. There has probably been a tendency in some past theory and research to focus on only one of these themes. Group process, for example, has been a favorite topic for study.

Figure 6.1 on page 138, from Campion, Medsker, and Higgs (1993) illustrates the nature of organizational tasks and workgroups that are likely

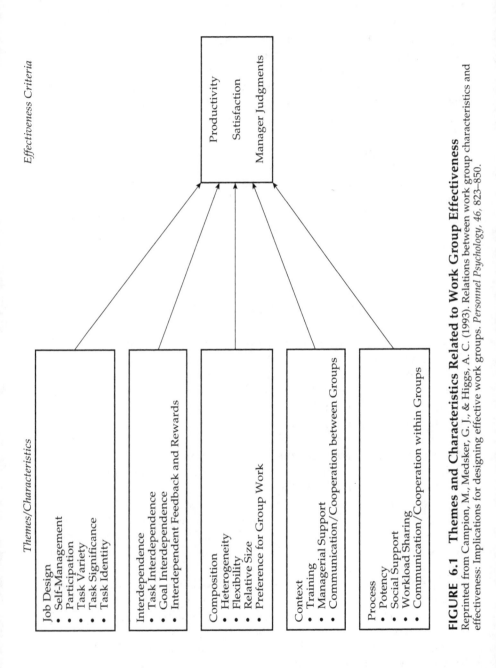

FIGURE 6.1 Themes and Characteristics Related to Work Group Effectiveness

Reprinted from Campion, M., Medsker, G. J., & Higgs, A. C. (1993). Relations between work group characteristics and effectiveness: Implications for designing effective work groups. *Personnel Psychology, 46,* 823–850.

to make them more effective. Effectiveness is defined in terms of both individual outcomes (satisfaction) and organizational outcomes (productivity and manager judgments about group effectiveness). Job design consists largely of the core characteristics of intrinsically motivating jobs or tasks. I noted in an earlier chapter that jobs with autonomy, variety, task signficance, task identity, and feedback tend to motivate individuals. The same principles seem to hold for people working in groups. In groups, the terms *self-management* and *participation* commonly describe autonomy at the group level. Figure 6.1 places feedback under interdependence rather than job design probably on the grounds that feedback usually comes from other people or groups. Groups are likely to be more effective if their tasks have these core characteristics for the same reasons individuals are: They will be motivated to work harder on these types of "enriched" jobs.

Interdependence among the group's members includes task interdependence, in which group members must work with each other to get the whole task accomplished. This is probably what we think of first when we consider interdependence. It also includes goal interdependence; individuals in the group must share a clearly defined group goal, and if they have some separate subgoals, these should be clearly linked to the group's overall goal for the group to be more effective. Interdependence of feedback or rewards means that each member's rewards must be linked in some way to the effectiveness of the group as a whole—the group's overall task or goal rather than or in addition to an individual's subtask or goal.

Composition refers to the make-up of the group. Some of these characteristics were subsumed under the earlier discussion of types of groups, most notably heterogeneity and relative size. As I noted earlier, heterogeneity seems to have some benefit when organizational outcomes are the effectiveness criteria and when the task requires creativity or problem solving. When individual outcomes such as satisfaction are considered or when other types of tasks are necessary, however, it is not clear whether this would be the case. Flexibility among group members, so that they can do each other's jobs, should make groups more effective. Regarding group size, the smallest number of people that can handle the task is usually the best size. Small groups keep people interested and require them to be responsible for part of the group's work, which should increase motivation and satisfaction; in addition, in organizational groups, using more people in the group than is necessary would seem to waste organizational resources. Campion et al. (1993) note that little research has been conducted specifically on the extent to which people in the group prefer group versus individual work, but it seems likely that some people simply prefer to work in groups and others prefer working as individuals. This would seem very important in their behavior in groups, which would affect group effectiveness.

The organizational context of the group is also likely to be important in the effectiveness of groups. Group training has often meant training in group processes, or interactions, but Campion et al. (1993) point out that technical or skill training is likely to be important for groups just as it is for individuals to complete their tasks. Additionally, although there has been little research on support of upper level management for group work, it seems likely that this is a necessity if group work is to be used, encouraged, and rewarded. Another aspect of an organizational group's context, although not present in most laboratory experiments on groups, is that there must be communication and cooperation between interdependent groups in the organization.

The final theme in Figure 6.1 is one of the oldest themes in group research and theory: Internal group process is important to group effectiveness. In the history of group research and theory, McGrath's (1964) input-process-output model is probably the dominant way of thinking about groups and effectiveness (Campion et al., 1993; Guzzo & Shea, 1992). In this way of thinking, the nature of the people composing the groups (their skills, personalities, demographic characteristics, etc.) influence group processes (leadership, communication, and other influence processes), and these group processes directly affect group effectiveness or outputs. This shows that group processes have historically been thought to be extremely important, because they directly change the level of group effectiveness. As I noted earlier, however, most of the research has been done in the laboratory, and this may reduce or eliminate some important effects that occur in ongoing organizational groups due to the organizational context.

Nevertheless, Campion et al. (1993) point to four group processes that they propose to affect group effectiveness. Potency is the group's belief that it can succeed, kind of a team spirit that might be similar to self-efficacy of individuals. Self-efficacy is an individual's belief that he or she has the general capability to succeed at important tasks and is in control of success or failure at them (Bandura, 1986; Hellervik, Hazucha, & Schneider, 1992). A second group process, social support, occurs when group members try to help each other and interact with each other in a positive, enthusiastic, or encouraging way. Workload sharing occurs when members are motivated to work hard and do their share because others in the group can identify their own part. Thus, the fact that group members will know about each other's efforts and accomplishments should motivate them to work hard. Finally, just as communication and cooperation between groups is important (as a part of group context), they are important within a group as well, if the group is to be effective.

Overall, if we wish a group to be as effective as possible, it is important to consider the elements of Figure 6.1. Campion et al. (1993) have done a nonexperimental field study of this model, among the mostly female employees of a large financial services company. They surveyed a random sample of five employees and the manager from each of eighty permanent, formal, organizational groups that averaged about fifteen members each. They each performed interdependent clerical tasks for one of five geographical units of the company. As expected, at least some characteristics within all five categories of group variables in Figure 6.1 were correlated with the individual and organizational effectiveness outcomes. The correlations were generally only medium to weak in strength, however (most of the statistically significant correlations did not exceed 0.30). Furthermore, it was interesting that, for at least one variable, the direction of the relationship (the sign of the correlation) was probably in the direction opposite from expectations. Group size was positively related to all three measures of effectiveness, indicating that larger groups tended to be more effective. This is one of the few studies to simultaneously examine real-life organizational groups, a large number of contextual variables, and multiple types of effectiveness. The results encourage the belief that paying close attention to the group variables in Figure 6.1 probably is important if we want organizational groups to be effective.

CONCLUSIONS

Organizational psychology's historical interest in groups is consistent with the value that interpersonal activities in organizations are important. It is difficult to come up with accurate, general statements about groups, their nature, their effectiveness, and their processes, however, because the nature of groups and their contexts vary considerably.

A major issue for organizations is the effectiveness of groups. Because organizational leaders often have some discretion about how to organize work, the issue is often the relative effectiveness of groups versus individuals. Most research has shown that groups are probably at least as effective as their average member would be but are not usually as effective as their best member would be. Most of this research has occurred in the laboratory with artificial groups instead of with actual organizational groups. Furthermore, the nature of the tasks investigated has been relatively limited, with an emphasis on cognitive tasks, such as creative problem solving. This casts doubt on the relevance of much of the research for the wide variety of organizational groups and tasks.

In organizational groups, context is likely to be important. That is, the group is not isolated but is embedded in some type of context partly supplied by the organization itself and partly by the larger environment. Although many laboratory group experiments have ignored this, many of the organizational psychology approaches to groups, for example in Homan's external subsystem, Tavistock's emphasis on technology, and Campion's context and job design features of groups, recognize this. Campion (1993) has offered a relatively complete listing of factors to consider when working with organizational groups to determine their effectiveness or to make them more effective. His five categories of variables are job design, interdependence among members of the group, composition of the group, external group context, and internal group processes. Past work has focused more on process than on the other categories of variables, but organizational psychology has been looking at many of these other variables in recent years.

Overall, two main questions about groups have repeatedly surfaced in the context of organizational psychology: Are groups more or less effective than individuals, and how do group members interact with and influence each other? This chapter has dealt more with the first question than the second. The next chapter focuses more on the second question. In general, group members influence each other through the use of ambient and discretionary stimuli, which cue and reinforce behaviors, attitudes, and thinking of other group members.

REFERENCES

Alderfer, C. P., & Smith, K. K. (1982). Studying intergroup relations imbedded in organizations. *Administrative Science Quarterly, 27,* 35–65.

Bandura, A. (1986). *Social foundations of thought and action: A social cognitive theory.* Englewood Cliffs, NJ: Prentice-Hall.

Benne, K. D., & Sheats, P. (1948). Functional roles of group members. *Journal of Social Issues, 4,* 41–49.

Campion, M., Medsker, G. J., & Higgs, A. C. (1993). Relations between work group characteristics and effectiveness: Implications for designing effect work groups. *Personnel Psychology, 46,* 823–850.

Cartwright, D., & Zander, A. (1968). Groups and group membership: Introduction. In D. Cartwright & A. Zander (Eds.), *Group dynamics* (3rd ed.) (pp. 45–62). New York: Harper & Row.

Guzzo, R. A., & Shea, G. P. (1992). Group performance and intergroup relations in organizations. In M. D. Dunnette & L. M. Hough (Eds.), *Handbook of industrial and organizational psychology,* Vol. 3 (2nd ed.) (pp. 269–313). Palo Alto, CA: Consulting Psychologists Press.

Hackman, J. R. (1992). Group influences on individuals in organizations. In M. D. Dunnette & L. M. Hough (Eds.), *Handbook of industrial and organizational psychology,* Vol. 3 (2nd ed.) (pp. 199–267). Palo Alto, CA: Consulting Psychologists Press.

Hellervik, L. W., Hazucha, J. F., & Schneider, R. J. (1992). Behavior change: Models, methods, and a review of evidence. In M. D. Dunnette & L. M. Hough (Eds.), *Handbook of industrial and organizational psychology,* Vol. 3 (2nd ed.) (pp. 823–895). Palo Alto, CA: Consulting Psychologists Press.

Likert, R. (1961). *New patterns of management*. New York: McGraw-Hill.

Likert, R. (1967). *The human organization*. New York: McGraw-Hill.

McGrath, J. E. (1964). *Social psychology: A brief introduction*. New York: Holt, Rinehart, & Winston.

McGrath, J. E. (1984). *Groups: Interaction and performance*. Englewood Cliffs, NJ: Prentice-Hall.

McGrath, J. E. (1991). Time, interaction, and performance (TIP): A theory of groups. *Small Group Rsearch, 22*, 147–174.

Michaelsen, L. K., Watson, W. E., & Black, R. H. (1989). A realistic test of individual versus group consensus decision making. *Journal of Applied Psychology, 74*, 834–839.

7

INTRAGROUP INTERACTIONS: LEADERSHIP AND INTRAGROUP COMMUNICATION

Chapter 6 raised the two major questions about groups: are groups more effective than individuals and how do groups affect their members? There I discussed effectiveness of groups and briefly noted that groups affect their members through ambient and discretionary stimuli. In this chapter, we will examine in more detail how groups affect their members; there are volumes of studies and theories about this, often under the rubric of group process, which one can consider intragroup interactions. Interpersonal influence is the crux of many observations about group work, and that influence often seems to lead to some form of conformity of group members with norms, expectations, or just with the behaviors of other group members.

Groupthink, or a drive to achieve consensus of opinion among group members that is so strong it can lead them to distort perceptions of reality and exercise poor judgment (Janis, 1968), would seem to be an extreme example of conformity due to group processes. In early writings about groupthink, many of the examples offered to illustrate groupthink were political groups making decisions that were risky and that turned out badly. In addition to groupthink, risky shift is another group decision-making phenomenon that was first observed a few decades ago. It, too, implied that groups had a tendency to make decisions that were risky—in this case, decisions that were more risky than the average individual in the group would make if acting alone (Brown, 1965). In hindsight, and after a good deal of further research and consideration, however, it is not clear that groups really do tend to make riskier decisions than individuals make (Whyte, 1989). Because of the well-known early work on these topics, however, we often run across the belief that groups prefer risk. Because this belief is probably erroneous, I will not dwell on group processes that might lead to risky group decisions. Instead, this chapter examines three types of interpersonal processes that seem particularly important for organizational groups: leadership, interpersonal perception, and communication.

LEADERSHIP

The essence of leadership is interpersonal influence. Leaders have an effect on their parts of the organization because they influence people around them to act in certain ways.

Researchers have studied leadership in various ways, especially (1) how people emerge from a pack of equals to become leaders and (2) how some leaders seem to be more effective than others. Regarding these two topics, most of the leadership research in organizational psychology has examined the effectiveness rather than emergence of leadership. The field has also focused on formal rather than informal leaders. That is, organizations have designated people in certain positions as being leaders (usually giving them titles such as supervisors, managers, or executives), and organizational psychology studies of leadership have usually examined these people and their subordinates. Most of our research on leadership could accurately be considered studies of supervision, because they examine how people supervise their immediate subordinates. There is, however, a concept of executive leadership, which focuses on the effects of someone who is at the very top of a larger organization and is expected to influence the entire organization rather than just a few immediate subordinates. The recently increasing study of charismatic and transformational leadership has touched on this type of leadership.

The Need for Leadership

A primary question that is probably not asked often enough is, why are leaders or supervisors needed at all? If people know their jobs, and if there is a reward system for motivating them to do the jobs, is it possible that leaders are unnecessary? Some organizations go through periods during which they downsize their leadership personnel (among others). One large manufacturing company I know, after years of the traditional use of foremen as first-line supervisors of production workers, eliminated all foreman positions several years ago. The company is functioning at least as well as ever. This can imply that these leaders were not needed. Obviously, there are cost savings when positions are eliminated, but there might even be other gains for the company as well. According to the job characteristics theory of intrinsic motivation (see Chapter 5), autonomy can induce many employees to become more motivated. There are many other theories that would make the same argument, replacing the term *autonomy* with a theory's own favorite term for it, for example, *participation, empowerment,* and *delegation,* and so forth.

This means that the employees might work harder and make up for less leadership or supervision; and it should also be obvious that a move away from close, direct supervision (or from any supervision at all) is consistent with the organizational psychology value or belief that people have high abilities and are trustworthy. They should be able to do the job themselves.

Still, leaders are probably useful in some situations. The organization that eliminated supervisors was an old, well-established organization with well-developed jobs and experienced people. Even in such a mature organization, however, there still is a need for some leaders, although the number of leaders needed and their best positions in the hierarchy are probably not clear. Why do such organizations need leadership? There are at least five reasons why leadership is necessary even in such organizations: (1) the incompleteness of organizational design, (2) the need for representatives of organizational groups across boundaries, (3) changing environmental conditions, (4) changes that internal organizational processes induce, and (5) the characteristics of the organization's members (Katz & Kahn, 1978).

The formal design of organizations and the accompanying formal job descriptions are never complete. That is, they cannot anticipate all events that will happen on a job. Leaders might be necessary, therefore, to explain, monitor, and enforce the unwritten, complex details necessary for people to perform their work well. If this tends to suggest that supervisors should look over the shoulder of workers and provide close, detailed supervision, however, this would conflict with the basic organizational psychology value or belief that employees tend to have high skills levels and are trustworthy. Even so, newer employees and employees encountering some situations for the first time might need direction from others. Of course, one might argue that they could get this from peers rather than from supervisors.

Regarding the boundary functions of leadership, it is apparent that many times someone is necessary to speak and act for an organizational group or department in dealing with other groups in the organization. Organizational groups are often interdependent in some ways, and they need to coordinate their activities. It would be inefficient if the entire membership of two groups had to get together to coordinate their every action. A designated leader usually has the authority to speak for, act for, and make some decisions for the group. It is possible that the entire group or anyone of its members could do this job quite well, but it is more efficient if the organization consistently designates one person to do it. The same argument would, of course, apply to representing the group to others who are entirely outside the organization.

A third obvious case in which leaders could be useful occurs when there is significant change occurring in the environment outside the organization. From time to time, organizations may have to deal with changes in suppliers, customers, competitors, laws affecting their activities, new inventions, and so forth. Specialized organizational groups might be set up to monitor such changes, but there needs to be some authority to decide whether and how to change the organization itself to remain or become effective in the face of change. While job descriptions and the structure and goals of the organization might reduce the need for leaders during stable times, these very descriptions, structures, and goals might need to change when the environment is unstable. Leaders are the people whose jobs give them the authority to make such changes in the organization itself.

Just as the organization's external environment can change and require effective leadership, the organization's internal environment is also changing or dynamic, even if there is no leader making the internal changes. Different parts of the organization often have somewhat different subgoals or tendencies, and people must negotiate them to avoid conflict that would be harmful to the entire organization and to prevent one part of the organization from getting its way too much at the expense of others. A good example is a potential conflict between production departments and human resource departments (Katz & Kahn, 1978). One goal or tendency of a production department is often efficiency. That is, it may try to make the product in good quantity and quality with as little cost as possible. One of these costs, however, is personnel or people required to make the product. Human resources or personnel departments also are interested in the human side of the organization; part of their function is to keep people in the organization, which can translate to reducing turnover. It would be handy for production departments to be able to pay people very little and to discard people on a moment's notice when fewer people can maintain adequate production. This would reduce their costs and make them more efficient. Such treatment, however, would make many people less likely to apply for jobs or to stay if hired and, therefore, would make the human resource department's job more difficult. Such conflicting tendencies can create tension and unhealthy competition within the organization. Furthermore, if one side manages to dominate the other too much, one or the other of the organization's functions will not perform as effectively as it should. Leaders can help to control these unhealthy tensions within the organization by keeping the good of the overall organization in mind and exercising authority toward that end.

The fifth reason for needing leaders in organizations, even in ones that are well-established, is the nature of people and the way they behave in organizations. People are not totally dedicated to the organization above all other interests and at all times. Although they are members of the organization, they have other interests, loyalties, demands on their time, affiliations, and memberships. Even if they are totally committed to the organization at one time in their lives, their situations can change in ways that have nothing to do with the organization. As people are less committed to the effectiveness of the organization, or at least their parts of it, they are less likely to do everything they can to make it function well. Some people, usually leaders, are necessary who will put the organization among the first priorities that they have in life; they will work harder and longer and pay more attention to the organization's effectiveness. They may not do this forever, as that is probably too much to expect from most people. If they wear out as leaders, for whatever reason, then the organization might replace them with new dedicated leaders. People are not solely organizational members at any one time, and they are not members at all times (e.g., they leave the organization for many reasons). But it helps if at least some people in the organization are especially dedicated to it at any one time.

For all these reasons, organizational leaders are necessary, but it is not entirely clear how many leaders are necessary. It may be that organizations emphasize leaders and leadership to a greater extent than is necessary, at least in our culture. Perhaps we like to think great people are responsible for good events and evil people are responsible for evil events, and so we look to the leaders of organizations to explain what is good or bad about the organization.

Leaders' Influence

There are probably many parts to leadership, such as paperwork, planning, and dealing with forces outside the group, but the parts of leadership that have interested organizational psychologists the most are the interpersonal influence processes between leaders and their followers. Based upon Hackman's (1992) approach to influence in intragroup behavior (see Chapter 6), we can look at leadership as the use of ambient and discretionary stimuli by leaders. The most obvious influence processes of leaders involve the presentation of discretionary stimuli to the subordinates in the group. If someone is doing a good job, the leader might present the employee with positive stimuli such as praise, pats on the back, or more formal and tangible organizational rewards. In addition, the leader might ask the subordinate for suggestions about the work, which the employee might experience as a stimulus suggesting that the leader respects the subordinate. When the subordinate is performing poorly, the leader might present more negative or aversive stimuli, or withhold positive stimuli.

Other discretionary stimuli include information. If the employee is performing poorly, the supervisor or other leader might provide advice about techniques for doing the job better. Directions are information also. The supervisor might schedule employees' work and direct them about what their assignments are from time to time. This would be discretionary, because the supervisor provides this information differentially to different employees at different, appropriate times.

Leaders also can use ambient stimuli. They, by their own interpersonal actions and demeanor (e.g., friendliness or distance), can set a group tone or climate to which people react positively or negatively. The leader can make personal changes in the physical environment, such as placing pictures or decorations in the workplace; he or she can also encourage or discourage other group members from affecting ambient stimuli this way. The way the supervisor dresses can emphasize differences or similarities between him- or herself and the subordinates (which might suggest less or more equality between the positions in the group). Organizational psychology has not usually considered leadership explicitly as the provision of discretionary and ambient stimuli by the leader, but it is that nevertheless. In the following, more traditional discussion of major organizational psychology approaches to leadership, readers can identify for themselves how one can interpret a leader's style as one of these types of group stimuli.

Leadership and Followership

If leadership is essentially the way the leader in a group influences the others, we can also consider this process from its other side: followership is just a different view of leadership. We often want to know what a leader is or does that influences the followers, but we instead could try to figure out why followers are influenced by the leader. One way organizational psychologists have considered this is the bases of power the leader has over the followers.

The members of a group who are followers or subordinates might be influenced by a leader for many different reasons, and there are five well-known categories of such reasons for followership: reward power, coercive power, legitimate power, expert power, and referent power (French & Raven, 1959). Obviously, the leader might influence people because he or she can provide rewards that they value, or because the leader can provide punishment, coercion, or outcomes that are aversive to them. Much of the common-sense thinking and some of the research on leadership emphasizes much reward and coercive power, and it is especially easy to see rewards and punishers in terms of discretionary stimuli that are provided based upon whether or not the subordinate is doing what the leader desires.

Legitimate power refers to a different reason why the subordinate is influenced by the leader. In this form of power, the subordinate complies with the leader's influence because the leader, by virtue of position in an organizational hierarchy, has the right to direct those who are in subordinate positions. When someone agrees to join an organization (e.g., takes a job in a company), that new employee is agreeing to follow orders of the supervisor. It is seen as legitimate or right, almost *morally* right, for the person to comply with the supervisor's request, and that is a reason for some followership.

In addition to reward, coercive, and legitimate bases for power, subordinates might comply with the leader's requests because they see the leader as an expert in key elements of the task. Thus, the leader would know what is best because of knowledge and skill in the very task the person is doing, or perhaps because the leader has knowledge of the bigger picture—why things are done this way and how this task fits in with other tasks elsewhere in the organization.

The fifth base of power, referent, means that people can follow the leader because they identify with him or her. The leader may be their friend, but at any rate the leader is someone they look up to and want to be like. They refer to the leader for some of their standards of good behavior. In this case, the subordinates' behaviors are influenced by trying to be like the leader or to do what they think the leader would like them to do.

A clear theme coming through in the literature on the bases of power is that expert and referent powers are the most effective of the five, although the actual research results are not always consistent. The mostly nonexperimental field studies have found that expert and referent powers are usually more strongly and more consistently correlated with important individual and organizational outcomes than the other bases of power are, and that the other bases of power are likely to have little good effect at all (Podsakoff & Schriesheim, 1985). Indeed, the typical criterion in organizational psychology for deciding whether a leader is effective is the response of subordinates. Leadership styles that are related to subordinates' job performance or satisfaction are usually considered effective. For example, expert and referent powers are especially related to subordinate's satisfaction with the supervisor (an individual outcome) and to the organizational outcomes of absenteeism and job performance (although less strongly). This goes, however, against some common sense and research in some other areas of psychology that would suggest rewards (reinforcement) and punishments can have strong effects on behavior.

Podsakoff and Schriesheim (1985) have noted, however, several problems with most of the studies on the bases of power. The research designs and methods used in studies comparing all five power bases have usually been nonexperimental field designs. As I noted in an earlier chapter, this suggests that the results might generalize well to the real world, but we are not sure whether there are any causes or effects occurring. If we add to this the fact that the bases of power are usually measured with *perceptions* of followers (i.e., a survey asks subordinates why they are influenced by the leader), we can see that people who like the leader (satisfaction) might answer expert and referent power for many reasons. One reason might be that it is socially desirable to say that someone you like is an expert or that you look up to them. In other words, it is possible that satisfaction caused the ratings of the bases of power instead of the bases of power causing the subordinate to be satisfied, as theory suggests.

For several reasons, Podsakoff and Schriesheim (1985) have argued persuasively that the measures for bases of power in most research have potential problems and errors. One is the use of rank-order rather than rating measures. Instead of asking people to rate each of the five bases of power separately, say on a scale from one to ten, researchers usually ask them to rank-order the five bases of power from the most important to the least important. This is unrealistic, because in fact some of them might actually be equally important as others. Also, it loses information, because it cannot be known from the rankings whether the first-ranked power base is much more important than the others or just a little more important. Finally, when things are ranked (instead of rated on separate scales), their scores are not independent from each other. Thus, if expert power gets ranked first and referent power second, the other three bases of power cannot get a score higher than three. There is a tendency for the five bases of power to be negatively related to each other. Although this is only a tendency, it might affect how they are correlated with other things, such as individual outcomes (e.g., satisfaction) and organizational outcomes (e.g., performance). If a power base is correlated strongly and negatively with an outcome, the others are less likely to be. This would tend to happen not because the concepts behind these bases of power are actually related to the outcomes differently, but just because of the way they were measured—by ranking.

Schriesheim, Hinkin, and Podsakoff (1991) demonstrated some of these problems with rankings in a study of secretaries, research scientists, and restaurant employees. They used both rankings and ratings (e.g., on Likert scales with a range of possible answers) so they could make comparisons. Consistent with expectations, the correlations between the bases of power and outcomes such as satisfaction, commitment, and motivation varied depending on which type of measure of power the researchers used. It is likely that ranking the power bases distorts the results. We probably should take the research results garnered by rankings with a grain of salt until research with better measures can confirm or deny them.

There are still other problems with the measurement of the bases of power in much of the research, but these examples illustrate why we must interpret the research results with caution. None of this, however, means the bases of power could not be important for understanding leadership. They do seem to make sense as a logical set of reasons for why leaders can influence the followers. The problems of research on the bases of power illustrate why it is important to have a basic understanding of research methods to be able to interpret and later to use research results wisely.

What is Leader Effectiveness?

One might infer from the bases-of-power approach to leadership that the amount of influence the leader has on the subordinate defines effectiveness of leadership. Organizational psychologists have usually advocated referent and expert powers on the grounds that they seem to be effective in getting subordinates to comply with the leader's wishes. This is a legitimate way to decide whether leadership is effective, but it is not precisely the way that has usually been used in organizational psychology approaches to leadership. Subordinate reactions of two types are usually indicators that the leader is effective: subordinate's job performance or work effectiveness and subordinate's job satisfaction—in other words, subordinate's reactions to leaders that one can consider organizational outcomes or individual outcomes.

Leader Traits versus Behaviors and Universal versus Contingent Leadership

There are many theories about how to obtain effective leadership, but most of them are in one of four categories, as in Figure 7.1. The top of the figure indicates that some approaches to leadership stress the traits, while others

	Trait	*Behavioral*
Universal	Personality Ability and Skill Physical	Work-oriented Worker-oriented
Contingency	Task Materials and Technology Subordinates	Clarity of Situation Leader's Knowledge Nature of Subordinates

FIGURE 7.1 **Current Approaches to Understanding Effective Leadership**

stress the behaviors of the leaders. That is, in response to our basic question, what makes a good (effective) leader, the answer sometimes describes what the leader is or is like (the traits), and sometimes it describes behaviors (usually behaviors toward the subordinates). Although traits are theoretically related to behaviors, different leadership theories have stressed one over the other, and each research project tends to measure or manipulate only one of these two types of variables—either the traits or behaviors of leaders.

The labels at the side of Figure 7.1 indicate that approaches to leadership can be either universal or contingent. A universal leadership theory holds that the same type of leader trait or behavior is appropriate and effective in all situations; it does not depend upon anything else. A contingent leadership theory, on the other hand, maintains that traits or behaviors that are effective in one situation might be unproductive in another situation; therefore, the nature of effective leadership is contingent on something else, usually something in the leader's situation. The entries in the bottom two cells of the table indicate aspects of the situation on which the effectiveness of the traits or behaviors in the upper part of the table might be contingent. Thus, for example, in the first column, the effectiveness of a leader with a certain set of personality characteristics might depend upon the nature of the subordinates he or she is supervising.

The dominance of each of these four leadership approaches in Figure 7.1 has not been equal historically or presently. Historically, the first popular approach was probably universal trait theory of leadership, followed by universal behavioral theory, then contingent trait theory, and finally contingent behavioral theory. They dominated the thinking of organizational psychologists in roughly this order. None of these approaches is likely to go away, however, and as long as we cannot explain leadership effectiveness perfectly and completely, all four will probably have some place in our thinking.

Currently, the relative dominance of the four approaches to leadership is roughly depicted by the relative size of the rectangles they occupy in Figure 7.1. Thus, universal trait theories are not currently very popular, while behavioral contingency theories are probably the most popular. Overall, leadership approaches emphasizing behaviors of leaders rather than their traits are thought to be more accurate. There is probably an even greater discrepancy between universal and contingency adherents; most organizational psychologists today are probably convinced that the best type of leadership depends upon the nature of the situation, making them contingency theorists.

Consistent with the organizational psychology belief that research has value, the popularity of these leadership approaches among organizational psychologists is largely based upon research and experience in trying to use these theories. It is not always obvious how one can tell if a leader is effective, but researchers must use a concrete, operational, measurable definition. As I noted earlier, organizational psychologists have usually decided that the responses of the subordinates best indicate leader effectiveness. That is, because the leader gets tasks accomplished primarily by getting the subordinates to do them, the subordinates' responses are the best measures of the leader's effectiveness. I have classified in earlier chapters two such types of employee responses as individually and organizationally relevant criteria.

The Universal Trait Approach to Leadership

The reader should infer from the size of its rectangle in Figure 7.1 that universal trait approaches to leadership are not currently very popular in organizational psychology. Traits or characteristics of leaders are usually in one of three categories: personality traits, ability or skill, and physical characteristics. There is especially a great deal of research and theory about personality traits of leaders, and much of it seems aimed at determining what traits differentiate leaders from nonleaders. The reader should note that this is not the same issue as what differentiates effective leaders from ineffective leaders.

Some research, however, has aimed at the effectiveness of leaders with different traits. Some of the traits that might be related to leader effectiveness include high levels of energy, tolerance for stress, integrity, emotional maturity, and self-confidence (Yukl & Van Fleet, 1992). While it is popular among nonpsychologists to think of *effective* leaders as possessing special qualities, authors long ago (e.g., Hollander & Julian, 1969) noted that the research does not support this view very strongly—at least not universally, in all leadership situations.

The Universal Behavioral Approach to Leadership

Organizational psychologists have considered two interpersonal behaviors important for group members and leaders, specifically, to help their groups be effective. They go under various names, but Figure 7.1 labels them work-oriented and worker-oriented behaviors. Work-oriented leader behaviors involve things such as scheduling subordinate's work, giving instructions, checking on their work, and giving feedback. Worker-oriented leader behaviors include, among other things, listening to workers' personal problems, being considerate and sympathetic to them, and generally exhibiting friendly behaviors toward them.

Within organizational psychology, perhaps the most dominant leadership theory of this nature came from the Ohio State Studies, although there are other similar theories. Soon after World War II, researchers at the Ohio State University studied the behaviors of leaders by administering questionnaires to their subordinates, asking the extent to which their supervisors acted in certain ways. Many of these studies were of military leaders and subordinates. Based especially on factor analyses, it appeared that there were at least two leader behaviors (1) that the subordinates consistently described and (2) that were more consistently related to subordinates' responses than others. In these nonexperimental field studies, the worker-related behavior (labeled consideration in the Ohio State approach) tended to be related to the satisfaction of the subordinates, and although less consistently, the work-related behavior (labeled initiating structure) tended to be related to subordinates' job performance (Stogdill, 1974; Yukl & Van Fleet, 1992). While there are no doubt other leadership behaviors that might be useful for leaders to use, versions of these two have dominated the universal behavioral theories of leadership.

The Trait Contingency Approach to Leadership

The cells of Figure 7.1 representing contingency theories of leadership are larger than the cells representing universal approaches to represent the dominance of contingency theories in the thinking of today's organizational psychologists. These theories explicity avoid arguing that the traits of the leader tend to result in good or bad subordinate responses all by themselves. Instead, the leader's traits interact with one or more things in the nature of the situation to determine the subordinate's reactions. Thus, the effects of any specific leader trait on subordinate reactions is contingent upon the situation.

Example characteristics of the situation that might affect the relationship of leader traits with subordinate reactions are the nature of the task the subordinates are doing, the physical materials and technology with which the subordinates work, and the nature of the subordinates themselves. Probably the oldest and best known of these theories is Fiedler's (1965, 1968) least-preferred coworker (LPC) theory. One can credited it with making organizational psychologists pay attention to potential contingencies in leadership effectiveness. The LPC is a variable one measures by asking leaders themselves to describe, using a list of adjectives in a questionnaire, someone with whom they would not like to work—a coworker with whom they least prefer to work. The score on this questionnaire is then taken as a measure of some characteristic of the leader. Leaders with high LPC scores basically say relatively nice things about their least preferred coworker, while leaders with low scores say very negative things about them.

If LPC is a kind of trait of the leader, the question of how this leader trait is related to subordinate outcomes is answered contingently. In this theory, LPC scores of leaders tended to be positively correlated with the performance of subordinates in some situations and negatively correlated with it in other situations. When three characteristics of situations were *either* relatively favorable or unfavorable for the leader to influence subordinates, the theory said that there was a negative relationship between LPC and subordinates' performance. When the three situational characteristics were only moderately favorable for the leader, however, there was a positive relationship between the leader's LPC score and subordinates' performance. The three situational characteristics were related to the subordinates' task (the degree to which it was clear how to do the task), the quality of the interpersonal relations among the subordinates and between the subordinates and the leader, and the formal power the leader had based on position in the organization.

Another trait-contingency approach to leadership is cognitive resource theory (Fiedler & Garcia, 1987). Cognitive resources are primarily skills or abilities (traits) that might be useful for leaders to have in dealing with subordinates. Basic intelligence and technical competence might be such traits, and experience would also be an indication of such skills. Leaders with these traits are likely to make better plans and decisions in the workplace; and, if they direct their subordinates according to these plans, the subordinates should perform well. We should usually find, therefore, a positive correlation between leaders' cognitive resources and subordinates' performance.

The effects of the leaders' cognitive resources on subordinates' responses might be contingent, however, upon the nature of task (e.g., does it really require much intelligence?), the nature of the subordinates (e.g., will they follow the well-laid plans of the leader?), and the amount of stress in the situation (e.g., will stress distract the leader from using his or her best judgment?). One quasi-experimental field study with Airforce personnel has not supported most of the contingency aspects of the theory (Vecchio, 1990), but the theory is relatively new and is likely to be still evolving.

The Behavioral Contingency Approach to Leadership

The behavioral contingency theories argue that the most effective leader behaviors depend on the situation. Figure 7.1 indicates that some of these theories look to the clarity of the situation, the leader's knowledge, and the nature of the subordinates for contingencies that determine what leader behaviors will be most effective.

One such theory is path-goal theory of leadership (e.g., House, 1971). It assumes that motivating subordinates to perform well is a primary task for leaders, and it explicitly uses expectancy theory of motivation to explain how to do this. From the discussion of expectancy theory of motivation (see Chapter 5), we can conclude that leaders will be more effective if they increase their subordinates' expectancies (beliefs that their efforts will lead to performance), instrumentalities (beliefs that their performance will lead to outcomes), and valences (values they place on the outcomes). This makes a good deal of sense, but it is not always clear how to increase these things. All three of these variables are internal states of the subordinates, and therefore, there is no simple, direct way to change these states.

Instead of being able to get "inside" the subordinate to change these variables, the leader can only operate from the outside. Supervisors, therefore, could make it clear how the subordinate should do the work by giving instructions or could increase skills through training. This should help to strengthen the effort-to-performance expectancy of the subordinates, because knowing what to do and having the skills to do it should make them more confident that they will perform well if they try. Path-goal theory is a contingency theory, because it may not always be necessary or helpful for the supervisor to give instructions and training. The subordinate may already have adequate skills and knowledge and, therefore, have a strong effort-to-performance expectancy. Actions by the leader aimed at improving it will have no effect. The most effective leader actions, therefore, are contingent upon the situation.

Similarly, the leader behaviors could try to influence the subordinates' instrumentality beliefs. By praising subordinates (an outcome) for good performance and by telling or showing them that their pay will be based on performance, for example, subordinates may come to believe that their outcomes are based upon performance. Of course, if pay is not based on performance, subordinates may not believe the supervisor's message; or, if they already know that it is, the message may not increase instrumentality beliefs. These leader behaviors, therefore, might be more effective in some situations than in others.

Leaders could also make subordinates more effective by having enough influence to actually change the organization's reward system so that pay really is based on performance, thereby increasing subordinates' instrumentality beliefs. Leaders could also garner more resources for subordinates to work with, potentially increasing their effort-to-performance expectancy (because they should believe that they can perform better if their resources are better). This would fit quite well with path-goal theory, but most of the research and theory so far has focused on the supervisor's interaction directly with subordinates.

A second well-known behavioral contingency theory of leadership is the normative decision theory, which Vroom and his colleagues (e.g., Vroom & Jago, 1988; Vroom & Yetton, 1973) largely developed. It focuses on one aspect of leadership, decision making, and especially on the dimension of participative versus nonparticipative decision making. A common organizational psychology value or belief (see Chapter 1) is that people have high abilities and are trustworthy. If the subordinates have sufficient information and have the organization's welfare at heart, then why not let them make some important decisions? The normative decision theory of leadership gets its name because it very specifically proposes norms about what types of decision making processes *should be* used contingent on the situation. Thus, it argues for a norm in the sense of what is right, best, and recommended for leaders do.

The theory is also consistent with the organizational psychology value regarding interpersonal interaction, because it specifically looks at group as well as individual decisions. In this approach to leadership, the most participative theory entails *group* participation, in which the leader and subordinates share information, interact about an issue or problem, and come to a group consensus about a solution. The second most participative decision making leadership style is one in which the leader consults the group to get the group's opinions about what should be done before making a decision. The third most participative leader style is consulting with the subordinates individually to get their opinions about what to do before making a decision. Because the main difference between this individual consultation and the group consultation (which is considered to be more participative) is whether the leader consults subordinates individually or as a whole group, the normative decision model considers interacting groups to involve inherently more participation than interaction between a supervisor and one subordinate at a time. Of the five styles of leader decision making, the fourth most participative (therefore, also the second most autocratic of the five) is making an autocratic decision after seeking relevant information from the subordinates—but not necessarily seeking their opinions about solutions. Finally, the most autocratic leader style occurs when the leader makes a decision without seeking either information or opinions about solutions from the subordinates (Vroom & Yetton, 1973).

The most appropriate of the five levels of participation in decision making depends on the nature of the situation, and the theory provides rules and even a decision tree to recommend which type of leader behavior is best in several different types of situations. Important features (Vroom & Jago, 1988) of the situation include

1. the degree to which the quality of the decision really is important
2. whether the problem is relatively structured
3. whether the leader has enough information about the problem to make a good decision alone
4. whether subordinates have relevant information
5. whether subordinates acceptance or belief that the decision is good is really necessary to motivate them to carry out the decision
6. whether subordinates are likely to accept an autocratic decision very well

7. whether subordinates share common objectives with the leader and the organization
8. whether the decision needs to be made quickly and the availability of subordinates
9. whether there are conflicts among the subordinates

In general, some of these situational variables are more relevant to the quality of the decision (e.g., being sure to get all possible information is likely to lead to a better-quality decision), and some are related to motivating subordinates to carry out the decision enthusiastically (e.g., to get them to accept the decision as their own and be more motivated to work on it).

Organizational psychologists developed and tested the normative decision model largely by asking managers to describe their decision styles in various types of situations, and it usually appeared valid there. In a recent experiment, however, when Field and House (1990) asked subordinates about the same real situations, decisions, and outcomes (success or failure of the decision) that their manager-leaders were asked, the data from managers, but not that from the subordinates, supported the model. This raises questions about the model, such as whether or not the leaders might be reporting situations, decision styles, and outcomes consistent with their own implicit theory of leadership rather than reporting objective reality. Of course, we should not assume that subordinates' reports are necessarily any more objective than that of the managers; but, if different people see things differently, we are hesitant to accept only reports from one set of people without other evidence that they are really the "correct" ones. Future research on this theory is likely to be interesting and should help solve this problem.

One other leadership theory in the behavioral contingency category has brought an important feature of leadership to the attention of organizational psychologists. Leader-member exchange theory (often labeled LMX theory) explicitly recognizes the fact that leaders do not treat all subordinates alike (e.g., Dansereau, Graen, & Haga, 1975). Other theories of leadership have largely ignored this seemingly obvious idea. The leader might, for example, treat more competent, trustworthy, and better-performing subordinates differently by allowing them more freedom regarding how they want to go about doing their jobs. The theory has suggested that this could even occur with subgroups of subordinates rather than with individuals, so that there might be an in-group and an out-group. It is not, however, clear whether the subordinates really do or should constitute true subgroups (Yukl & Van Fleet, 1992). The theory is still evolving, but no matter how it ends up, making us think more seriously about leaders treating different subordinates differently could be one of its important, lasting contributions.

Social Perception

Perceptions about other people in the workgroup are important determinants of how people treat each other. One can see this in leadership. The LMX theory reminds us, for example, that the way the leader perceives subordinates (e.g., as more or less productive, loyal, and trustworthy) might determine how he or she treats them. The same is true for others in the group. That is, the way that the subordinates see each other (and see the leader) affects the way they treat each other. Social perception, or perceptions of other people, therefore, can influence the interactions or dynamics in the workgroup.

When different people look at somebody's characteristics and behavior, they can perceive them differently, because perception involves some interpretation as well as some more "objective" information. Attribution is a key concept in social perception in organizations in two ways: (1) we attribute characteristics to other people and (2) we attribute causality to the results of their work. Thus, people in workgroups attribute characteristics or traits to each other, such as timidity or boldness, recklessness or caution, congeniality or aloofness, being achievement-oriented or indifferent to achievement, high ability or low ability, and so forth in an endless array of personal traits. What we think they are like then influences what we say to and how we treat others in our workgroup. We might be more likely to take coworkers into our confidence if, for example, we think they are like us in important ways.

The second form of perception that seems relevant in organizational groups is the perception of causality. As with personality traits, causality is an inference or attribution we make about a situation; it cannot be seen directly. Industrial/organizational psychology has frequently studied one set of causal attributions—attributions about the causes of job performance. Social psychologists long ago observed the "fundamental attribution error" (e.g., Ross, 1977). When we see someone's behavior, we can attribute the causation of that behavior to the person, the environment, or some combination of both. We have a common tendency, however, to attribute causation of other people's behavior to the person, probably more than we should.

When the behavior is poor performance, we might attribute the cause to the person (e.g., the person has little skill or did not try hard) rather than to the situation (e.g., there were not enough resources for the person to do the job correctly or the task was too difficult for anyone to do successfully). If the person making this attribution is the supervisor, performance appraisal ratings can be affected. If the cause of poor performance is attributed to the person, for example, a supervisor might be more inclined to give a poor performance rating than if the supervisor believes that poor performance is not the fault of the person. While we might attribute the causes of our own successful performance to our own efforts and abilities and the causes of our own poor performance to the situation to protect our own self-image, we are not as likely to do that for other people. If there is a fundamental error in the perception of other people, it is probably the over-attribution of negative traits to them when they perform poorly. Just as with our own performance, however, sometimes it is simply not the fault of the person.

COMMUNICATION IN WORKGROUPS

The organizational psychology value that interpersonal activities are important (see Chapter 1) obviously implies that communication within workgroups is important. Communication is a very common form of interpersonal interaction and is almost synonymous with it. One person in a group may talk, write, or simply gesture to another in an attempt to communicate ideas, instructions, influence, or even just idle thoughts.

Theory about communication has long held that the process of communication involves a source, a message, a channel, a receiver, some effects, and a feedback loop back to the source (Berlo, 1960). In a communication episode in a workgroup, the source would be one of the people in the group who has a message to communicate to one or more others in the group (the receivers). The channel represents the means or medium through which the message is communicated, for example, face-to-face oral communication. When a source member of the workgroup tells a coworker that he or she needs to cut ahead in line to use the copy machine because of a rush job, the coworker will react by allowing or not allowing this request. The coworker's reaction is an effect of the communication, and the source person experiences it as feedback. This example represents the process of communication. In organizational psychology, the message itself is obviously at least as important as the process through which it is delivered. When we consider communication as a topic, however, we seem to examine the contents of the message much less often than we focus on the process.

Organizational psychologists have probably not studied communication as intensively as they have studied many other organizational phenomena (e.g., leadership and job design). Other social scientists, however, have studied communication intensively; in fact, communication may be seen as a separate discipline all by itself. It is largely from this other discipline that we derive information about communication and apply it to organizations.

Structures of Communication Networks

Within a group, there is a communication structure or network. That is, each person might communicate with certain group members more than others. Figure 7.2 diagrams a hypothetical communication structure. One can identify the groups in the organization by the proximity of the people (circles) to each other. There is a top group of three people, second level groups of (from left to right) four and five people, and bottom level groups of six, four and seven people. In addition, one person near the bottom seems to "belong" to either both or neither of the six- and four-person groups at that level.

One may conceive group structure to be a pattern of relationships among the group members, and there are many types of important relationships among people in organizational groups (communication, status, authority, influence, workflow, friendship) (Brass, 1984; Krackhardt & Porter, 1985). There is some tendency in organizations for types of relationships to go together; that is, where there is a communication relationship between two people there is also likely to be interpersonal influence occurring between them. Research and theory about social networks sometimes blends the relationships together, making it somewhat difficult to talk only about our topic here, communication within (and between) organizational groups.

Looking at the lines of communication within groups, groups can consist of different numbers of people; even in the same organization, every group is not usually the same size. There are different structures of communications within a groups. Everybody can talk to everybody else, as in the four-person group in the upper left of Figure 7.2, or communication patterns can be more restricted—that is, not everybody talks to everybody else.

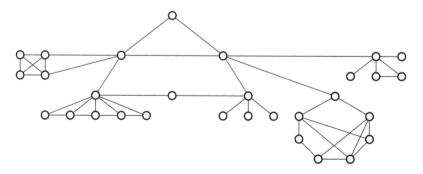

FIGURE 7.2   A Hypothetical Communication Structure in a Small Organization

There are some common principles about such within-group communication structures. For example, people who occupy certain positions in the structure are more likely to be satisfied than others. Those who are more "central" are the group members who are in contact directly with a larger percentage of the people in the group (e.g., Bonacich, 1987; Freeman, 1979; Friedkin, 1991). They tend to be more satisfied than the others are. Those who are more "peripheral," or are more on the edge of the group in the sense that they communicate directly with fewer people (there are fewer lines in the drawing connected to them), tend to be less satisfied than the others. Furthermore, groups in which more people are in contact with each other (e.g., at the extreme, the lower right group in Figure 7.2) tend to have greater average satisfaction than other groups.

In addition to satisfaction, group morale, or other attitudes, organizational psychologists have been interested in the effects of such communication structures on group performance effectiveness. The results, however, have often been confusing and ambiguous. There is a general belief that factors such as the nature of the task and the nature of the other relationships among the group members might influence the group's effectiveness at accomplishing its organizational tasks. For example, Leavitt (1951) suspected long ago that, for tasks requiring complex analysis and decision making, the more "decentralized" networks with more channels (such as the group in the lower-right of Figure 7.2) might be more effective. On the other hand, for fairly simple, straightforward tasks, groups with more centralized communication structures (such as the four-person group in the middle of the bottom of the figure) might more quickly accomplish the task.

Intergroup relations are the topic of the next chapter, but Figure 7.2 shows that organizational groups are usually not totally connected with each other. Instead, it is as if parts of the groups are connected, as the lines between only one or two members of different groups depict. This indicates that, in the drawing, only one person or a few people in each group usually communicates with people in any given second group.

CONCLUSIONS

Consistent with the organizational psychology value placed on interpersonal behavior, intragroup interactions have been a long-term interest area in the field. The interactions of people within their workgroups are the essence of organizational groups. Such interactions by group members usually aim at influencing each other. One set of such interactions usually concerns formal roles in organizational groups. One group member in organizational groups is usually the leader (or supervisor, manager, chair, director, etc.). Interactions involving influence attempts by this person are usually part of leadership. In principle, it may be possible even for an organizational group to function without a formal leader, but leaders usually perform certain functions, such as representing the group to outsiders and taking care of unexpected situations. For that matter, just by being more dedicated to the organization and group than others the leader can be useful—by catching potential problems and correcting them before they cause trouble. In principle, nearly all the leader's responsibilities can probably be taken care of by someone who is not formally designated as a supervisor, but in practice, a formal group leader is usually named in organizations.

Anyone in the group, including the leader, can use discretionary and ambient stimuli to influence group members. One could argue that the implementation of some formal organizational policies are simply the institutionalization of such stimuli. It is easiest to see this in the case of discretionary stimuli such as promotion systems providing advancement only for people who are productive. This is a group-level phenomenon when the supervisor of the group is asked to participate in deciding who gets promoted—because the leader is a member of the group. The organization can also formalize some ambient stimuli. For example, a department (a formal organization group) dress code requiring business attire might set the tone for formality and dignity in the group.

The reactions of a leader's followers, either task performance or satisfaction usually defines the leader's effectiveness. By this way of thinking, the leader is certainly dependent upon the subordinates, and so it is important to know why they would be influenced or allow themselves to be influenced by the leader. Even though organizational psychologists interested in leadership have not always clearly recognized it, it seems obvious that the so-called bases of power are intimately linked to a leader's effectiveness, thus making "followership" and leadership two sides of the same coin.

Organizational psychologists have probably not given interpersonal perception as much attention as it deserves. It seems likely that the way people in organizational groups treat each other is closely linked to the way they perceive each other. There has been little study of the perceptions of leaders' about the causes of good and bad job performance of their subordinates, but perception is probably important in work groups in more ways than that. We tend to attribute characteristics to people sometimes based on only a little information. Then our attributions about them can affect the way we interact with them. There is probably much more happening in organizational groups due to these perceptions than most of us understand at present. Communication within groups is usually based in part on interpersonal perceptions. Communication and social perceptions are basic characteristics of intragroup interactions. We need more research before we will understand clearly what their impact is on organizational groups, but we have made a start.

REFERENCES

Berlo, D. D. (1960). *The process of communication: An introduction to theory and practice.* New York: Holt, Rinehart, & Winston.

Bonacich, P. (1987). Power and centrality: A family of measures. *American Journal of Sociology, 92,* 1170–1182.

Brass, D. J. (1984). Being in the right place: A structural analysis of individual influence in an organization. *Administrative Science Quarterly, 29,* 518–539.

Brown, R. (1965). *Social psychology.* New York: The Free Press.

Dansereau, F., Jr., Graen, G., & Haga, W. J. (1975). A vertical dyad linkage approach to leadership within formal organizations: A longitudinal investigation of the role making process. *Organizational Behavior and Human Performance, 13,* 46–78.

Fiedler, F. E. (1965). Engineer the job to fit the manager. *Harvard Business Review, 43,* 115–122.

Fiedler, F. E. (1968). Personality and situational determinants of leadership effectiveness. In D. Cartwright & A. Zander (Eds.), *Group dynamics: Research and theory* (pp. 362–380).

Fiedler, F. E., & Garcia, J. E. (1987). *New approaches to effective leadership: Cognitive resources and organizational performance.* New York: Wiley.

Field, R. H. G., & House, R. J. (1990). A test of the Vroom-Yetton model using manager and subordinate reports. *Journal of Applied Psychology, 75,* 362–366.

Freeman, L. (1979). Centrality in social networks. *Social Networks, 1,* 215–240.

French, J. R. P. Jr., & Raven, B. H. (1959). The bases of social power. In D. Cartwright (Ed.), *Studies in social power* (pp. 150–167). Ann Arbor, MI: Institute for Social Research.

Friedkin, N. E. (1991). Theortical foundations for centrality measures. *American Journal of Sociology, 96,* 1478–1504.

Hackman, J. R. (1992). Group influences on individuals in organizations. In M. D. Dunnette & L. M. Hough (Eds.), *Handbook of industrial and organizational psychology,* Vol. 3 (2nd ed.) (pp. 199–267). Palo Alto, CA: Consulting Psychologists Press.

Hollander, E. P., & Julian, J. W. (1969). Contemporary trends in the analysis of the leadership process. *Psychological Bulletin, 71,* 387–397.

House, R. J. (1971). A path-goal theory of leader effectiveness. *Administrative Science Quarterly, 16,* 321–339.

Janis, I. L. (1968). *Victims of groupthink.* Boston: Houghton, Mifflin.

Katz, D., & Kahn, R. L. (1978). *The social psychology of organizations* (2nd ed.): New York: John Wiley & Sons.

Krackhardt, D., & Porter, L. W. (1985). When friends leave: A structural analysis of the relationship between turnover and stayers' attitudes. *Administrative Science Quarterly, 30,* 242–261.

Leavitt, H. J. (1951). Some effects of certain communication patterns on group performance. *Journal of Abnormal and Social Psychology, 46,* 38–50.

Podsakoff, P. M., & Schriesheim, C. A. (1985). Field studies of French and Raven's bases of power: Critique, reanalysis, and suggestions for future research. *Psychological Bulletin, 97,* 387–411.

Ross, L. D. (1977). The intuitive psychologist and his shortcomings: Distortions in the attribution process. In L. Berkowitz, (Ed.) *Advances in experimental social psychology 10.* New York: Academic Press.

Schriesheim, C. A., Hinkin, T. R., & Podsakoff, P. M. (1991). Can ipsative and single-item measures produce erroneous results in field studies of French and Raven's (1959) five bases of power? An empirical investigation. *Journal of Applied Psychology, 76,* 106–114.

Stogdill, R. M. (1974). *Handbook of leadership.* New York: Free Press.

Vecchio, R. P. (1990). Theoretical and empirical examination of cognitive resource theory. *Journal of Applied Psychology, 75,* 141–147.

Vroom, V. H., & Jago, A. G. (1988). *The new leadership: Managing participation in organizations.* Englewood Cliffs, NJ: Prentice-Hall.

Vroom, V. H., & Yetton, P. W. (1973). *Leadership and decision making.* Pittsburgh: University of Pittsburgh Press.

Whyte, G. (1989). Groupthink reconsidered. *Academy of Management Review, 14,* 40–56.

Yukl, G., & Van Fleet, D. D. (1992). Theory and research on leadership in organizations. In M. D. Dunnette & L. M. Hough (Eds.), *Handbook of industrial and organizational psychology,* Vol. 3, (2nd ed.) (pp. 147–197). Palo Alto CA: Consulting Psychologists Press.

8

RELATIONS AMONG
ORGANIZATIONAL GROUPS

Organizational psychologists extend the value they place on interpersonal activities to intergroup activities. Interactions between organizational groups have been the subject of a great deal of interest in organizational psychology. Not only do individuals in organizations have to interact with each other, but groups also must interact with other groups in the organization. They can do so in mutually beneficial ways, ways that promote the organization's overall goals, or ways that promote one group's goals over the other's. Although Chapter 6 noted that there are a great many types of organizational groups, interactions between formal groups have been the subject of more literature in organizational psychology than interactions between other types of groups. Any theorizing or empirical research about the classic management principle of coordination, for example, is usually focusing on coordination of activities between two or more formal organizational groups.

The word *organization* implies some harmony among its parts; otherwise, it would be disorganization. For the most part, organizational groups that come into contact with each other (not all groups in a large organization even have any contact) interact harmoniously. We have paid much less attention to this commonly found harmonious intergroup activity than to problems between groups, however, probably because intergroup problems are more interesting than intergroup harmony.

In addition to interdependent action, groups also can be responsible for constraints on each other and can be in actual conflict (e.g., Brett & Rognes, 1986). An example of a constraint placed on an organizational group because of its interface with another group would be a production department (group) not being able to produce more than 10,000 items per month because the procurement and purchasing department (another group) cannot buy enough materials and supplies for them to produce any more than that. Intergroup conflict usually means that two or more groups who depend on each other disagree about how each is supposed to behave. Of the three group interface issues (interdependent action, constraints, and conflict), organizational psychologists have spent the most time and effort working on conflict. This is probably because it is the interface issue that is both the most interesting and the biggest problem in organizations.

SPECIALIZATION AND COORDINATION

Because of their size, very small organizations often have few formal groups within them. A very small organization might even act as a single group, which performs all functions for the organization. As organizations become larger, however, they tend to develop specialties within them. A single person might perform these specialties if the organization is still rather small. For example, an organization might hire a bookkeeper who specializes in nothing but accounting and keeping records on everything in the organization. As organizations become even bigger, however, eventually they usually have more than one person performing each function, and these people are in a group under a single supervisor forming a formal group within the organization.

We can consider some generic organizational functions to be production, production support, maintenance of the organization as a human system, adaptation, and management (e.g., Katz & Kahn, 1978). Formal groups tend to form roughly around these functions. Thus, we might find production departments that produce the main product or provide the main service that defines the industry classification in which the organization is (e.g., meat packing departments of a company in a meat packing industry). Production support groups might include departments that purchase raw materials and ship out the finished product (purchasing and shipping departments). A personnel or human resources department often performs the maintenance function. This formal group is responsible for maintaining the human organization through such activities as recruiting, selection, and training. As you might expect, it is the one in which psychologists have shown the most interest, because expertise about people comes into play the most here. Organizations periodically must adapt to changes in their environments (e.g., changes in consumer demands and preferences, new technology), and some groups or departments might specialize in research about the necessary changes and development of new products or ways of doing things. Finally, of course, there is usually a management group overseeing all of the others.

Because these different groups tend to focus on getting different parts of the organization's work done, it is not surprising if they operate somewhat differently, independently, and in need of coordination. Even within the production division of the organization, there are often subgroups or departments. In an automobile plant, for example, there might be a painting department in addition to one or more assembly departments. The output from one department often becomes the input or materials with which the other department will work. Thus, one department might be dependent upon the other in this way. Some means of coordination are necessary to prevent problems in one department from becoming a problem for the next one. In short, specialization often leads to problems of coordination; therefore, it is common for formal organizational groups to come into conflict with each other.

Because specialization of function often leads to a need for coordination, there are many ways of coordinating the different groups' work. Chapter 7 mentioned that different groups in a network may be tied to each other only loosely. That is, there might be only one or a few points of contact that normally occur. Only one or a few individuals in each group have direct contact with others, and this infrequency of contact can be a block to effective coordination between the groups. In an ordinary hierarchically structured organization, the responsibility for coordination traditionally is seen as the responsibility of someone higher in the organization. Figure 8.1 illustrates this. Each supervisor and all direct subordinates might be considered an organizational group, and the responsibility for coordinating their efforts falls to the next highest supervisor in the hierarchy. Thus, the responsiblity for coordinating the activities of groups 1 and 2 belongs to the person occupying position A, and the responsibility for coordinating the efforts of groups 3 and 4 belongs to the person occupying the top spot, B.

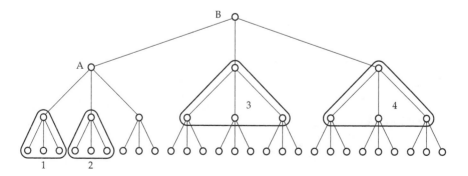

FIGURE 8.1   Traditional Hierarchical Responsibility for the Coordination of the Work of Interdependent Groups

The matter of *how* to coordinate their efforts is often left to the supervisor who is responsible. A traditional way built into the system, however, is for that person to use the authority and power formally built into his or her position and *order* the supervisors below to do their work in some specific way that the upper level supervisor believes will lead to better coordination of the work.

There are other ways to use the formal organizational structure to promote coordination between formal organizational groups or departments. They do not usually rely upon the power of the higher level positions in the hierarchy, however. Some of them involve specific roles in a communication network. Figure 7.3 illustrates this. It is reproduced with some new notations as Figure 8.2.

Position A in Figure 8.2 illustrates the traditional use of the hierarchy to direct and coordinate the work of those below (in this case, those below are illustrated as individuals rather than groups). One alternative to that traditional method is position B, a liaison position. The person occupying position B is in direct contact with two groups, in this case, with the formal leaders of two groups. A liaison person might, alternatively, be in contact with multiple members of each group. It is important in the illustration that the liaison role is neither higher nor lower than the groups whose work it helps to coordinate. If it were higher, it would imply that the person in this role has formal power over the two groups; in this case, it would not be very different from a higher level supervisor and would probably work very much like the traditional, hierarchical way of coordinating the groups below. If it were lower, it might have so little status, respect, influence, and power that the two groups would pay little attention to the person's efforts to coordinate their activities.

The liaison person passes information between groups and uses personal (rather than formal) powers of persuasion to get them to coordinate

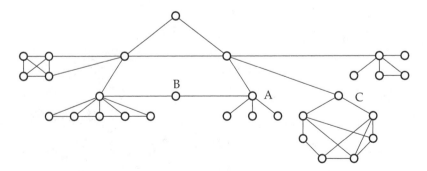

FIGURE 8.2 Formal Means of Coordination between Interdependent Groups

their activities. To be successful, the liaison person must have the respect of each group; this type of respect, however, is more a characteristic of the person rather than the position. The two groups must be willing to listen to and be influenced by the liaison person. Therefore, not only is the creation of the formal position important, but it is just as important *who* is occupying the position. In traditional, formal, bureaucratic types of organizational hierarchies, the nature of the specific person occupying a position should not matter very much; instead, it is the formal authority and duties of the position that matter. The successful use of liaison roles often incorporates some characteristics of the person that are outside the formal hierarchy.

Positions A and C illustrate another important type of position affecting coordination. They are positions that can act as gatekeepers. Anyone who is in a position to receive and send all communications between the group and any other groups can perform the gatekeeper function. One can identify the other gatekeeping positions in Figure 8.2 by looking closely. A gatekeeper allows some pieces of information but not others to pass between groups; therefore, he or she can either help or hinder intergroup coordination. By preventing irrelevant information from passing between groups, information overload might be avoided; this will help the group avoid wasting time on unimportant things. By passing important information to the people who need to have it in a timely manner, the gatekeeper improves coordination between the groups. If the gatekeeper blocks important information about other groups, however, coordination will almost certainly suffer.

Two other formal ways of improving understanding and coordination among groups are (1) to use a specific form of job rotation and (2) to physically relocate one or more members from each group. If people are periodically rotated from one group to another, members of both groups should understand better what the functions of the other group are and have better communications with the other group. Their experience with the functions of the other group should lead them to know how to coordinate their work better with that group. Furthermore, because they have worked with the people in the other group, it is easier for them to make contact and communicate directly with them when necessary. It is usually easier to deal with somebody one knows personally than with a person one has never met.

Similar results might occur by relocating one or more members of each group so that they are physically close to the other group. Frequent contact with members of the other group might make for better communication and understanding—and, therefore, coordination. Of course, this will work better for some types of jobs than for others. For office work in which one's own work can largely be contained within one's own office, it might work better than for production work, for example, in which the employee would have to remain at a given spot on the assembly line. A professor of one discipline could move to a floor of a building in which there are primarily professors of another discipline (group) and still accomplish the job fairly well. Such a location, however, would almost certainly lead to more be-tween-group contacts for this person. When a department meeting is held (within only one discipline), his or her presence means that there will be some understanding of the other discipline at the meeting, and this might help between-group coordination when decisions are made.

In nearly all of the ways of inducing better coordination among groups via the use of formal structures, organizational psychology has an implicit assumption: that increased contact and communication between the groups will lead to better coordination. This assumption, however, is not a neces-sary part of the use of the traditional hierarchical way of coordinating groups. In that case, the person in the hierarchical position above the two groups gathers the information and uses it without necessarily passing it on to the groups themselves. Such hierarchically structured organizations often use a phrase to describe the way it decides whether or not to pass informa-tion to subordinates: Information is provided on a need-to-know basis. This usually means that people are given the least information possible. While the other extreme of providing all possible information to every person in the organization is probably unnecessary and might lead to information overload, the need-to-know approach is often too restrictive for the effec-tiveness of the average organization and might lead to reduced coordina-tion. For some reason, it seems as if the need-to-know approach inevitably fails to provide some information that would help people to do their jobs better.

Throughout the history of organizational psychology, it seems that there has been a preference for investigating coordination and conflict res-olution techniques that increase communication between and information received by the groups themselves. Perhaps this is consistent with two of the organizational psychology values I noted in the first chapter: a prefer-ence for interpersonal interaction and a belief that people have high abili-ties and are trustworthy. After all, communication is a form of interaction, and having people work on their own coordination implies that they have the ability to coordinate their work and that they can be trusted to do so.

CAUSES OF INTERGROUP CONFLICT

Aside from lack of coordination, groups in organizations can also be in states of downright conflict. Most of the theory and research about coordi-nation concern formal groups in the organization, but conflicts can occur be-tween almost any kinds of organizational groups, not just those that the ones who design the organization formally recognized and explicitly formed.

Many of the conflicts between formal groups originate in the process of dividing scarce resources among the groups (e.g., Salancik & Pfeffer, 1974). Organizations typically have only a limited amount of money or other resources that can be budgeted among the different departments, divisions, and other formal groups. A group obtaining more to meet its goals, therefore, might mean that another group receives less to meet its goals. Once we recognize this, we should not be surprised by conflict in organizations. Instead, it is probably inevitable. To try to get rid of all intergroup conflicts within an organization is probably fruitless. In any case, all conflicts might not be bad. Sometimes they might help us to consider new alternatives and to see that there are other points of view.

Some person or group representing the authority of the whole organization is usually required to resolve such conflicts about scarce resources. In an organization in which this comes down to budget allocations, conflicts over budgets often occur annually and are among the most intense conflicts occurring each year. These conflicts are lessened when an organization is enjoying good economic times, that is when the overall budget is expanding, and they are probably worst when the organization is contracting. In the former case, the issue is who is going to benefit most from the good times, while in the latter case, it might be a matter of who survives at all.

While conflict between formal organizational groups over scarce resources is an obvious source of intergroup conflict and has been studied quite a bit, it seems likely that there are other potential sources of conflict that have received less attention. Organizational psychologists might do well to consider more seriously conflict between groups other than ones the organization formally designates and to consider conflict that may have its source in things other than competition for scarce resources. As I noted in Chapter 6, groups that those in charge of the organization do not intentionally form can form around many different issues. One type of these, identity groups, can comprise people who share a common identity because of their earlier history; that is, biological and demographic similarity or common past experiences might bring people together.

Managers who all received their MBAs from the same prestigious university (a common historical experience for them) might form an identifiable group in an organization. Furthermore, if they are dominant in the organization, they might form an in-group, while other managers are part of an out-group. These managers might even be in a variety of formal departments so that this informal group cuts across many formal groups. Conflicts between identity groups could be simply interpersonal, that is, they do not like or respect each other very much. This, in turn, can lead to serious organizational problems if the members of the two groups have to work together and coordinate their efforts.

Often, conflict between such informal groups can begin in part as a conflict over scarce resources, but it is not always very clearly so. If the two groups compete for promotions, for example, this can be seen as a competition over scarce resources. In this case, promotions are the resource, and they are scarce for most organizations once people get into middle management, because of the pyramid shape of most organizations. Aside from formal promotions, controlling the policies and directions of the company are often important to managers, and conflict can occur between identity groups over this. The resource here is power and influence, whether formal or informal. Many managers desire such influence, and it usually is scarce.

Even though many instances of such nonformal group conflicts may be conflict over scarce resources, some instances of intergroup conflict between them might be harder to conceptualize that way. Some sources of intergroup conflict may be personal rather than organizational. Even if only by mere chance, it is likely that there will be instances in which the make-up of the groups' members is a source of conflict. If they met as people outside the organization, they still would be in conflict; they simply do not like each other. In this case, the cause is not due to anything in the organization. Sometimes people can be so flexible that they can still work together to achieve organizational goals, perhaps out of a feeling of obligation and duty. There may be no notable problem for the organization. While in their organizational roles or jobs, they are expected to act in a certain way toward each other, and they do it. In such cases, some professions might be concerned about the situation and desire to work on the problem. Perhaps a clinical psychologist might be willing to do individual or group therapy (if the people themselves ask). Because it is a personal or interpersonal problem rather than an organizational one, however, the organizational psychologist would usually not be concerned. This is an instance illustrating one of the differences in different fields of psychology.

Of course, it is also quite possible that interpersonal conflicts between groups also damage the functioning of the organization. The problem between people in the two groups might lead to lack of coordination, for example, simply because they avoid each other when they need to be communicating. In such cases, the organizational psychologist would try to help, not by doing psychotherapy, but by taking one or more approaches to improving communication and coordination. The goal is not necessarily to get them to like each other, but to get them to work effectively.

AN ORGANIZATIONAL INTERGROUP THEORY

In some ways, knowledge about both group and intergroup processes in organizations may have come more from practice than from research as traditionally and narrowly defined in psychology. That is, much of the literature has come from people who are actively engaged in trying to change group, or in this case, intergroup relations, attitudes, and behaviors. Sometimes by simply reporting their impressions based upon consulting cases, and sometimes by incorporating elements of traditional research into their practically oriented activities, a literature has evolved about intergroup relations in organizations. Although there is no single dominant intergroup theory, one of the leading writers and theorists in the specific area of intergroup relations in organizations is Alderfer (e.g., Alderfer, 1971, 1986; Alderfer & Smith, 1982).

Research Methods in Intergroup Theory

Perhaps as a result of this emphasis on application in the intergroup area of organizational psychology, the research methods used tend to be different from those most used and recommended elsewhere in the field. Many organizational psychologists in other topic areas would judge some of the methods experts use (e.g., participant observation, reports of what has been learned from consulting cases, researchers' and group participants' observations made in a less standard form than is usually recommended in classical research) in intergroup theory as providing only weak evidence on causality and generalizability—the two main aims of organizational psychology research (see Chapter 2).

Perhaps because of a tendency of traditionally oriented researchers to discount research methods frequently used in the intergroup domain, explanation and advocacy of the specific methods used has become part of intergroup theories. Ethnocentrism is an influential concept in intergroup theories, and it plays a part in the research methods that are considered appropriate. Groups tend to be ethnocentric, viewing their own people, culture, values, ideas, and accomplishments as the most important and correct. One then tends to judge other groups by the extent to which they conform with one's own group. An important point for many intergroup theorists is that researchers are members of groups just as much as anybody else is. That is, there are small and large collections of researchers that have common views of the world. Furthermore, due to ethnocentrism, like the views of any other group, researchers' views will affect the way they see the worlds in which other groups live. The important point is that subjects of research are other groups and that the researchers' own group membership causes them to misunderstand, to varying degrees, the world of the subjects. This presents a serious problem, because a researcher's avowed intent is to understand the groups and their world accurately.

An example concerns the common use of questionnaires in traditional, nonexperimental field studies in organizational psychology. The questionnaires, or at least large parts of them, are usually standardized, that is, exactly the same questions are used in many different organizations and in many different groups within an organization. One then assumes that each person answering the questions means the same thing by the answers, regardless of the group to which that person belongs. Intergroup approaches to organizational psychology in particular assume that group members influence the way that each other sees the world and the way that group members will understand, interpret, and respond to specific questions. The assumption, therefore, that the same questionnaire items mean the same thing to all people in an organization, regardless of their group membership, is rejected, making the use of standardized questionnaires suspect. It is easy to see at the extremes, such as cross-cultural research. It is very difficult to translate an organizational psychology questionnaire into another language and to be sure it means exactly the same thing in another culture. Often, the best efforts still end with a questionnaire that has, for example, lower reliability than the original questionnaire used in the culture and language for which it was originally developed (e.g., Kauffman, 1990). Although less extreme, it seems possible that similar effects might occur with different groups in the same organization.

Intergroup theory, therefore, recommends that researchers be more reflective about their own membership in a group of researchers and how that membership might distort their understanding of other groups—namely, the groups they are studying (Alderfer, 1986). By studying one's self (e.g., one's own biases), the researchers might be in a better position to understand and lessen the ways that they misunderstand the behavior and thoughts of the groups they study. This takes on a clinical flavor at times. Alderfer, for example, (1) notes a possible correspondence to the concepts of transference and countertransference as distorting factors in a relationship between a psychotherapist and clients and (2) labels his preferred methods of intergroup research "clinical methods."

Alderfer (1986) also notes that many previous studies of groups in organizations have had a fundamental flaw. They did not take place at the group level and, therefore, have not really examined groups very directly. Instead, sometimes they have investigated phenomena at the individual level. This might occur if we administer personality tests to the members of the group and then assume that the sum or average of their personality scores clearly indicates something about the group. An example concerns the concept of efficacy. Self-efficacy has recently become a popular concept at the individual level of organizational psychology. To study group efficacy, for example, we might ask each group member, "To what extent do you believe that you are capable of performing your tasks well?" If we average the scores of all the members of the group and assume that this is a measure of group efficacy of the entire group, this is not necessarily a measure of group efficacy. The issue at the group level is whether the group as a whole is capable of performing the group's tasks. It would be more appropriate, therefore, to ask the group members, "To what extent do you believe that your group is capable of performing its tasks well?" Summing these items may very well yield a different result that is more meaningful as a group-level variable. Furthermore, one might argue that it would be better still to have the group come to a consensus about its efficacy instead of summing individuals' opinions about it.

Social psychology, which has long had an interest in groups, houses several different approaches to research, most of which I described in Chapter 2 on research methods in organizational psychology. Perhaps the dominant research method in social psychology is the laboratory experiment. As I noted in Chapter 2, the dominant method in organizational psychology is probably nonexperimental field research. Because both social and organizational psychology are interested in multiple group interaction, it is not too surprising that there does not seem to be a single dominant research approach on this topic. I described in detail the laboratory experiment in Chapter 2. Suffice it to repeat here that the social psychologist using this approach tends to study college students in a well-controlled setting and as a result has better evidence about the nature of causality than about generalizability. Nonexperimental field research on organizational groups observes (watches, records, or interviews) naturally occurring events in the field. The advantage here, of course, is better generalizability, but the weakness tends to be evidence about causality.

A third research method, which I discussed as a hybrid research method in Chapter 2, is a set of quasiexperimental methods. This method of studying intergroup relationships attempts to increase our faith in generalizability and not lose too much evidence for causality. Here, the researcher manipulates variables in real-world organizational groups, and as much as possible, controls other variables either "physically" or statistically. As I noted earlier in this chapter, practice and application has had a strong influence on organizational psychology at the intergroup level. Often, in trying to resolve or prevent intergroup problems (implying an intervention or manipulation of one of more variables), researchers have collected some data. Because these instances rarely include very strong controls, they are not true field experiments (one method type in Chapter 2). Instead, they are quasiexperimental designs of varying degrees of rigor.

Alderfer (1986) argues, in his organizational intergroup research, that he favors a fourth kind of research, one I did not cover in Chapter 2. He labels it "clinical methods." The word *clinical* does not refer to clinical psychology topics so much as to the clinical research method in mental and physical health topics. In this method, the researcher takes systematic observations during the course of applied work, usually in cooperation with the group members themselves. Ideally, both the researcher and the group members are explicitly aware of the researcher's own group membership (a member of a research group) as well as the group memberships of the study groups. Group members, not just the researcher, help to study and

interpret their own reactions. Thus, the roles of the researcher and the subjects of study are closely and purposely intertwined.

The biggest difference between this approach and quasiexperimental
field methods is that the researcher, far from trying to remain aloof and,
therefore, objective, purposely becomes involved with the study groups to
understand them better. All researchers, not just intergroup clinical researchers, recognize the potential problems of researchers contaminating
their studies by not being objective. The traditional solution is to minimize
contact between researchers and subjects as much as possible and to stan-
dardize what contact is left. Alderfer's intergroup method's solution is to
acknowledge that there will be some problem and, therefore, to try to be
aware of the researcher's potential contaminating influence, to let it occur,
but to let all parties help to interpret it. Instead of reducing bias, the attempt
is to understand what the effects of the researcher's biases are.

Traditional researchers and intergroup researchers with Alderfer's approach tend to be quite critical of each other. I contend here, however, that
neither is probably as good as they think nor is the other as bad. Many traditional researchers do quite a good job of reducing the possible effects of
their own biases. One would have to examine each study separately to
judge how successful it was at bias reduction; however, all are not equally
successful. Furthermore, once the decision is made to enter the field (and
eliminate laboratory experiments as a method), problems of control of many
biases arise. As Alderfer notes, it probably is impossible to get rid of all of
them. It is not necessary, however, to have a great deal of researcher bias in
the study. As an example, regarding the use of standardized questionnaires
that are written from the researcher's rather than the subjects' point of view,
many traditional organizational psychology researchers are willing to com-
promise the standardization of the questionnaire (1) by writing new questions based on input from preliminary interviews with the people in the
organizational groups and (2) by altering or eliminating questions that
members of a specific organization are likely to misinterpret. For his part,
Alderfer's own research is not the most extreme form of nonstandardized
research we can find on organizational group processes. He does sometimes
use specially tailored questionnaires for everybody in the organization (i.e.,
it is standardized for everyone in a single study), and he does sometimes
use inferential statistics to try to get an overall "objective" summary of the
results of the study (e.g., Alderfer & Smith, 1982).

Embedded Groups

A key context issue of groups in organizations is the nature of their embeddedness in the organization. Organizational groups are embedded in a
surrounding consisting of other groups. Each of these groups has its own

values, culture, and view of the local situation and world at large. These characteristics of the other groups, or taking a perceptual approach, the focal group's perception of them, determines some of the group's attitudes, activities, and expectations. If two groups are in competition and both are embedded within the same organization, the organization provides an important context. For example, if the organization surrounding the groups favors one over another for any reason, then this affects the outcome of the competition. If one group believes that the larger organization favors its competitor, then the group might (1) be resentful and try to leave the situation (turnover) or even take quasi-legal efforts to get justice (e.g. file grievances in some form or other), (2) be demoralized and not compete very hard, or (3) be angry and compete even harder. The point is that the surrounding organization in which the groups are embedded can affect the nature of group interactions. Traditional intergroup research has often overlooked the nature of the embeddedness in organizations and the effects this embeddedness might have. Groups in organizations rarely interact in isolation, and theories, methods, and applications that ignore their organizational context will not be fully successful.

Identity and Organizational Groups

Chapter 6 noted that there are many possible classifications of groups. Alderfer's (1986) intergroup theory provides two broad classes of groups in organizations: organizational groups and identity groups. Given the emphasis on practical treatment of intergroup problems in organizations, Alderfer might have chosen these two broad group classifications because they are often evident in common organizational problems. Organizational groups consist of people who share roughly equivalent organizational positions. Because of this, they tend to see and interpret things similarly to each other.

In the typical hierarchical organization, the positions of members of an organizational group are usually similar in that they are formal groups that are located horizontally or vertically in the organization. Organizations have vertical hierarchical levels, such as bottom-level production workers, first-level supervisors, middle managers, and senior officers. One can conceive the people at any one level as constituting an organizational group. Their hierarchical position means that they have much in common: similar amounts of responsibility, authority, prestige, and so forth. These experiences tend to make people develop a similar world view about what is good, fair, necessary, and important. Horizontally, organizations are usually segmented by functional specialization or division of labor. Thus, an organization may have a personnel department, an accounting department, a marketing department, and one or more production departments.

Membership in one of these formal groups means that, to some extent, people are treated similarly and think similarly. They are not all exactly alike, but their similar positions tend to make them more similar to each other in important ways.

The horizontal and vertical organizational groups are usually semi-stable as long as people are in the organization. The organization may eventually transfer or promote people (or occasionally demote people), but the employees tend to stay in one place for a while before these things happen. There is another type of organizational group, however, that is explicitly temporary. Task forces or committee assignments are examples of formally designated organizational groups that may not last very long and whose members might change more frequently than the typical, stable horizontal and vertical organizational groups. A task force might even form so that its membership purposely includes people from a variety of vertical and horizontal positions in the organization. Such a task force, therefore, would be an organizational group that cuts across many other organizational groups.

Furthermore, the reader should note that the organizational groups are *all* linked together by overlapping membership. At a minimum, each supervisor is a member who links his or her group of subordinates to a group above it in which the supervisor is a subordinate. Instances of this are in both Figures 8.1 and 8.2. Formally, the people who are members of more than one group are linking pins (e.g., Likert, 1967) and should reduce the incidence of intergroup problems between organizational groups.

Identity groups, on the other hand, are not dependent upon one's formal position in the organization and are not formal groups. They consist of people who share important common features such as demographics or biology (e.g., age, sex, race), or history (attended same college, were members of the same sorority, fought in the Vietnam War). Because of their common characteristics, treatment, and experiences, they tend to have common views of the world, including their views of the organization—what is good, necessary, and important for it. The organization does not determine the identity group, and the identity group is independent of it. People belonged to their identity groups before they were members of the organization and will be members of them after they leave the organization. Just as organizational groups tend to overlap, so do identity groups. For example, people are simultaneously members of a racial group, a gender group, and an age or generational group.

Identity group membership and organization group membership tend to be related in most organizations. The common expression, "glass ceiling" sometimes refers to the fact that just men (an identity group) seem to reach the top level (an organizational group), at least in many organizations. Although organizational and identity groups are related, their relationships are usually far from perfect. Therefore, just as with overlaps among organizational groups and overlaps among identity groups, overlaps occur between types of groups. That is, some people of different identity groups are often present in some organizational groups. The civil rights laws regarding employment from the 1960s through the 1990s have helped to increase this overlap. On the surface of it, all the obvious overlaps among the various types of groups should tend to reduce intergroup conflicts. One interesting question when intergroup conflict occurs, therefore, is why conflict between these particular groups? This question is not clearly answered, but one likely answer goes back to the concept of scarce resources. One such resource is promotion to higher positions in the organization and the power and privileges that come with those positions. An organizational group such as the finance department might compete with the production department managers for promotions to the top positions and power in the organization. This is not an unusual phenomenon.

Keeping in mind that all groups are embedded in the organization, the upper illustration in Figure 8.3 on page 184 shows an example in which both organizational and identity groups are embedded in each other. The women members of a certain workgroup are an identity group, and all the other groups within which they are embedded are organizational groups. This figure even includes the society in which the total corporation is embedded. That embeddedness will influence the behavior of the whole organization, although that is a topic reserved for Chapter 9. The women in a particular workgroup of managers are embedded within their total workgroup (which includes some men); the workgroup is part of a department (e.g., sales); the department is embedded within the whole corporation; and the corporation also has a surrounding context (society). If the researcher sees this embeddedness, it might help him or her to understand the attitudes and behaviors of these women.

Because intergroup theory argues that organizational psychologist can best understand the reactions of groups by knowing about their own perceptions, however, the part at the bottom left of Figure 8.3 is even more useful for understanding the reactions of the women in this workgroup. Here we see the women's own perception of the situation regarding their ability to gather scarce resources (e.g., their likelihood of getting promoted or of influencing important decisions in the organization). Their own group is unshaded, and the shadings of the other groups in which they are embedded reflect their perceptions of the favorableness of those groups to their women's subgroup. Their workgroup as a whole is shaded, indicating that they do not believe that it is favorable to their promotions or for them to exercise influence. This group might consist of a majority of males who simply do not value the women's work and ideas. These women see the next

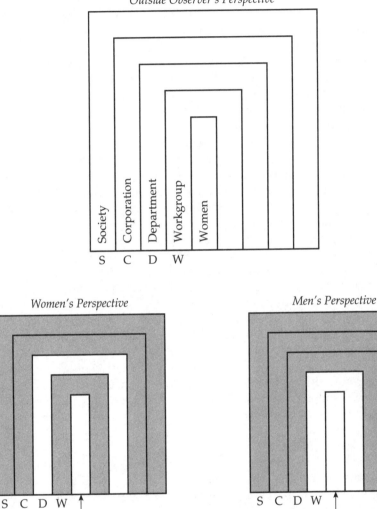

FIGURE 8.3   **Embedded Identity and Organizational Groups**

level, however, as being favorable to them. The department might be headed by a woman who they perceive as being favorable to women's work and ideas. Their view of the corporation and society as a whole, however, is that these larger contexts in which they are embedded are not favorable. Instead, they might believe there is a pro-male bias among those who

control the organization and in society as a whole. Certainly, it seems that
to understand actions of this subgroup of women, their view of the world
in which they are embedded would be very important.

This group of women is in competition with the men in their workgroup
to gain promotions and to influence the policies and decisions the workgroup and the department make. Just to flesh out this intergroup situation,
the lower right diagram in Figure 8.3 shows how the subgroup of men in
this same workgroup might perceive the situation. The reader should note
that the men might not agree with the women's view on everything. In this
case, they both agree that the workgroup favors men and the department is
more favorable to women, but they disagree in their perceptions of the corporation and the society in which they are embedded. The men might believe, for example, that affirmative action programs in the corporation and
laws in society favor women, while the women believe that traditional values of bias against women in the workplace prevail there. To understand
fully the intergroup competition between the men and women in this workgroup, the nature of its embeddedness and the way each group perceives
the situation is important. In this case, the organizational groups within
which they both are embedded and each identity group's perception of that
embeddedness affects the relations between two identity groups.

CONCLUSION

Interpersonal activities in organizations are important to the effectiveness
of the organization and the well-being of its members, and such activities
include intergroup activities. Compared to other areas of organizational
psychology, practitioners have played a somewhat stronger role in developing our knowledge of intergroup relations. Perhaps related to this, there
has also been some focus on problems rather than on harmonious intergroup relations. Problems between groups might be due to competition, especially competition for scarce resources, and they lead to conflict and lack
of coordination between the groups. Organizational intergroup theory has
focused on two types of groups: identity groups and organizational groups.
To understand events at interfaces between groups in organizations, however, we need to consider the context. The context consists of the way in
which the groups are embedded in larger groupings of organizational roles
and even in society itself.

The research methods the intergroup domain often uses have tended to
be either quasi-experimental field methods or else more impressionistic
judgments of researcher-consultants and the group members themselves.
There is a strong belief that the views of the group members themselves
need to be understood to learn about intergroup attitudes and behaviors.

REFERENCES

Alderfer, C. P. (1971). Effect of individual, group, and intergroup relations on attitudes toward a management development program. *Journal of Applied Psychology, 55,* 302–311.

Alderfer, C. P. (1986). An intergroup perspective on group dynamics. In J. Lorsch (Ed.), *Handbook of organizational behavior* (pp. 190–222). Englewood Cliffs, NJ: Prentice-Hall.

Alderfer, C. P., & Smith, K. K. (1982). Studying intergroup relations embedded in organizations. *Administrative Science Quarterly, 27,* 35–65.

Brett, J. M., & Rognes, J. K. (1986). Intergroup relations in organizations. In P. S. Goodman (Ed.), *Designing effective workgroups* (pp. 202–236). San Francisco: Jossey-Bass.

Katz, D., & Kahn, R. L. (1978). *The social psychology of organizations,* 2nd ed. New York: John Wiley & Sons.

Kauffman, J. R. (1990). *Implications of U.S. and Mexican national culture for the job characteristics model.* Mount Pleasant, MI: Unpublished master's thesis, Central Michigan University.

Likert, R. (1967). *The human organization.* New York: McGraw-Hill.

Salancik, G. R., & Pfeffer, J. (1974). The bases and use of power in organizaitonal decision making: The case of a university. *Administrative Science Quarterly, 19,* 453–473.

9

MACRO ORGANIZATIONAL PSYCHOLOGY

The most macro level at which one can consider organizational psychology is the organizational level. Here, we usually consider organizations as single entities having characteristics of their own and dealing with characteristics of their external environments. We could, therefore, compare one organization with another. Even thinking at this level entails some transformation for most psychologists, because they are used to thinking about individual differences, or at most group differences, instead of organizational differences. Indeed, when organizational psychologists work at this level, their work tends to blend with sociology and occasionally even economics (O'Reilly, 1991). Probably fewer organizational psychologists work consistently at the organizational level than at the group or individual levels, and this is reflected in the fact that only one chapter (Chapter 9) of this book is on the organizational level. Lest we think that the organizational level is unimportant or is not relevant to organizational psychology, however, we only need to look at volume three of the *Handbook of Industrial and Organizational Psychology* (Dunnette & Hough, 1992), which contains chapters about organizational level topics such as organizational-environment relations and a whole section of chapters about the design of organizations.

The basic organizational psychology value that empirical research and theory are valuable is relevant at the macro level as well as at the individual and group levels. Some special research problems, however, become apparent very quickly to researchers at the organizational level. If we use the same types of research designs I described in Chapter 2, some of them seem to imply an enormous amount of work. For example, if the organizational psychologist wants to do a field experiment, he or she would need to choose many organizations, randomly assign them to experimental or control groups, manipulate the independent variable with the organizations in the experimental group, and then measure the dependent variable in all organizations. To do a nonexperimental field study, the organizational psychologist should obtain a large sample of organizations, measure their crucial characteristics, and compute inferential statistics. One of the keys here is the phrase *large sample of organizations*. Furthermore, the organizations should ideally represent some known population. They might, for example, all come from a single industry.

Simply getting the cooperation of one organization for conducting organizational psychology research at the individual or group levels is often a difficult task for the researcher; to obtain the cooperation of many organizations is much more difficult. Still, it has been done. Some alternative approaches in research that is generally considered relevant to the organization level are: (1) doing a laboratory experiment or even a quasi-experimental field study in which artificial, temporary organizations are created and studied; (2) studying subunits of a large organization, sometimes on the grounds that they are autonomous enough to constitute separate organizations; (3) studying variables that are organizational level characteristics, even though they occur within only a single organization.

Perhaps a result and symptom of this difficulty in doing research that is truly at the organizational level is the existence of a subfield of the organizational sciences called "organization theory." Organization theory is a major organization-level subfield usually found in business and management fields. The interesting point for our purposes is the use of the word *theory* in the label for the field. While theory and research are integrated at the micro level, we might infer from this label that the macro level is primarily theory rather than empirical research. In organizational psychology, we value both research and theory, but at the macro level, perhaps we are somewhat more able to work with theory than with empirical research relative to the other levels. To whatever extent this is true, it is probably due to the sheer difficulty of conducting rigorous research at the organizational level compared with the micro levels of organizational psychology.

We now examine the nature of organizations as entities to outline the scope of macro-organizational psychology. This means describing the myriad variables that are of interest at the organizational level as a way of providing a feel for this level. Then I will describe well-known forms of organizations, each of which puts together groups of these variables in different ways. Finally, I present an overarching theory, systems theory, that purports to encompass all forms of organization to provide a partial integration of the forms.

THE NATURE OF ORGANIZATIONS

Chapter 3 described the nature of individual human beings. Chapter 6 defined and described groups. I have saved attempts at defining organizations at the organization level for this chapter. Just as in defining groups, there seems to be no one, clear, precise, uniformly acceptable definition of organizations. There is no lack of definitions of organizations, but any specific definition is usually open to exceptions and criticisms. Traditionally, definitions of organizations have included the following elements: Organizations are collections of people who have banded together to coordinate their efforts toward the accomplishment of their common, explicit goal(s) and have grouped themselves according to both specialized tasks or activities and a hierarchy of authority and responsibility. One thing that differentiates organizations from both large masses or collectivities of people (e.g., a crowd or a mob) and from most small social groupings (e.g., a party or a group going to a movie) is formality. A second is order. There is usually an orderliness about organizations that is less apparent in other types of human collectivities, although it may simply be that the orderliness is more apparent because it is more explicit and formal. This orderliness is represented in the traditional definition of organizations by the word *coordinate*. The coordination may break down as I implied in the previous chapter on intergroup activity, but it does seem to be necessary for organizations to exist over a long period of time. Both the organization's structure of roles (e.g., similar roles are often grouped into departments or hierarchical levels) and the rules that determine the organizational member's actions are known, explicit, and formalized. In many organizations, they are even written down somewhere. This amount of formality is usually not present in groups of people that one would not consider to be organizations.

This traditional definition of an organization especially fits the classical way of organizing, which I will discuss shortly. One can easily quibble, however, with some or all parts of the definition other than formality and order. Consider the following parts of the traditional definition of organizations: (1) collections of people, (2) common goals, (3) groups according to specialization of tasks (a "horizontal" division of the organization, sometimes called division of labor), and (4) hierarchical levels.

Instead of collections of people, some would argue that the organization is really a collection of roles that anyone may occupy. This view implies that the rules governing the roles or positions in the organization determine the important organizational actions, and not the people themselves. To define the organization, therefore, as consisting of people rather than of the rules governing their roles misses an essential feature of organizations. Furthermore, instead of either roles or people as the basic building blocks of organizations, one could argue that actions or even the energy used in those actions are the essence of organizations (e.g., as Katz and Kahn imply, 1978).

One can also challenge a second part of the traditional definition of organizations, common goals. The traditional definition seems to imply that people join together voluntarily because of their common goals. While this may be true of some organizations, especially those we label as voluntary organizations, it is not clearly true of all members of all organizations. A large manufacturing company, for example, might have people join it with various degrees of volition. Maybe some employees prefer to work elsewhere, but they are not able to obtain a job where they would want to. Furthermore, at the extreme, we could consider the work of prison labor and even slave labor. These seem to be work in organizations, but they certainly do not seem voluntary. If everyone does not join the organization in a totally voluntary way, then it comes as no surprise that everybody probably does not have the same goals for the organization. Some people may simply want the organization to survive forever, while others would be quite satisfied for it to survive for a few more years until they retire. Some members of the organization might want it to make profits at all costs, while others would rather see it shut down than commit crimes or pollute the local area with waste products to make a profit. Some want it to pay as much as possible to laborers, while others want it to pay as much as possible to the owners. In short, the goals of different organization members can be diverse and conflicting, rather than common.

One can question the third part of the traditional definition of organizations, the horizontal division of labor by function. It is true that most organizations seem to have some specialization of labor, and if they are large enough, to have formal divisions or departments in which are people doing the same type of work. We often find, therefore, production departments, marketing departments, personnel departments, and so forth. The question, however, is whether this type of division is a *necessary* characteristic of organizations. Classical organizations definitely tend to operate this way. This type of division tends to occur in organizations in various countries. There are exceptions however, and as we will see shortly, there are even organizational theories advocating different ways of organizing the work the organization does. In a so-called "matrix" organization, for example, division of the organization is accomplished at least as much along project or product lines as along functional lines. One way of looking at the so-called "organic" organizations is to consider them as organizations that are less specialized or divided. Both of these I describe more later in this chapter. This horizontal differentiation along functional lines seems to be extremely common, but it may not be a necessary part of organizational life.

The fourth and final part of the traditional definition of organizations that one can challenge is the concept of hierarchy. As with the horizontal division of the organization along function lines, if we look around at most organizations of any size, we will see vertical distinctions among organizational members in a hierarchy of authority and responsibility. Probably because of this, the traditional definition of organizations assumes that this is a necessary part of organizational life. Indeed, at least some distinction of organizational roles along such lines might be universal, but there are extremely large variations in the extent to which this characteristic is present in different organizations. In addition, less hierarchy is sometimes advocated for organizations, either for reasons internal to the organization such as to motivate and satisfy employees or for reasons external to the organization such as to allow employees at all levels to adapt their work to new environmental situations as necessary.

As with defining groups in organizations, precise and clearly acceptable definitions of organizations are hard to come by. We are left with a somewhat loose definition in which only three general elements seem always to apply: There are a number of people involved (although it may be better to define an organization as being composed of roles or of activities rather than of the people occupying the roles or performing the activities), there is formality, and there is some order. Many other characteristics are very common, but probably not necessarily very dominant in all organizations: common goals, horizontal division of labor by functional specialization, and vertical or hierarchical division by authority and responsibility. There are probably still other characteristics that are common to many organizations, and some of them may become apparent in the rest of the discussion of organizations in this chapter.

Organization-Level Topics

In addition to defining organizations, another way of getting an overview of the organizational level of organizational psychology is see what topics are often relevant in the thinking at this level. Table 9.1 on page 192 lists many of the topics that researchers and theoreticians often study and with which consultants at this level attempt to work.

The first column in the table includes organization-level topics that are generally characteristics of the organization, while the second column contains characteristics of the organization's external environment. Organization-level theories and research usually focus on one or more elements of the first column and try to relate them (1) to a criterion such as organizational effectiveness (also in the first column), (2) to some of the individual-level variables that I discussed in earlier chapters (e.g., job satisfaction, commitment, absenteeism), or (3) to one or more of the environmental variables in the second column. If theory or research suggests a causal relationship, one usually assumes that causation goes from outside inward or from more

TABLE 9.1 Common Organizational Level Topics

Characteristics Inside the Organization	Characteristics Outside the Organization
Technology	Technology
Structure	The economy
Size	Legal environment
Climate and culture	Cultural setting
Top management	Competition
History of the organization	Scarcity/munificence
Decentralization and participative decision making	
Control systems	
Organizational effectiveness	

macro to more micro. Although it can be done, it is harder to explain how the organization's size, for example, can affect the environmental variables such as the economy than to explain how macro variables such as the economy can affect the organization's size. Similarly, one usually assumes that the organizational level variables are more likely to affect the individual level variables than the other way around. This presumed causal influence of the organization level on the lower group and individual levels shows the importance of the macro level for organizational psychology. Organizations can have powerful effects on the lives of their members; therefore, we can probably rightfully criticize most organizational psychologists for trying to understand people in organizations while confining their work to the more micro levels.

Characteristics of the Organization

Table 9.1, includes technology in both columns. Technology has long been defined as the basic techniques or methods of doing the work (e.g., Woodward, 1965). While technology often invokes images of complex machinery, the actual definition says nothing about machines or tools. Instead, the way of doing work includes the way that humans behave as well as the tools they use. The tools and machinery might require, however, certain types of actions by the humans who use them. Traditional assembly line work is a type of technology in which people may have to remain in one place and repeat the same actions every few minutes. Continuous processes technologies, such as those in some chemical companies, might require operators to monitor dials or other displays, be alert for problems, and turn some valves or other controls once in a while. Banks or insurance companies might have mediating technologies in which people must mediate between two "customers" by obtaining something (often money) from one source (e.g., a bank depositor) and transferring it to another source (e.g., a borrower) for a fee (e.g., interest). These are all technologies, even though the last example does not seem to focus on tools or equipment. As Table 9.1 notes, technology is both internal and external to the organization. The technology the organization uses is thought to affect the organization's members, and technologies also are invented in and exist in the organization's environment. Competitors can use them, or one's own organization can adopt them; in either case, they might influence the organization.

A structure in Table 9.1 is a pattern of relationships, and organizational structure is a pattern of relationships among the parts of the organization. As I noted earlier, the parts of the organization might be people, roles, or activities. To make it easy to understand structure, I will discuss only one of these, roles, or positions. Structure can still be more than one thing, however, because a pattern of relationships among positions in an organization can focus on any of several types of relationships. Positions can be related to each other in terms of power, communication, status, or responsibility. If we had chosen to treat people as the basic parts of the organization, we would have to add more relationships, more personal ones, including liking and respect. While people might like each other, however, roles or positions do not. An organizational chart or drawings of communication networks (see figures in Chapters 7 and 8) illustrate structures of one sort or another.

A well-known idea at the macro level is that technology moderates the relationship between structure and effectiveness (e.g., Miles, 1980). That is, structure causes effectiveness, but the same structure does not always lead to effectiveness in every situation. Instead, the effects of structure on organizational effectiveness is contingent on the technology of the organization. For example, if the technology is one in which an organizational member or a small group produces a whole product (e.g., task identity, in terms of an intrinsic motivation theory at the micro level in Chapter 5; Hackman & Oldham, 1980), then a structure that is less hierarchical (e.g., has fewer levels of supervisors and management) might be more effective than a more hierarchical structure. This contingency theory means that there is no one universally best way to organize (i.e., to arrange organizational structure) in all situations.

Size of the organization (Table 9.1) usually means the number of organizational members to an organizational psychologist. One should note, however, that there are other ways of measuring the sizes of organizations. Other disciplines, such as finance and economics, consider some of them to be more important. Net financial worth, dollars of sales, number of a product manufactured per year, profits, or net dividends can be a measure of organizational size. Size, at least in terms of number of people, has often been related to structure. When there are more people, there is more opportunity to divide the organization into subparts that have relationships to each other. Larger organizations are likely to have more departments, and, therefore, problems of coordination of the activities among the parts are more likely to occur.

Some organizational psychologists interested in the organizational level focus on top management, another entry in the first column of Table 9.1. The reason is that top management, because of its power, may have important effects on the whole organization. They help determine the structure of the organization and make decisions that might influence other organizational level factors, such as the use of technology and the size of the organization. In addition, organizational climate or culture is often set by the top group of executives or managers (Schein, 1990).

Climate is an older term and *culture* a newer term in organizational psychology. In spite of attempts by some culture researchers to deny any overlap between the two concepts (Denison, 1990), some people see little difference in the two, perhaps because each is somewhat ambiguous. Culture and climate seem to be a feeling that one might get about the organization after becoming very familiar with it, that is, by working in it for some time. Each term is macro because it describes the nature of an entire organization. One major and obvious difference has been for researchers of climate to rely more on questionnaires and empirical data analysis and for culture researchers to rely more on nonstandard observations (Schein labels them "clinical" observations, 1990) made after becoming familiar with the organization through applied consulting contacts, perhaps especially with top management (Denison, 1990). Thus, the research methods that "climate" researchers use tend to be more mainstream and traditionally acceptable in the larger organizational psychology area than the methods "culture" researchers use. A typical set of topics of interest to climate researchers, culture researchers, or both is attention to people, tendency to take risks, task orientation, trust in people, and formality in relationships.

Culture research and theory tend especially to focus on implicit, unquestioned assumptions or values that people have regarding the way that things should be (Schein, 1990). Usually the organization has some history during which these assumptions were developed. Practices based upon these beliefs were successful for the organization in the past, and now people do not even question or think about them; instead, they just assume them to be true. The organization might select new employees, or new people may aspire to join because they think the same way. Socialization after the newcomers are in the organization helps to further remove any deviant thinking.

Organizational history and decentralization of authority are also related to culture and climate. Culture theorists argue that historical events in the company influence the nature of the dominant culture in the organization today. As I noted already, certain ways of doing the work of the organization have been successful in the past (history), and the organization has institutionalized them as being right, correct, and perhaps even morally superior. The organization's history, therefore, has led it to its current cultural state.

Decentralization, under one label or another, has long been a favorite theme for organizational psychologists at the macro level. It refers to decentralization of power, influence, or authority in the organization. Centralized power is concentrated in one or a few places, almost always quite high in the organization's hierarchy. Organizational psychology has often promoted decentralization, or spreading decision-making power around in the organization, although there may be some controversy regarding exactly what constitutes the best type of effective participative decision making (e.g., Cotton, Vollrath, Lengnick-Hall, & Froggatt, 1990; Leanna, Locke, & Schweiger, 1990). In general, this usually means having people at lower levels participate more in making some of the important decisions. The degree of centralization or decentralization sometimes is considered a part of organizational structure, because power represents a type of relationship among the parts of the organization. A pattern of power relationships can, therefore, be part of an organization's structure.

Control systems, the next entry in the first column of Table 9.1, refers to the control of the behaviors of the members of the organization. Theories of control are usually based on feedback, especially negative feedback (Hellervik, Hazucha, & Schneider, 1992). An individual organizational member can control personal behavior by getting feedback about work quantity and quality; if someone discovers a deficiency, the employee can correct it. At the organizational level, there is usually a system (or subsystem) for controlling other subsystems, and it too involves feedback. The control system for a whole organization would consist of (1) departments that monitor and collect data about the activities of the other departments, especially data about costs and effectivess, and (2) departments that exert pressures or control efforts toward these other departments. The former might include accounting and finance departments and any record keeping units (including personnel, which keeps records of some personnel-related costs, e.g., absenteeism), and the latter includes payroll and decision making units (usually somewhere in higher level management) that might decide to reward or punish various other units (e.g., by increasing or decreasing budgets, by elimination or creation of whole departments, or by rewarding or punishing key leaders of departments).

Organizational effectiveness, the final element in the first column of Table 9.1, is a key element because it is basically the criterion that determines the degree to which the organization is successful. Because it has such pivotal importance, one might be surprised to find that what it is or how to measure it is not always clear. If we want to know the extent to which specific combinations of variables, e.g., a certain type of technology with a certain type of environment, are most effective, we must know what we mean by effectiveness.

Some common ways of thinking about organizational effectiveness include focusing on profit maximization, on goal attainment, on functions performed for the larger system, and on sheer survival. Profit maximization, obviously, could only be a goal in profit-making organizations and would not apply to the nonprofit sector of society. The goal attainment approach assumes that organizations have goals inherent in them, but this is really not true. The question one must ask, is "whose goals?" (e.g., Miles, 1980). Organizations are not really thinking beings with goals; instead, people have goals for the organization. Some of these people might officially obtain power at any time to have their goals accepted as the organization's goals, but other people who are constituencies of the organization will still have other goals. In fact, the profit maximization view of organizational effectiveness is a specific type of goal-oriented approach to organizational effectiveness. The owners of the organization receive the profits, and some of them surely have the view that profit maximization is the appropriate operational definition of organizational effectiveness. As I noted in Chapter 8, other people who are constituents of or stakeholders in the organization might think other goals are more important for the organization.

A functional approach to organizational effectiveness argues that each organization is a subsystem that performs one or more functions for the greater system within which it is embedded, society at large. A manufacturing organization produces goods that benefit the larger society, an educational institution embues students with knowledge and skills that allow them to adapt and thrive in society, and a police organization maintains order and protects the public. Each organization fulfills a major function for society, therefore, its effectiveness is the extent to which it performs this function.

Survival is another common answer to the question, what is organizational effectiveness? In this view, simply lasting a long time is a sign of effectiveness. The news media widely report that young organizations have a particularly high failure rate. One can argue that the ability simply to survive is a sign of an effective organization.

Before moving on to examine the organization's environment, the elements of the second column of Table 9.1, the reader should note that many of the characteristics of organizations in the first column of the table have parallels at the individual or group levels. Individuals and groups use the technology of the organization, groups at least have structure and size, individuals and groups adhere to culture and climate, groups have their own "top management" and history, decentralization and participative decision making seem related to individual's autonomy, and the concepts about types of data collection and feedback in the organization's control systems are basically adapted from what is known about the way individual behavior is controlled and motivated. By returning to Chapters 3 through 7 about the individual- or group-level, readers can find many parallels. As I noted earlier in this chapter, one way of thinking is that the organization level influences the individual level. Therefore, for example, participative decision making at the organization level might result in many individuals experiencing job autonomy. One might also surmise that there would be problems if the levels were too inconsistent. If, for example, the organization structure is very tall and narrow, so that each supervisor has very few people to supervise, this might conflict with attempts to implement autonomy in individual jobs. When supervisors have little to do other than supervise a few people, they might supervise, criticize, and instruct them very closely, which would tend to take away autonomy.

Characteristics of the Environment

Just as the organization level needs to be consistent with the individual level, the organization also needs to be consistent with its environment. This is because the organization interacts with the environment and must be ready to adapt to it if necessary (Miles, 1980). When the environment is rapidly changing or is very complex, it often has the description of "an uncertain environment." This requires the organization to be very adaptable or to adopt some ways of dealing with or reducing the uncertainty. Uncertainty has been a key environmental concept in organization-environment theories (Davis, 1992).

The first element in the right column of Table 9.1 is technology. I noted earlier that technology is also a characteristic of the organization itself. Many of the technologies an organization uses, while the organization might have adapted them for use, were probably invented elsewhere. When new technologies again arise, and before the organization imports them, they are part of the environment. If society is seeing rapid technological advances in areas that are important to the organization, this makes the technological part of the organization's environment quite complex and uncertain.

Likewise, the other elements in the environment (and in the right column of Table 9.1) can also vary in terms of their complexity and uncertainty. The relevant economic environment, whether local, national, or international, can be good or bad, but there are times when it is uncertain, uncontrollable, and complex. The legal environment refers to the laws governments pass (again local or national, but even international at times) that affect the organization. These could include laws about employment (e.g., minimum wages, payroll taxes, required health insurance, retirement), occupational safety, pollution regulations, truth in advertising, corporate income taxes, and collusion with competitors. The potential for such laws is unlimited. Ideally, laws should make the environment much more clear; laws are intended to be clear rather than confusing, so that people and organizations will know what they must do. Sometimes there is room for interpretation of the written law, therefore making it less certain. In addition, laws can change this year or next, making the future legal environment uncertain.

Organizational psychology has not always paid much attention to the cultural setting of the organization as an environmental factor, but it has probably always affected organizations. At a minimum, the culture affects the nature of the workforce available to the organization and the nature of its potential customers. This has become far more obvious in recent years, with the globalization of many markets and international competition. When organizations start to deal frequently and on a large scale with cultures that are very different from their own, the effects of culture on organizations become more obvious. Hofstede (1980; 1984) in his well-known studies reported that average values, a basic element of culture, differ in different nations. People in some nations tend to value individualism more, for example, while others value collectivism or being with and sharing with other people. His other dimensions of culture are power distance (acceptance of the fact that power may be distributed unequally), desire to avoid uncertainty, and masculinity-femininity. Workforces from different cultures may, for example, expect and desire more or less participation in decision making in their organization due to cultural values about power avoidance.

Perhaps to a lesser extent, subcultures within a large nation such as the United States are also important for organizations. Leaders of organizations sometimes recognize this when they make statements about parts of the country where they would like to place their organization and about the nature of the people residing there. An officer of a corporation might note the antiunion culture in some parts of the country, and army officers might talk about a military-friendly culture in some places.

The competition, another element in the environment (Table 9.1), usually refers to other organizations offering the same product or service. Obviously, if they offer it better in some way (more convenient, better quality, or lower cost), then the organization will suffer by comparison. Some organizations exist in wide-open competition, while many others exist in an environment of restricted competition. The legal environment can function to restrict competition (e.g., by granting public utilities the sole right to offer a service) or to enhance it (e.g., by antimonopoly laws). If an organization is the first to offer a product or service in a geographic area (e.g., the first fast-food franchise in town), it faces little competition, but this will probably change over time.

The final example of a characteristic of the organization's environment in Table 9.1 is scarcity versus munificence of resources in the environment. Obviously, if the environment that is relevant to the organization has very little of the organization's needed resources (e.g., raw materials for its product), the organization will have a much more difficult time and face much more uncertainty than it will if the environment has plenty of readily available resources. Resources can also include the labor, or potential members of the organization. Labor is a valuable type of resource for organizations.

The variations in environments are one set of factors influencing the characteristics or forms that organizations take. These forms can be of several basic types.

FORMS OF ORGANIZATION

There are several forms of organization or ways of organizing to get work done and goals accomplished. This means that many of the characteristics of organizations can differ from one organization to another. The principle of equifinality means that there are usually more than one way to get to the same final goal (Katz & Kahn, 1978). Each form of organization combines some of the variables noted in the previous section of this chapter. There are many possible forms of organization, including four well-known variations: classical, humanized, organic, and matrix.

The Classical Form of Organization

The classical form of organization, or variations on it, is probably the most common form in the world today, and its roots are perhaps the oldest of any form of organization. Historically, the development of bureaucracy was the beginning of this organization form. The German sociologist, Max Weber (1947) described long ago some of the basic principles of a bureaucratic organization. They include

1. A hierarchy of authority
2. Impersonality
3. Rational-legal authority
4. Personnel decisions on the basis of technical competence
5. Reimbursement of organizational members with money

6. Limited terms of office
7. Managers separate from ownership
8. Higher level office holders committed to their careers in the organization

Weber (1947) described well-known and effective organizations in Europe, including the military and the church. He argued that these organizations had found the most effective way of organizing and that it was so effective that all other organizational forms would disappear in trying to compete with them. He may have largely been right; one can now consider bureaucracy and its variations classic in the sense that they are well-established.

A hierarchy of authority refers to the vertical differentiation of the organization as I described earlier in this chapter. Impersonality is inherent in some of the other principles of bureaucracy; it means that the organization is conceived as composed not of people but of offices (roles or jobs). Because there are rules governing the behavior of people holding the jobs, in theory it matters very little who the person is holding the office. One person is pretty much replaceable with another, and the organization remains unchanged without any important difference. This view metaphorically compares the organization to a machine; therefore, theories concerned with bureaucracy and classical forms of organization are sometimes described as machine theories (e.g., Katz & Kahn, 1978; McKenna & Wright, 1992).

Rational-legal authority refers to the existence of written rules governing the behavior of people in each office. Power of one office over other offices in the hierarchy is explicit and formal. It is also limited, however, because if it is not written down that a superior can order a subordinate to do a specific act, then the power does not exist. This is sometimes seen as a protection of the workers from management abuse.

Managers, those who actually run the organization, are not its owners in a true bureaucracy. Like the military and the church, outsiders (e.g., stockholders), not the managers themselves, often own the modern corporation. Officeholders or job holders do not get their office for life. The organization hires them to do the tasks the office requires based on their technical competence for the specific tasks. The job holders can be released or may leave on their own accord at the end of a contractual agreement. They are paid with money rather than in the goods the organization makes or in company script. This seems obvious today, but it was not always the case before the rise of bureaucracy. Finally, the higher-level office holders tend to see working in the organization as a career to which they are committed. It is a very important part of their lives; they tend not to work elsewhere on a second job and are even reluctant to move to another organization. They have the good of this organization at heart.

In addition to bureaucracy, two other early approaches to organizations helped form today's version of the classical organization. Both came to the fore in the early 1900s. The first, scientific management, focused on the lower-level jobs in organizations, especially production organizations. It argued for determining the one best or most efficient way of doing the work and making that the standard procedure for everyone to work. On production jobs, this often entailed studying jobs with stopwatches to see what is the fastest way to do them, determining when and how many rest pauses lead to the most output in a given period of time (such as a day), and then paying workers on a piece rate so that they would be motivated to produce as much as possible. Fredrick Taylor (1947), one of the primary proponents of scientific management, argued that the same principles should be used on nonproduction jobs, including management. This was pretty much rejected in practice, however, as managers decided to use the principles only on lower-level jobs. Wherever used, however, it can easily be seen as an extension of a machine view of organizations. People are similar to the parts of a machine (the organization) to be used as efficiently as possible for productivity.

The other early approach to organizations that helped to elaborate the classical organization form was administrative management (Gulick & Urwick, 1937). Administrative management provided additional details and principles to the bureaucratic ones used in forming organizations in the classical manner. Some of these included

1. The division of labor along functional lines
2. The need for coordination among these divisions
3. A limited span of control (the number of people any one person supervised)
4. Unity of command (any organization member only has one immediate supervisor)
5. The scalar priniciple (there is one clear line of authority from any one position in the organization all the way to the top and back down)
6. The staff principle (experts in specialty areas outside the main production or service area of the organization should usually be in staff or advisory roles rather than in positions in direct control of main parts of the organization)

Overall, many of the principles of classical organization imply or directly concern issues regarding the formal organizational hierarchy or structure, the amount of centralization, and control systems in organizations (elements of the first column in Table 9.1). Classical organizations can be efficient and effective, but they also tend to have some persistent problems, especially the loss of enthusiasm and willingness to work hard by members of the organization, too little coordination among the functional parts of the organization (often resulting in a tendency for large organizations to become overloaded with managers to try to increase coordination through hierarchical control), and difficulty in adapting to environmental changes. While not every classical organization has all of these problems equally, they seem to be quite common. Other forms of organization arose after the classical form, and they are attempts to deal with one of more of these problems of classical organizations.

The Humanized Form of Organization

The humanized types of organization are responses to certain problems of classical organization styles that their resemblance to machines embodies. The classical organizations tend to treat people as interchangeable, replaceable parts of a machine. Sometimes a great deal of uniformity and conformity is required, probably more than many people want. This dehumanizing treatment tends to make people dissatisfied and does little to motivate them internally. There are two main subtypes of the humanized form of organization, human relations and human resources. The first seems to focus more on increasing job satisfaction, and the second on increasing internal motivation.

Human Relations Organizations
Perhaps springing historically from the Hawthorne studies' observations that paying more attention to people seemed to make them happier and more productive, the human relations organizations humanize the organization by treating people in ways that show caring for them. There is no one way of doing this, but examples might include supervisors listening to their personal problems; providing clean, comfortable, and attractive working conditions; and instituting outside of work activities such as company picnics or company-sponsored social events (e.g., bowling teams). This seems likely to satisfy some personal needs, such as social and comfort needs, and, therefore, satisfaction with job and with the company overall should increase. There is sometimes a belief that motivation and, therefore, job performance will also increase. There is little theoretical reason to believe this, however, and this belief might be due to the common misunderstanding of the difference between satisfaction and motivation I noted in Chapters 4 and 5.

Human Resources Organizations
The label human resources refers to the idea that human beings have many resources that are typically unused during their organizational activities. These include unused skills, abilities, energy, and effort. The approach here

is to get people to use more of their abilities and skills in productive work, and the way to do this is usually some variation on organizational decentralization. That is, people are given more authority and responsibility to do their work. The organizational psychology belief that people have high abilities and are trustworthy is especially apparent here. The historical roots of the human resources approaches are not as old as those of the human relations approach; in fact, human resources organizations may have developed after there was a recognition that the human relations organizations were better at improving human consequences such as job satisfaction than they were at improving organizational consequences such as job performance.

Early advocates of the human resources approaches to organization included McGregor (1960) with his Theory Y, in which managers were urged to assume that people were naturally hard working, wanted to have more responsibility, and were trustworthy, and Likert (1961) with his System 4, which urged much the same except that it advocated giving groups rather than individuals more responsibility. Each of these theories also had a label (Theory X and System 1, respectively) for the more traditional style of management, which tended to treat people as if they were untrustworthy and had little ability. If we return to Chapter 5 on motivation, we can see that a person's so-called higher-order needs (e.g., needs for achievement, and esteem) have the possibility of being satisfied in human resources organizations by accomplishing important and challenging tasks for which one is responsible. In terms of the characteristics of organizations in the right column of Table 9.1, there is more decentralization, less reliance upon formal control systems, and a culture and climate top management fosters including trust.

As with the other organizational forms, there are many variations on the human resources organization. Whenever we hear about organizations practicing decentralization, participative decision making or participative management, delegation of authority, empowerment, and similar concepts, this is a sign that the organization is trying to practice a form of the human resources approach to organizing.

The Organic Form of Organization

The organic form of organization is also a reaction to problems encountered in classical-style organizations. Contrasts are often made between organic and mechanistic (machine-style or classical) organizations, especially regarding differences in their adaptability. Adapting to environmental uncertainty and change that cause problems for classical organizations is supposed to be the strength of organic organizations. McKenna and Wright (1992) note that the organism is a common metaphor to which organizations are often compared. When this metaphor for organizations is used, the focus is usually on living organisms' abilities to adapt to their environments to survive.

The organic organization replaces the relatively rigid hierarchical structure with one that is able to change easily and rapidly to adapt to changing environmental situations. While it is usually relatively easy to diagram the hierarchical structure of a classical organization or even a humanized organization, it is less clear how to diagram an organic organization. Even if it might be possible to diagram one's structure of roles at any one time, it might change relatively quickly.

A brief account of an assignment I used to give to my classes in organizational psychology is one way to illustrate an organic organization in a concrete way. To see the contrast between some of the elements of classical organizations and organic organizations, I instructed students to go to one of the well-established, fast-food chain restaurants in town during a busy weekday lunch hour. Because of the relatively small size of the workforce and because the work areas were relatively open to sight from the customers' dining area, it was possible to observe many of the physical activities people did as part of their jobs. For comparison, there was a local "mom-and-pop" restaurant that was of similar size and number of employees, menu, and layout, and at lunchtime it seemed to do roughly the same amount of business as the fast-food chain restaurant.

At the classically organized chain restaurant, employees stayed pretty much in one place and did one thing over and over again, such as pouring drinks, flipping hamburgers, putting ketchup and mustard on hamburgers, taking orders from customers and saying them aloud into a microphone, or taking payment and making change for customers. There also appeared to be a supervisor overseeing all of these routine, repetitive, simple, low decision-making responsibility, one-best-way jobs. It was very easy to observe the structure of the work.

At the mom-and-pop restaurant, on the other hand, an observer had great difficulty identifying roles and organizational structure. Over time, any one worker appeared to be changing tasks frequently and usually without instruction to do so. A single organizational member, within a twenty-minute period, might take a customer's order, write it on a piece of paper, and put the paper in a place where someone could read it and cook the food, move to the dining room and clean some tables, pick up some food from the grill area and give it to a second customer, put some hamburgers on the grill for a third customer, take payment from a fourth customer, take an order from a fifth customer, take hamburgers off the grill and put them on a tray or in a bag for a sixth customer, and move back to the dining room area with a broom. Watching another organizational member would reveal them doing many of the same things but in a different order, dealing with some of the customers the first person dealt with, but not others. In short, it was difficult to identify roles and relationships among them (organizational structure). This might be because the roles were constantly changing; another way to explain it is to assume that nearly everyone had the same role, but that the role was complex. The role of each person might entail the simple instruction that the person is supposed to see what needs to be done and then to do it. This was probably an opportunity to observe the physical manifestation of an organic organization.

While the organic organization might tend to have its roles structured in a way that provides a lot of responsibility, the stimulus for and philosophy behind this organizational form is not exactly the same as that behind the human resources organization. Instead of promoting more empowerment because of an understanding of the nature of human beings and trying to get them motivated to use more of their skills (as in the human resources approach), the reason for the organic organization is more of a concern that environmental complexity, uncertainty, and change requires an organization that is flexible and adaptable.

The development of organic organizations was accompanied by an explicit attention to the concept of contingency, because classical organization forms seem quite appropriate as long as the environment is stable, predictable and certain, but organic organization seems better for organizations in more complex and uncertain environments. The nature of the most effective organization form, therefore, is probably contingent on the environmental situation.

The Matrix Form of Organization

In contrast to the organic organization, the matrix organization can be diagrammed very clearly, and usually is. Its actual working relationships, however, often seem less clear than classical organizations. Classical organizations are divided horizontally by function, that is they might have departments for production, finance, marketing, personnel, and other functions. When organizations become large and complex, however, they often diversify their product (or service) lines. Then a logical choice would be to divide or differentiate by product instead of by function. That is, there might be a separate department for each product. This is easy to see in very large organizations such as General Motors. Although they have reorganized many times over the years, one common way to organize has been according to their products. Therefore, there might be a relatively autonomous division producing Chevrolets, another producing Cadillacs, and so forth. Each of these divisions might do its own production, finance, marketing, and personnel tasks.

A matrix organization usually is structured or divided along more than one dimension. In manufacturing companies, for example, a matrix organization might be organized along both functional and product lines. Figure 9.1 illustrates how it might look. One or more positions could fill each box in the matrix. There might be fourteen people working on production of Product A, for example, or over one hundred working on production of Product D. There might be three people working in finance for Product B and only one finance employee working on Product E. There is a head or manager in charge of each function for all products, and there is a head or manager overseeing each product who has some say over each function as it pertains to that product. The matrix is thought to alleviate problems of

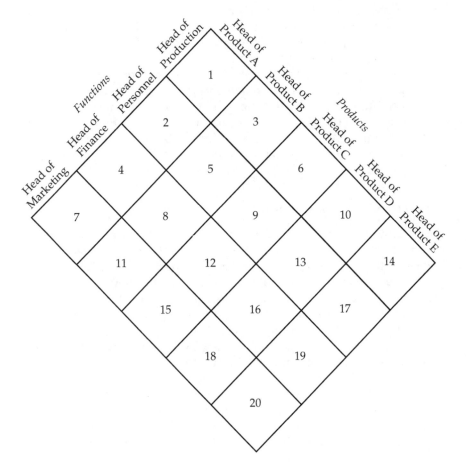

FIGURE 9.1   Matrix Form of Organization

coordination among departments and divisions that occur in classical organizations by increasing contact and communication among people in different functions and products.

One major implication for this is that each person, no matter where he or she is located in the matrix, has both a product and a function supervisor. This is a very different structure from classical organizations, and it even directly violates some of the classical organization principles, notably unity of command. Because of this, one would expect that there would be a lot of conflict in the organization. In one study of an organization changing from a more classical form to a more matrix form organization, however, role conflict did not seem to be a serious problem. In addition, the quantity of communication among organizational members increased, as expected, but the quality of those communications seemed worse (Joyce, 1986).

Obviously, this type of matrix cannot be appropriate for organizations that are small or that have only one product. Furthermore, not all organizations have products; some are service organizations. The basic idea of a matrix is that the organization is formally divided along more than one line, but the lines do not have to be product and function. Other lines of division might include, for example, services rendered or geographic regions in which the organization works. Also, one should not infer that all parts of the matrix are necesssarily occupied. It may not be cost effective, for example, for anyone to work full-time on personnel for Product B in Figure 9.1 if it is a very small department; or, it may not be sensible for anyone to work on marketing for Product E if it is still being developed and is not close to being ready for production and sales.

Although the classical organization is oldest, all of these forms have been around for a while now, and there are many hybrid combinations of them. There are probably few organizations that fit purely one form of organization without violating any of the form's principles. Nevertheless, understanding these forms can help us to understand typical organizations, their strengths, weaknesses, and purposes.

SYSTEMS THEORY

Systems theory of organizations, one assumes, often applies to all organizations, regardless of their form. Most organizational psychologists now believe in systems theory of organizations, but they do not always agree just what organizational systems theory is. Katzell (1994) notes that there is a "meta-trend" in the field toward calling every model and theory about organizations a systems theory. It sometimes seems common to draw a figure with boxes containing labels indicating organizational psychology variables, to draw arrows between most of the boxes proposing that they are causally related to each other, and then to call it a systems theory. A systems theory means more, however, than simply that everything is related to everything else. Katzell has argued that a systems theory of organizations probably should incorporate most of the features of Katz and Kahn's (1978) original descriptions of organizations as systems to be considered a true organizational systems theory. Katz and Kahn noted ten principles of open systems, which Table 9.2 arranges into five categories: three openness principles, two survival principles, two self-correction principles, two subsystem principles, and one principle of equifinality.

The three openness principles emphasize that organizations are open to their environments. Their boundaries are at least semipermeable, in that some things can pass through them selectively in either direction. Katz and Kahn (1978) considered energy, in many different forms, to be the prime element of organizations. Things we think of as energy, such as human physical and mental labor and electricity or steam power, were included. Other things that enter the organization can also be conceived as energy, however, usually stored energy. Raw materials, ore for a steel mill for example, are forms of stored energy, because they represent the expenditure of energy used to transform them to their present state and transport them to the mill. These inputs pass into the organization because it is open to them. Other things do not enter, because the organization is selective by trying to allow only useful things to cross its boundaries and enter. Throughput refers to the primary processes the organization goes through in working on its main product or service, for example, turning ore into steel, and output refers to the fact that this final product or service exits the organization, usually to go to a customer or user. Just as with the input, the output may be conceived as stored energy. The raw materials that were considered stored energy have now been worked on with the expenditure of more energy within the organization, and so the product now represents the sum of even more energy than the raw materials did.

The next two principles of systems in Table 9.2 show that one assumes survival to be a major goal of open systems. To survive, the cycles of events

TABLE 9.2   Ten Principles of Systems Theory of Organizations

Three Openness Principles	Two Survival Principles	Two Self-Correction Principles
Importation of energy	Systems as cycles of events	Information input, negative feedback, and the coding process
Throughput	Negative entropy	
Output		
		Steady state and dynamic homeostasis

occur that allow renewal of necessary resources for the organization. In a modern business organization, money is usually the link between most of the stages of the cycles. Organizations, therefore, use money to buy and import raw materials, labor, and other necessary energy. Money pays to transform the raw materials into a final product or service (throughput) and to export it to the environmental consumers (output). The consumer then pays money to the organization to be used for more raw materials, labor, and other energy. Thus, the cycle can start again. Without this cycle being completed, the organization could not survive.

Negative entropy, the other survival principle in the table, is a term borrowed from the natural sciences, and it recognizes the fact that organizations require some energy just to stay organized. The patterns of relationships representing organizational structure, the coordination of activities, and everything that separates organization from disorganization does not happen by chance. There is a tendency for organizations to become disorganized (and, therefore, not to survive), and some energy must be expended to prevent this entropy or tendency toward disorganization. In business organizations, money is one force serving this purpose (by now you might have guessed that money is one representation of energy); for example, it brings people into the organization and keeps them from leaving, and it keeps them following instructions that coordinate their work to complete the throughput activities. Money, however, is not the only factor fighting entropy. We can return to Chapter 5 about motivation to find additional reasons why at least some people in some organizations are willing to work in a coordinated fashion to achieve output for the organization. Furthermore, if we took the time to analyze organizations of very different forms, for example, voluntary organizations, we would discover that, while all organizations need to fight entropy, not all of them do it by distributing money.

The next two principles in Table 9.2 illustrate the organization's use of information to keep its activities relatively constant and steady. Information is essential if the organization is to know that it needs to change. When

TABLE 9.2 *(continued)*

Two Subsystem Principles	One Equifinality Principle
Differentiation	Equifinality
Integration and coordination	

something is going wrong that threatens the organization's effectiveness, (negative) feedback about it is necessary for it to know it must make alterations. Changing markets, the changing nature of its own workforce, changing laws affecting the organization, changing technology, and many other changes in the environment can affect the organization. If it receives feedback and understands the relevance of the feedback, the organization can attempt to alter its activities, structure, raw materials, technology, or whatever the feedback suggests to be more effective. It is through the use of this corrective feedback that organizations can maintain their normal steady state.

I have addressed previously in this chapter the two subsystem principles in Table 9.2. As organizations age and especially if they grow, they tend to specialize or differentiate themselves. Typically, they usually split into horizontal and vertical parts. The horizontal divisions or departments, in classical organizations especially, tend to represent different functional areas. Katz and Kahn (1978) note that every organization must perform five functions. Four of these generic functions often become housed in separate horizontal subsystems of classical organizations: production, support, maintenance, and adaptive functions. Although these functions are usually easiest to identify in classical organizations because formal divisions often represent them, every organization must somehow perform these functions. An extreme organic organization must also perform them, but there may not be any clear formal division for each of them.

The production function, of course, refers to the main work for which the organization is identified. Support subsystems directly support the production function by interacting with the environment on its behalf, for example, by purchasing or otherwise bringing needed inputs into the organization and by selling and or transporting the finished output into the environment. The maintenance function refers to the need to preserve the organization or system itself. This largely concerns procuring and keeping human beings as members of the organization and keeping their energies directed toward accomplishment of organizational effectiveness. The organization uses a whole range of rewards and occasionally punishments for this purpose. The final function that is usually identifiable as a formal horizontal division in classical organizations is the adaptive function. Classical organizations often have specific departments (e.g., research and development, market research, product research departments) whose aim is to sense change in the environment and recommend or show the organization how to adapt to it so that it will continue to survive and thrive.

A vertical division of labor in classical organizations usually represents the fifth function, management. Because of differentiation of the classical organization into separate subsystems performing the other four functions, there is a potential for lack of coordination. Separation of the four functions, which almost always occurs in larger organizations, reduces contact and communication among them. The response of most organizations is to try to coordinate through the use of hierarchical control: Someone is placed "above" these subsystems who has the authority and responsibility to direct them in ways that aim at coordinating their energies. As I noted earlier in this chapter and in other chapters, there are other ways of coordinating organizational activities besides the use of the vertical hieararchy (e.g., the use of liaison roles). Integration specifically refers to a very different way to solve the same problems, but it is probably only feasible in small organizations. It happens because everyone in the organization is able to understand what needs to be done, to be committed to helping the organization, and to take necessary action. The example of a restaurant using an organic style organization, which I described earlier in this chapter, illustrates integration. Regardless of the means, the organization must somehow perform the coordination and integration function.

The final principle of organizational systems theory is equifinality. It is the basic principle that there are many ways to reach the same end, and many of them can be equally viable. While there may be some ways of organizing and doing work that might not be effective, there is usually more than one way that can be effective.

CONCLUSIONS

Macro organizational psychology has received less attention than the group or individual levels have from organizational psychologists. This might be because they are uncomfortable thinking at the organizational level; training in psychology rarely prepares us for this very well. It might also be because of the relative difficulty of conducting rigorous empirical research at the organization level compared with the "lower" levels. Nevertheless, characteristics of and events occuring at the organization level are likely to be extremely important for understanding happenings at the individual and group levels. The lower levels do not exist in a vacuum. The organization level not only interacts with the group and individual levels, but it also interacts with the external environment—an even greater macro level.

Many of the topics at the organizational level get their influence in some way from the classical form of organization. Because it is by far the dominant form of formal organization in our world, many of its characteristics are taken for granted in our research, theories and applications. In many ways it is the background against which all of our thinking is cast. We tend to compare other organizational forms with the classical organization, we wonder whether our new theories about participative management will work in a classical organization, and we propose contingency theories in which new innovations will work better in some situations and classical principles will prevail in others. The influence of the classical organization form on organizational psychology is perhaps part of the culture of organizational psychology, because in Schein's (1990) terms, many of its principles have become unquestioned assumptions.

Whether organizations take the classical form or not, they must perform some generic functions to survive and be effective. In addition, the principles of systems theory are widely acknowledged today as inherent in any organization. To understand and work with organizations, one must understand the five types of systems principles, as applied to organizations: Systems are open to their environments, they tend to seek survival, they are self correcting, they tend to have subsystems that can cause problems of coordination, and there is probably more than one viable way for an organization to be effective.

REFERENCES

Cotton, J. L., Vollrath, D. A., Lengnick-Hall, M. L., & Froggatt, K. L. (1990). Fact: The form of participation does matter—a rebuttal to Leana, Locke, and Schweiger. *Academy of Management Review, 15,* 147–153.

Davis, G. F. (1992). Organization-environment relations. In M.D. Dunnette & L. M. Hough (Eds.), *Handbook of industrial and organizational psychology,* Vol. 3, (2nd ed.) (pp. 315–375). Palo Alto, CA: Consulting Psychologists Press.

Denison, D. R. (1990). *Corporate culture and organizational effectiveness.* New York: John Wiley & Sons.

Dunnette, M. D., & Hough, L. M. (1992). *Handbook of industrial and organizational psychology,* Vol. 3, (2nd ed.). Palo Alto, CA: Consulting Psychologists Press.

Gulick, L., & Urwick, L. (Eds.) (1937). *Papers on the science of administration.* New York: Columbia University.

Hackman, J. R., & Oldham, G. R. (1980). *Work redesign.* Reading, MA: Addison-Wesley.

Hellervik, L. W., Hazucha, J. F., & Schneider, R. J. (1992). Behavior change: Models, methods, and a review. In M. D. Dunnette & L. M. Hough, (Eds.), *Handbook of industrial and organizational psychology,* Vol. 3, (2nd ed.) (pp. 823–895). Palo Alto, CA: Consulting Psychologists Press.

Hofstede, G. H. (1980) *Culture's consequences: International differences in work–related values.* Beverly Hills, CA: Sage Publications.

Hofstede, G. H. (1984). The cultural relativity of the quality of life concept. *Academy of Management Review, 9,* 389–398.

Joyce, W. F. (1986). Matrix organization: A social experiment. *Academy of Management Journal, 29,* 536–561.

Katz, D., & Kahn, R. L. (1978). *The social psychology of organizations* (Revised Ed.). New York: John Wiley & Sons.

Leanna, C. R., Locke, E. A., & Schweiger, D. M. (1990). Fact and fiction in analyzing research on participative decision making: A critique of Cotton, Vollrath, Froggatt, Lengnick-Hall, and Jennings. *Academy of Management Review, 15,* 137–146.

Likert, R. (1961). *New patterns of management.* New York: McGraw-Hill.

Katzell, R. A. (1994). Contemporary meta-trends in industrial and organizational psychology. In H. C. Triandis, M. D. Dunnette, & L. M. Hough (Eds.), *Handbook of industrial and organizational psychology,* Vol. 4, (2nd ed.) (pp. 1–89). Palo Alto, CA: Consulting Psychologists Press.

McGregor, D. (1960). *The human side of enterprise.* New York: McGraw-Hill.

McKenna, D. D., & Wright, P. M. (1992). Alternative metaphors for organization design. In M.D. Dunnette & L. M. Hough (Eds.), *Handbook of industrial and organizational psychology,* Vol. 3, (2nd ed.) (pp. 901–960). Palo Alto, CA: Consulting Psychologists Press.

Miles, R. H. (1980). *Macro organizational behavior.* Santa Monica, CA: Goodyear Publishing.

O'Reilly, C. A. III (1991). Organizational behavior: Where we've been, where we're going. *Annual Review of Psychology, 42,* 427–458.

Schein, E. H. (1990). Organizational culture. *American Psychologist, 45,* 109–119.

Taylor, F. W. (1947). *The principles of scientific management.* New York: Norton.

Weber, M. (1947). *The theory of social and economic organization* (translated by A. M. Henderson & T. Parsons and edited by T. Parsons). New York: The Free Press.

Woodward, J. (1965). *Industrial organization: Theory and practice.* London: Oxford University Press.

10

APPLICATIONS OF ORGANIZATIONAL PSYCHOLOGY

Organizational psychology research and theory, as I have discussed in the previous chapters, leads to some obvious recommendations for changing and improving organizations. Sometimes these directions for change are explicit, but other times they come from research and theory that only implicitly indicate how to improve things. This is true at each of the three levels of organizational psychology: individual, group, and organizational. Anyone studying the previous chapters should be able to come to some conclusions regarding ways to improve organizations: readers should not necessarily wait for others to figure it out.

There are whole fields of application-oriented organizational psychology, sometimes using their own labels. Rather than calling it the application of organizational psychology principles, the fields sometimes use labels such as organization development or planned change. Much of this chapter uses material from these applications-oriented topics. Rather than borrow a definition of fields such as organization development, let us define applications simply and broadly based upon previous discussions in this book. Simply put, we are interested in applications of principles of organizational psychology that aim at improving organizations. A common definition of organization development is the use of behavioral science knowledge for the improvement of both the individual and the organization (e.g., Porras & Robertson, 1992). We will go further than this and try to narrow the definition in an obvious way. We will consider only applications of organizational psychology research and theory, not all behavioral sciences. We do define organizational psychology in ways that are somewhat inclusive, but the reader should note that the applications in which we are interested do not include those that have traditionally been limited to personnel psychology, e.g., selection, performance appraisal, and job analysis. Training, another application of personnel psychology, however, seems to cut across both personnel and organizational psychology. A broad definition of many applications of organizational psychology can include types of training. Another type of behavioral science based knowledge that would not be applicable is knowledge that belongs in the vocational counseling area. As I noted in Chapter 1, individual-level actions that encompass career counseling are not usually part of organizational psychology applications.

The idea that the purpose of these interventions is to improve individual and organizational situations requires that we go back to one of the basic values of organizational psychology in Chapter 1: The person is as important as the organization. The reason for phrasing it that way, rather than simply saying that the individual and the organization are equally important, is to focus on the difference between organizational psychology and one of its closest sister fields; personnel psychology. The history of industrial psychology before organizational psychology came along was largely that of personnel psychology, and that history showed a clear preference for improving the organization more than the individual. Selection and performance appraisal, for example, aim at improving the effectiveness of the organization, and one can only secondarily argue that the individual's welfare is an aim.

Because the person is as important as the organization, then the goals of changing the organizations using organizational psychology principles are usually to improve both parties and not just one. The chapters on individual and organization outcomes showed what the indicators of the individual's and organization's welfare are. How to improve them is the question asked in any organizational psychology application.

The other three organizational psychology values in Chapter 1 are also important here. "People have high abilities and are trustworthy" is the second value implicit in much of organizational psychology, and it is also evident in many applications. There is a history of attempts to provide more influence for the individual over the behaviors in the organization, especially his or her own behaviors. One would only recommend and attempt such interventions if there were a strong belief in the individuals' abilities and motives. The third value is that interpersonal activities are important in organizations. This value is easy to see in many of the interventions or applications that attempt to improve personal interactions. This would include leadership or supervision changes, group and intergroup process consultation, and several forms of team building. The fourth value of organizational psychology is that research and theory have value. This implies that organizational psychology applications are based on the results of research and strong theoretical principles. Porras and Robertson (1992) noted, however, the applications side of the field has tended to emphasize action over research and theory. This means that when there is a problem in an organization, somebody is going to do something about it, and often quickly. Unfortunately, this emphasis on quick action often tends to mean that (1) the intervention is not thought through very well and is often not consistent with the best research and theory, and (2) evaluation research is usually not considered soon enough or seriously enough to proceed in a rigorous manner. Thus, much of the application side of organizational psychology is more divorced from research and theory than we would like. When this happens, it violates a basic value of organizational psychology, the one regarding the value of research and theory. Because of the relative lack of rigorous research on the interventions or applications of organizational psychology, we know less about its effectiveness than we know about the viability of some of the theories tested in other areas of the field.

ROOTS: SURVEY FEEDBACK AND GROUP PROCESS INTERVENTIONS

Although we cannot hope to discuss all of the possible applications of organizational psychology, we will look at them in two ways. First, we will consider two of the historical roots of practice in the field, the use of surveys for a variety of purposes and the examination of group processes in organizations. Subsequently, we will consider examples of applications derived from what we know about each of the three levels of organizational psychology: the individual, the group, and the organization.

Survey Feedback

Organizational psychologists have used surveys of employees for research and application purposes almost since the beginning of the field. I discussed surveys as research methods previously in Chapter 2. Here we are interested in their use for application or improvement for both individual and organizational situations. The most common, traditional use of employee surveys is probably to provide information upward in the organization's hierarchy. The structure of typical organizations is characterized by power, authority, and status at the top, with less and less of these important characteristics as one comes down the hierarchy. If people want to rise in the organization and become one of the more powerful, respected, and usually more wealthy people, it is wise to look good and to curry favor among those above them. One negative consequence is that they are often reluctant to bring bad news to the attention of the leaders of the organizations. Quite the contrary, in fact, they may be rewarded for success but seldom for failure of their parts of the organization. Thus, everyone in the organization has a part in a conspiracy to hide bad information from and bring good information to those at the top. Employee surveys are used traditionally as a means of increasing the quantity and accuracy or quality of upward communication in the organization. By doing an anonymous survey of the lower level employees (anonymous so that they will feel free to provide honest information even if it is unfavorable), upper level decision makers will be better informed when they make their decisions.

This simple use of surveys is not usually a very sophisticated application and is not usually a form of organization development. In fact, many modern organization development practitioners often contrast their techniques with this old-fashioned use of surveys. Practitioners often argue, and my own nonsystematic observations would agree, that top management rarely uses effectively such information after receiving the survey report. For whatever reason, management does not often act on this information alone. The question, then, is how to use surveys in a way that will be more effective for the improvement of the organization and its members.

Some early organization development approaches used surveys heavily, and the best known of these was probably the set of approaches labeled survey feedback to organizational groups (Mann, 1961). Although there are many variations on this theme, the basic idea is to focus on both surveys and groups. The focus on groups illustrates the value that personal interactions are important. Typically, every person in the organization is surveyed, and a questionnaire is used rather than an interview, which helps to keep costs low. The content of the survey may include almost anything, but it usually includes at least some questions on group processes, such as descriptions of the supervisors' leadership styles, communications within and between groups, interpersonal interaction styles, and attitudes toward group members. The researchers then summarize the data by group. The data provides a description of each natural group in the organization's hierarchy. The data for each group is then "fed back" to the group itself in a group meeting. Information that the group members provide about their own degree of cooperation with each other, for example, becomes the basis on which the group decides how to improve that cooperation. The understanding of group processes is important in such a meeting, and I often recommend that a group process consultant or expert be present in the group when this takes place to help the members understand and work with the information about itself. There are probably endless variations on this theme, but the principles are (1) that the group needs information about itself to change itself, and (2) that only people in the group have this information. Getting them to provide it honestly is likely to be difficult, however, if the information is seen as sensitive. The survey, therefore, is a springboard to get them started considering how they work together.

One generally acknowledges that a group may have difficulties changing everything that might need to be changed, therefore, all groups in the organization should undergo such survey feedback. Furthermore, because the people at the higher levels of the organization are likely to be influential with those at lower levels, one common recommendation is to start providing feedback to the groups at the top and, somewhat sequentially, work down. Obviously in a big organization, if each group took this seriously, then it would take a long time and could be very expensive.

Group Process Interventions

Besides employee surveys, another root of the applied field of organizational psychology lies in group process interventions In this root, practitioners once were active in the use of T-groups for changing organizations. Under various labels (e.g., T-groups, encounter groups, sensitivity training), practitioners made efforts to improve the understanding that people in organizational groups have of themselves and of each other. The idea is that they might benefit from this understanding by becoming psychologically more healthy. The organization might also benefit because the people could then work together more effectively. Such groups vary a great deal, but some of their common qualities include a tendency to be somewhat unstructured (having little in the way of a formal, active leader or other assigned and formal roles), being unfocused on a clear task in the beginning but ending by focusing on the perceptions by group members of themselves and each other, and by communications focusing on these perceptions.

Few actual groups of this type occur today, but there are clearly some descendants of them in any work on group processes such as leadership, group teamwork and cohesiveness, and interpersonal and group communications training. Campbell and Dunnette (1968) and others found that true T-groups provided very little benefit to organizations. There have been changes, therefore, in the practices at the group level, as I will discuss shortly. Nevertheless, many (but not all) of today's organizational psychology applications can be traced to one or both of the two roots: employee surveys and T-groups.

INDIVIDUAL, GROUP, AND ORGANIZATIONAL LEVEL INTERVENTIONS

To organize this book, I have used the common division of organizational psychology into individual, group, and organizational level phenomena. One can also characterize organizational psychology interventions in this way.

Applications at the Individual Level

Many potential applications of research knowledge at the individual level of organizational psychology are readily apparent. Two examples are job redesign and organizational behavior management.

Job Redesign

In job redesign, we examine a job for its potential to motivate and satisfy the employee. The work of Hackman and Oldham (1980) is the best known in this area, with its emphasis on the motivating potential of a job, which is due to a combination of autonomy, variety, task identity, task significance, and feedback. Although their theory conceived feedback as emanating from the job itself, in a job redesign program it need not come from there. It could come from agents or people as well as from the job itself. The reason that the Hackman and Oldham theory focuses on feedback from doing the task itself is that they were developing a theory of task (job itself) characteristics.

Logically, before attempting to redesign a job, one would want to know whether it needs it. A diagnosis, therefore, is necessary. The aptly named Job Diagnostic Survey (JDS), which is available in the Hackman and Oldham (1980) book, is often used for this purpose, although others may do just as well. As an aside, a common mistake in applying organizational improvement programs is not undertaking a thorough and systematic diagnosis before deciding what applications to attempt. In addition to deciding *what* applications to use, it is just as important *where* one should use them. The diagnosis might reveal that a job or jobs in a single department need improving but not jobs in other parts of the organization. In addition to the survey of job incumbents (e.g., by the JDS), it is also wise to diagnose with more than one method. Luckily, this might be relatively easy in the case of job redesign. One can also survey supervisors to get their opinions of their subordinate's job characteristics. In the JDS, there is a companion instrument, the Job Rating Form (JRF), also available in the Hackman and Oldham book. Again, however, someone who is relatively skilled in both organizational psychology and job redesign can easily enough survey supervisors by methods other than this one instrument. Diagnosis might reveal that the job is fine on autonomy but is weak on variety or task feedback. In this case, it might be wasteful of time and effort to work on increasing the job's autonomy. Instead, efforts should focus on weaker parts of the job's design.

As part of the diagnosis, one would also want to determine the employees' readiness for change (Hackman & Oldham, 1980). They should *desire* more responsibility. Organizational psychologists have often not paid enough attention to the diagnosis of the individuals in the job. Perhaps this is due to one of the values the psychologists hold, that is, that people have high abilities and are trustworthy. This is consistent with increasing responsibility in jobs, but some people may not be as trustworthy or as able as others. While this seems self-evident, it has not always been part of the diagnosis in organizational psychology.

Finally, as part of the diagnosis one would also want to determine the extent to which the organization itself is going to accept the redesigned job. The technological system, the control system, and the personnel system might be either consistent or inconsistent with the proposed changes (Hackman & Oldham, 1980). For example, with a technology such as an assembly line, it might be almost impossible to increase variety, autonomy, task identity, or any of the job characteristics very much without changing the technology. While this might be worthwhile in the long run, especially if workers become more intrinsically motivated from the job changes, in the short run it might mean massive alterations in the technology. Scrapping or drastically redesigning assembly lines to change the nature of jobs might be too costly in any short period of time. It would take some time to recoup the increased cost of new technology, and management might not be willing to undertake such costs.

This is closely related to control systems or the system used to provide feedback to the decision makers, usually higher-level management. The control system might include record keeping of production, expenses, and sales. Based on such information, management makes decisions to reward (or sometimes punish) people in various parts of the organization. The control system information is the type of information that the employee gets as part of feedback in redesigning a job. There is an inherent conflict in the concept of higher level management using this information to control the employees versus the employees using it to control their own job performance. Increasing autonomy of individual employees in their work is very consistent with the organizational psychology value or belief in employees' abilities and trustworthiness, but it is very *in*consistent with the traditional hierarchical use of control by upper-level management. Some organizations simply may not be able or willing to make the necessary changes in the job to increase the motivating potential of the job.

The personnel system may also be inconsistent with the efforts at job redesign. Personnel systems and the sister field of personnel psychology have usually worked very hard to develop clearly defined jobs with clear authority of one position (supervisor) over another, have selected employees to fit those jobs, and have trained them to do the jobs in the current way. In a few instances, contracts with unions may also have made these job designs even more rigid than they would otherwise be because it might take new bargaining to obtain agreement about changes. While the personnel system might be able to change or be flexible enough to allow for the necessary changes, it often is not.

As an example, Griffin (1991) reported a job redesign effort in a bank. A survey of tellers indicating that they were relatively dissatisfied with their jobs and a recommendation from an operations task force that the bank should introduce more automation into the teller jobs prompted the work. There was obviously more going on in the organization and in the jobs than just this job redesign for intrinsical motivation purposes. Management decided to redesign the nature of the job itself by increasing its responsibility, authority, and accountability. In addition to the tellers' former functions of cashing checks and accepting deposits and loan payments, (1) they now also handled commercial and travelers' check customers and recorded the transactions at their new on-line computer terminal, and (2) they were given autonomy to do this even for withdrawals over 100 dollars, which previously had required the signature of the supervisor. Feedback improved when management allowed the bookkeeping department to notify the teller of errors via computer as soon as they were detected. Previously, the tellers learned of the errors only at the end of the day. Finally, a message at the bottom of each transaction slip gave the customer the teller's name and advised the customer to contact that particular teller in case of any questions about the transaction. This was designed to increase the interactions between the teller and the customer, a recommendation by Hackman and Oldham (1980) aimed at increasing a sense of responsibility. Obviously, there were a great many changes in the tellers' jobs, and it would be impossible to know if only one or two had the effects on the dependent variables of work improvement and satisfaction, but that is usually the case in the real world.

Management excluded one bank in the large banking system from the changes, because the management had decided to sell this bank, although the employees did not know that at the time. This bank, therefore, served as a control for the banks receiving the changes. Unfortunately, management did not randomly choose the bank; therefore, it was not a true control group, but comparison with it nevertheless was helpful in judging the success of the job redesign efforts.

It took two months to complete all the changes, showing that such changes are not simple events. Measurements of some variables in the evaluation study were taken just before the changes occurred, then six months after, twenty-four months after, and forty-eight months after the intervention. There seemed to be no effect of the intervention on measurements of absenteeism or intention to quit the job, but there were varying effects on some other variables. Job performance, as measured by supervisors' ratings, did not change at first, but over the long run they improved. Job satisfaction and organizational commitment improved immediately but then returned to their previous levels and stayed there. The perceptions of the nature of the job, as measured by the JDS motivating potential score, improved immediately and stayed there, indicating that the tellers did perceive the changes to have occurred. There was, therefore, improvement in the nature of the job according to job redesign theory, and the employees noticed the changed nature of the job. The only "permanent" improvement to outcomes, however, was to one organizationally valued outcome, job performance (Griffin, 1991). One can at least say that such large-scale changes can affect performance.

Organizational Behavior Management

Organizational behavior management (OBM), the common name of the systematic use of reinforcement principles in organizations, has had some effects on some employee behaviors (O'Hara, Johnson, & Beehr, 1985). The basic idea is to determine an employee behavior that is in need of changing, to examine the behavior in detail to understand exactly what it entails, and to arrange consequences (usually reinforcement) for the behavior. Consistent with Porras and Robertson's (1992) approach to organization development, OBM explicitly maintains that improvements in the organization can only occur through changes in behavior. One should note, therefore, that improvements in many of the individually valued outcomes, such as job satisfaction, are not usually considered important, because they are not observable behaviors. Thus, OBM has had a tendency to favor organizational outcomes (only the ones that are behavioral, however) over the individual outcomes.

For a long time, OBM was largely confined to usage in psychologically oriented organizations, such as school systems and mental health institutions. In the last couple of decades, however, there has been an increase in its use in private sector organizations as well (O'Hara et al., 1985). There has been a tendency to use it for fairly simple employee behaviors that are easy to observe and to count. It has, for example, reduced absenteeism and increased production quantity. For more complex behaviors, a common tactic is to reinforce the final outcome of successful performance rather than the specific behaviors that lead to it. This assumes that employees will perform whatever complex behaviors are necessary to ensure successful performance (O'Hara et al., 1985). In this case, however, OBM begins to look like any other incentive system, such as rewards based on dollars of sales.

Applications at the Group Level

I noted earlier that the history of organization development has included many group-level approaches. Any training in interpersonal skills or in leadership borders on organization development if it applies behavioral science knowledge, and such training programs are common in organizations. Rather than routine use of the group-level types of training, however, we usually reserve *organization development application* as a term for unusual applications; this would include times when particular problems are acknowledged among existing members of the group or, for example, when the organization is about to undertake a new direction in its overall methods of working.

Group Process Interventions

Many interventions are in some way group process interventions. One explicit approach, which Schein (1987) advocated early, involves observing, in person, a natural work group interacting in its natural setting doing its work. The task is basically to help the group to understand its processes, as I described in Chapters 6 and 7, so that it can avoid miscommunications and other problems that are due to poor group processes. To do this, the observer must at some point offer the observations and conclusions to the group itself for its consideration. The group will then learn about its process. For that matter, so may the observer, because the group may show him or her to be somewhat mistaken in the original conclusions about the process. The assumption is clear that knowing about one's processes will help a group to improve them and also that improving its processes will lead to better outcomes for the individual and the organizations. Schein's early process consultation work came to the conclusion that it was more important to help the processes of the top group in the organization (e.g., the top officers of the organization) than other groups, because they strongly affect the rest of the organization.

Leadership Training

Most leadership training that goes under the rubric of organization development probably occurs in the context of the work group the leader supervises. Thus, rather than taking leaders or supervisors out of their groups and conducting some training with them alone, the recommended approach is usually to have the training conducted as part of group process, a very important part to be sure. There is often an emphasis on understanding one's own leadership style before one can change it in any way or use it more appropriately. The parallel with group process work in general is obvious. When leadership training is conducted in the context of the group, however, the group is likely to have some input about their perceptions of the leaders' style and to have some influence on how best to alter that behavior. Although there is often an emphasis in the literature on diagnosing the situation and trying to make the leaders' styles appropriate to the situation, in practice it sometimes seems as if it is more common to try to increase leaders' support or consideration behaviors than their task emphasis. One can surmise that most situations just happen to require this type of leadership style or that this may be a bias of organizational psychology.

Giving subordinates more influence is, after all, consistent with the organizational psychology value that people (subordinates, in this case) have high abilities and are trustworthy.

Team Development

Team development and practices under the formerly more popular name team building, consist of a wide variety of activities with naturally occurring groups in organizations. The aims for group members are to learn, usually through experiences in structured situations, their own dynamics and to increase their skills for effective teamwork, especially with an emphasis on problem-solving effectiveness (e.g., Liebowitz & DeMeuse, 1982; Neuman, Edwards, & Raju, 1989). As in the formerly more popular T-groups, the group itself examines the group processes, usually with a trainer or consultant, and one assumes that insight leads to more effective use of the group processes.

Eden (1985) presented one interesting example of a team-building situation. He conducted a field experiment to test the effects of the team development applications. The researcher randomly assigned logistics groups in the Israeli defense forces either to receive team development or not. The team development interventions consisted of a three-day workshop, including an initial diagnosis with the group leader, discussion of mutual expectations between the leader and the group, diagnosis by the team, team building activities, and writing new descriptions of how the team would work henceforth. The actual team building activities consisted of conflict resolution exercises, problem-solving exercises, surfacing and releasing interpersonal frictions, renegotiating role expectations with each other, and, therefore, redefining the group members' roles.

Eden surveyed the team members who had been through the workshops and those in the control groups, before and after the workshops took place, on group processes including leaders' behaviors, team functioning, team efficiency, and problem solving. The researcher found, however, no difference due to the team-building workshops in the surveys of group processes. In addition, Eden conducted a survey of the subordinates of the leaders in these command groups to see whether the effects of team development with the command groups could have a positive effect on the groups the leaders commanded. If the effort were successful, positive effects should filter down to lower levels of the organizations. These surveys included measures of the leaders' behaviors, unit coordination and communications, peer relations, satisfaction, and general management style. They showed no improvement either, however, which may not be surprising, because command units who had actually been through the programs showed no change in the first place.

These were very rigorous ways of looking at the effectiveness of the team-building development program. A field experiment method (see Chapter 2) such as this is an ideal way to examine organizational psychology issues. As a comparison method, Eden also asked the people who had been through the team-development program to evaluate simply and directly the workshop. Many of the participants reported that the workshops were a success, and three-quarters of them recommended that other teams go through a similar program. This is a very poor way to evaluate an intervention, only using perceptions of the people who had been through the workshop, no control group, no before and after measures, etc. One can hardly trust the results very strongly, and yet it was the only positive set of results in the study. Unfortunately, in practice, many of the team-building efforts seem to use primarily these kinds of evaluations. This is reminiscent of the comment by Porras and Robertson (1992) that organizational psychology research has not kept up with practice and that the field of organization development tends to favor action over any systematic and serious evaluation. Unfortunately, as long as we, as practitioners, do not make sure we evaluate our practices rigorously, we may be fooling ourselves about our effectiveness. It will be hard for the field to advance very far unless we take a serious look at our effectiveness through rigorous, no-nonsense evaluations. Studies such as Eden's (1985), are among the best reported so far. They are useful, because they can help us understand what has and what has not worked well in our organizational psychology practice.

Applications at the Organizational Level

It is almost axiomatic for some practitioners that true organizational change or development must take into account the *entire* organization. Some definitions of organization development even include this as a common element by indicating that it is "system-wide" change (e.g., three of the eight definitions from the literature review by Porras and Robertson, 1992). This is consistent with systems theory, which suggests that everything may be related to everything else. If so, then changing one part of the organization might only create a need to change the other parts of the organization with which that one was interdependent. Otherwise, the new part might not fit any more.

An example of this problem comes from a study by Lawler, Hackman, and Kaufman (1973). In applying one of the individual-level techniques, job redesign, they increased the motivating potential of the jobs of telephone operators in a phone company. Before this, the operators had poor job satisfaction and high absenteeism, and a diagnosis indicated that their jobs were too low on things such as autonomy and variety. They were able to improve the job design and thereby reduce the operators' dissatisfaction and absenteeism, but a new problem then arose. The supervisors of the operators seemed to have become dissatisfied and were even interfering with the operators' job functioning. At the simplest level, what may have happened is the failure to realize and account for the interdependence among parts of the organization's (operators' and supervisors') jobs by improving one part at the expense of the other. In a sense, the operators' increased autonomy, responsibility, and variety had taken parts of the supervisors' jobs away. Subsequently, the supervisors may have had too little to do, making their jobs boring, unproductive, and unfulfilling. This is a very simple and clear illustration of the principle that the parts of the organization are interrelated and that one must account for this interrelationship in any organizational improvement effort. Many times the interrelationships and their consequences are not so clear. Then, the problematic results of change efforts seem confusing and difficult to understand.

Another example comes from a well-known case study about women workers in a toy factory, the "fictitious" Hovey and Beard Company (Dalton & Lawrence, 1971). Their jobs were also rather unmotivating and unsatisfying, and with a consultant's help and their supervisors' eventual enthusiasm, their jobs were given more autonomy. Their production and morale increased dramatically, even though the technology (assembly line) remained basically the same. In this case, their increase in autonomy seemed to rub the job-design experts in the company (industrial engineers) the wrong way, because the women were allowed to decide, to a small extent, how to design their own jobs. In addition, because they were paid on a piece rate, their increased productivity meant that their pay increased to the point that they were making more money than people in the company who had more prestigious jobs and whom most people thought should be making more money. Eventually, this led the company to force the women to go back to doing the job the old, less productive way, which led to making less money and the women being less satisfied and less enthusiastic. Presumably, people in other parts of the organization then become happier. Again, the problem with the intervention was not that it did not work on its own immediate target (the production workers performance and morale), but instead the problem was its unintended effects on other parts of the organization. Most of the women and the supervisor, because they became disillusioned with reverting to the old job design, eventually quit their jobs.

What then, can be done to make an intervention truly consider the organizational level? From my observations and talking to many other organizational psychologists over a few decades, I think true organization-level interventions are actually quite rare. Instead, many interventions that might be primarily at either the individual or group levels claim to be organizational level in one way or another. In the previously mentioned group-level intervention of survey feedback to organizational families, for example, the theory is to start with the top group and then to work one's way down to the bottom groups in the organization. Actually doing this is probably rare, however. Schein's process consultation, in which the organization's top group improves its process, can be considered an organizational-level intervention because the top group is responsible for the entire organization. In theory, therefore, some other interventions can claim to be organizational level. While this indicates that the need for organizational-level work is important, it is not always clear that the interventions do it in practice. What interventions can be done that are truly organizational level, then?

Intergroup Interventions

Interventions at the interface between two or more groups might be considered organizational level interventions. I discussed the intergroup interface in Chapter 8 on organizational level because it is certainly at a level greater than the single group level. One of the major intergroup practices concerns conflict resolution. Because the potential for conflict between groups in organizations is great, this can be a very useful activity.

Strategies for resolving conflicts between groups have been well-known for a long time. There are many variations, but the basics are usually common (Porras & Robertson, 1992). The program is legitimized by having the officer to whom both groups report call a meeting and to have the groups' members know what is expected and how important it is. A series of meetings then takes place under the direction of a consultant from within the organization but from neither group or from outside the organization. The meeting may take place off-site, that is, not on the organization's property. This is supposed to loosen people up and allow them to interact more freely without interruptions and without all the organization's trappings reminding them of their usual, old ways of interacting (which they are supposed to shed).

There may be several phases of the subsequent meetings. First, in their separate groups, the members develop written perceptions, often in the form of lists, of important things such as their views of themselves and of the other group and how they think the other group sees them. In some form or other, the two groups then share their lists and try to discuss and come to conclusions about their perceptions. They then focus on problems that involve the groups at work. Again, they develop lists within each group, and then the lists are shared in some manner. In one variation Porras and Robertson (1992) noted, representatives from the group, rather than the whole groups, work together to consider the lists while other members of the groups watch the process.

People then form problem-solving groups that include members of each original group to work on the different problems. These problem-solving groups develop proposals, and the proposals are shared with the entire membership of the two groups. Agreements are then sought for ways to implement the solutions. This process should get people to see each other in more personal and human terms, increase understanding and trust, and (re)focus the attention of the people on the problems rather than on each other. It is primarily a start, and it is up to the groups to continue to work cooperatively rather than antagonistically. Getting the groups to undertake such treatment and getting the cooperation and approval from higher-level management is often as big a problem as conducting the program itself, but it can be done.

Changing Cultures

As I noted in Chapter 9, culture has become a popular topic at the macro level in recent years. One recent literature review listed changes in culture or values of the organization as part of most of the definitions of organization development (Porras & Robertson, 1992). It is not clear how to change cultures, although some possibilities seem obvious. If one wants to change to a more participative culture in which people are valued for their ideas and inputs, consistent with the principle that people have high abilities and are trustworthy, one way of doing this would be to trust people to help make this cultural change. In other words, it might make sense to make the change to another state by using as much of the other desired state as possible in the process of change. To become a more participatively managed organization, for example, it might make sense to conduct this change in a participative manner. This can be a paradox, however. It might be difficult to use participative techniques to change from an authoritarian culture to a more participative one. If the organization knew how to participate efficiently, it might already be doing it.

As I was writing this chapter, a series of articles appeared in the newspaper about a major corporation whose management had publicly decided to change to a more participative culture in which employees will be empowered to take charge of things about which they know and to take more responsibility for getting things done in the best way. Apparently, some managers were not moving very clearly or quickly in this direction, and a high-level executive who is in charge of the process sent an e-mail message to all of these managers telling them to change to the new cultural way of thinking or else they would be on their way out. One can interpret this as an authoritarian memo aimed at forcing people to become democratic. The reporter who wrote the article contacted various organizational consultants, and they gave various opinions, with a slight majority appearing to maintain that this way of becoming a more participative culture was likely to backfire.

Companies purposely and successfully changing their cultures have probably been rare, and the success of such large-scale organizational changes is usually not subject to close or methodologically rigorous evaluation. Nevertheless, culture has become a hot topic in organizational psychology in recent years, and we suspect that more companies will either (1) attempt such changes or (2) start saying that many changes they are making are changing corporate culture. There may be some truth in this. It is not entirely clear how one goes about changing an organization's culture, although some have tried to do so.

In addition, one can argue that some group-oriented techniques actually work at the organizational level when the top management group or preferably all of management is involved. The argument is that top management establishes the culture anyway, and if they change their own culture, then the way the rest of the company or organization works will also eventually change.

Sociotechnical System Changes

Organizations' production systems work through the interaction of the technology and social arrangements. Typically, management develops production systems primarily with the technical features in mind, perhaps too often ignoring the social aspects of the system. As the name implies, sociotechnial systems approaches to organization development explicitly consider and work with both of these systems. There is no one clear way to do this, no step-by-step process through which sociotechnical systems changes are made. This is because each organization may have a very different set of technical characteristics (and social characteristics, for that matter). Technology consists of the tools, machines, and the working processes through which the product flows as it is made or assembled. The word *technology* usually conjures up images of either large machines or electronics, but every organization doing a task has technology. At a fast-food franchise, for example, the bottle one uses to squirt the ketchup onto the hamburger is part of the technology. The *act* of slapping the top hamburger bun onto the hamburger, after the condiments are on it, is also part of the technology, even though the workers use hands rather than machinery. Technology, basically, is the way of doing the task.

Using the restaurant example, we might find that members of our workforce enjoy each other's company and react well to opportunities to see and talk to each other. We could, therefore, arrange the workplace so that every worker could see every other worker, and customers must keep quiet so workers could talk to each other better. We could arrange the ketchup bottle so that it takes two or more people to work it thereby promoting group work. This might optimize what we know about our social system. Alternatively, we could focus solely on the available technological system, using the most innovative, complex, and up-to-date technology. This might result in putting blinders and ear plugs on the employees, putting the customers on a conveyer belt and asking them to eat within twelve minutes (when the conveyer belt comes to the restaurant's exit), or having the ketchup in a large overhead barrel with a tube leading to the condiments table.

In one case we have considered only the social system, and in the other case we have considered only the technological system. The former case wastes potential technology, and the latter case underutilizes the social system. No real-world example uses either of these approaches. No real-world organization focuses on one to the total exclusion of the other. It seems, however, that some organizations, especially in manufacturing industries, treat technology as primary, while they misunderstand and seldom use effectively the social system. This might be due partially to the training of industrial engineers. Their expertise is largely in the development and use of new technology, often with the consideration of human capabilities and limitations, but rarely with the understanding of the total human being or the systems they form when working together. Many organizations, therefore, probably especially manufacturing ones, have a poor fit between the technical and social systems. These organizations develop the technology with a *theoretical* view of human qualities in mind rather than with consideration of the actual social system in the organization.

The first steps, then, are to understand the entire range of technologies available for completing the necessary tasks and to understand the entire range of social systems to which the organizations' members can adapt. Bringing these together into a good fit is the task, and it takes ingenuity, innovativeness, and insight. One common tool or technology for the person making this type of change is the use of participative decision making in one form or other. In other words, one can use input from the organization's members and from experts in industrial engineering.

Generally, a sociotechnical approach to organizational change begins with some sort of diagnosis of the social and technical systems and some insight that the two are not optimally meshed. The task, then, is to improve the integration of the two systems. If the technology is leading to low employee motivation, high rates of turnover, and low morale, management needs to design changes that can improve these human reactions. The term *social system* implies that the problems and solutions are not at an individual level. Because any set of social and technical systems may be different from another set (e.g., in another organization), one cannot specify very well in the abstract the exact tools and aims of sociotechnical approaches to changing organizations. It requires a great deal of insight on the part of the consultant or change agent, and if the effort is participative, on the part of the organization members also. Typical examples often cite technology such as traditional assembly lines that reduce the contact people have with each other, reduce the individual's control and intrinsic motivation, and require high degrees of coordination and control activities by managers or experts of various sorts. The typical solution is to arrange the work so that groups of workers have autonomy, increased control, and interaction with each other while doing a larger piece of the work (increases in task significance and task identity).

This might be done by keeping the assembly line concept but having the workers work as a group, with each group member doing tasks as the group decides, perhaps changing from time to time. The whole group would do more than any one person on a normal assembly line. The group members, therefore, work on more parts of the product than they would on a normal assembly line. How to accomplish this is limited only by the imagination of the people and the practicality of their ideas. For example, the group of people might "ride" along with the product for a while to work on it for a longer period of time, the assembly line might simply have a U-shaped curve in it with the group of workers primarily working inside the U so that they are near the product longer than usual, or the product might by tipped in various ways so that the group can work on various parts of it from their normal stations. The main issue, however, is to consider that the people working in an organization form one or more social systems, and that the social system can cause problems or facilitate work depending in part on the relations it has with the technology of the organization.

There are, of course, many other potential organizational level applications of organizational psychology. One obvious set of them is changing the structure of the organization. We will leave it to your imagination and a rereading of the section on structure from Chapter 9 to figure out how one might decide to introduce liaison roles, flatter organizational structures, different communication links, and so forth. Now we turn to the difficult task of explaining how effective the applications of organizational psychology typically are.

EFFECTIVENESS OF ORGANIZATIONAL PSYCHOLOGY APPLICATIONS

How effective the various organizational psychology interventions are has been very difficult to ascertain, in large part because one rarely evaluates them very objectively. Most often, as in Eden's (1985) "weakest" evaluation, the participants are simply asked whether they thought it was good. This type of evaluation according to Campbell et al. (1991) is almost worthless because of the many threats to its validity. In addition, it is likely that the interventions going under the same name (e.g., team development) vary quite a bit in their implementation, so that they might work in one situation and not in another—not because the program might not work, but because it is not the same program.

Porras and Robertson (1992), after a very large review of the literature evaluating organizational psychology interventions, concluded that about 38 percent of them have had positive effects, about 53 percent had no effects, and about 9 percent had negative effects on the dependent variables they were attempting to affect. By this count, over all intervention programs and over all dependent variables, we might conclude that these programs are only mildly effective. On the positive side, we can say that at least some of them are effective. Furthermore, sometimes the criterion or dependent variable that is the aim of the intervention is quite different (job satisfaction versus job performance) even though, in general, organizational psychology values both individual and organizational outcomes.

Another large-scale evaluation of the organizational psychology interventions was a meta-analysis by Neuman, Edwards, and Raju (1989). They calculated the average effectiveness of interventions that the literature had already reported. In this study, however, they focused on only one kind of criterion or dependent variable in these programs, individual attitudes. In the 126 studies they examined, they found that group-level interventions were the most effective at changing attitudes, that is, team building and laboratory training, followed by goal setting interventions. Over all the interventions they studied, however, there was little or almost no average effect. There was, therefore, substantial variation in the effectiveness of different interventions. From both the Porras and Robertson (1992) review and the Neuman et al. (1989) review, there is probably a minority of instances in which the organizational psychology applications have helped the organization, the individual, or both. Nevertheless, some effectiveness is apparent, and the task is to determine how to increase the number of "hits" or instances in which the programs are effective.

Two elements are probably important for organizational psychology applications to be effective: diagnosis and evaluation. Both of these require some time and effort in planning and may be missed in the action orientation of most organizational development programs which Porras and Robertson (1992) noted. Instead of relying on hunches that we know what is wrong and, therefore, what needs to be fixed, a systematic diagnosis should ascertain with some confidence the causes of the problem, often a criterion variable such as poor performance or dissatisfaction. One of the biggest advantages of the job-redesign approach of Hackman and Oldham (1980) is simply that they developed a diagnostic tool (the JDS) that can look for the most likely types of job characteristics that need change. Not all approaches have done this.

Some of the best research in organizational psychology journals reports the effectiveness of organizational psychology practices without including adequate or any diagnoses. This does not appear to be so on the surface, for nearly all the studies included a pretest of the organizational conditions before the conditions were changed. The point of a diagnosis, however, is not simply to make an assessment before making changes but also to base the changes on that assessment. Eden's (1985) study of team development, for example, which I praised for its methodological rigor, did not do a true diagnosis from a practical standpoint. If it had, it would have done the diagnosis to decide what type of changes to make and in which groups to make them. Some groups might have needed more team building, and some less or none at all. Eden, correctly from the standpoint of knowing whether this intervention had any effect, randomly assigned the groups to treatment or no treatment. What he did not know, however, is whether any of the groups needed any treatment or team development at all! In the Griffin (1991) study, the organization had apparently decided that job redesign was necessary. As far as we know, there was no systematic diagnosis, determining need. Someone with power in the organization must have thought there was a need; therefore, some sort of implicit diagnosis occurred. Many times, I have the impression that consultants make changes to organizations that are more consistent with the consultant's background, philosophy, experience, and expertise than with the organization's particular needs. Some consultants are likely to do team building, job redesign, goal setting, or organizational behavior management (behavior modification) regardless of the organization. This suggests that diagnosis is not taken seriously. If it were, then each consultant might be more likely to do one intervention in one organization and a different intervention in another organization, consistent with the organization's needs rather than with the consultant's habits. Before leaving this topic (diagnosis), I should note that practitioners often advocate that a beginning step is to have the organization's members participate in diagnosing the organization. Many of the more "participative" approaches to improvement of organizations do this. Therefore, one could argue that many of these do have a diagnosis imbedded in them. Again, based on my own observation, however, many times the diagnosis is not very systematic and thorough.

The other major need of organizational development, in general, is use of more objective and rigorous evaluation of the organization's projects. To some extent, no matter what the type of project, the whole field can benefit from better evaluation. At least then we will know more about the success of different kinds of projects in different kinds of settings, and we can all benefit from this knowledge in future practices. In essence, good evaluation is not much more than good research. Chapter 2 explains how such evaluations can take place. Because an intervention or change is occurring, this means there is a manipulation or independent variable; therefore, researchers may use experimental rather than nonexperimental designs. When the evaluation takes place in the field, a field experiment can often occur. Because of local and idiosyncratic conditions, such as too few subjects or constraints on randomly assigning people or groups to treatment versus no treatment conditions, true experiments, however, are difficult to implement in these settings. It seems that many people are, however, too willing to jump immediately to the conclusion that the experiments cannot be done at all; therefore, they do not try very hard to do as rigorous an evaluation of the project as possible. The task is to do an evaluation that comes as close as to a true field experiment as possible, if we really want to know how effective the project has been. Cook, Campbell, and Perrachio (1990) have provided one of the best descriptions of how to design such quasi experiments in the field.

Figure 10.1 illustrates the process of applying organizational psychology for the improvement of organizations and groups and individuals within them. Consistent with the value that organizational psychology uses theory and research, these elements play an important part. For the diagnosis the elements of the organization are not just randomly chosen. The diagnosis does not measure and evaluate every element of an organization, although that may seem useful. Instead, organizational psychology has given us hints about what might be wrong and how it might be improved based upon theory and research.

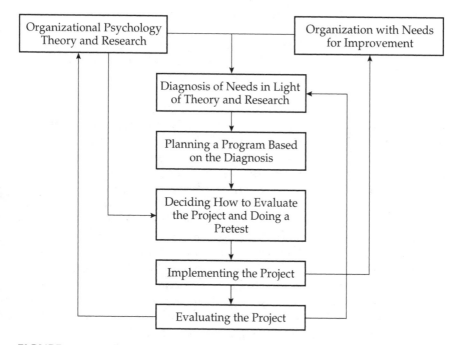

FIGURE 10.1 The Process of Applying Organizational Psychology

Even though this book just highlights some of the main parts of the field, the previous chapters show that the number of variables available for diagnosis at the three levels of organizational psycyhology is extremely large. One may be wise to diagnose all of them, but this is unlikely to be practical. In practice, the best that people usually do is to make educated guesses or hypotheses (whether they call them hypotheses or not in the application side of the field) about what might be wrong and to diagnose the relevant parts of the organization.

If there is a high turnover rate, for example, one may check the literature, which is full of studies on turnover and its causes. This might lead one to diagnose elements of pay, individual differences, organizational tenure, comparisons or equity with other relevant organizations, overall job satisfaction and facet satisfaction, and several other organizational aspects. An excellent diagnosis might include all this. The average practitioner, however, probably does considerably less in the way of diagnosis. That practitioner might simply diagnose the organizational aspect in which he or she specializes and knows the most, for example, supervisors' styles. Unfortunately, a more thorough diagnosis might be necessary to uncover the potential causes of job dissatisfaction and to be confident about it. Based on a thorough diagnosis, then, two things might be especially important in planning a program to meet the organization's needs. We would look at (1) the relationships between the potential causes of turnover and actual turnover (perhaps in this case using the surrogate variable, turnover intention, in place of turnover) and (2) the degree or strength of these causes. If a theoretical cause of turnover is unrelated or is barely related to turnover in the organization, it seems unlikely that it could be a serious cause of turnover there.

Maybe the result would be that supervisor style variables and a job design variable such as autonomy are the only ones strongly related to turnover. In this case, then diagnosis would look at the actual strengths or levels of these variable in the organization and in various parts of it. This is usually simply a look at the mean or average levels of these variables, but it is very useful if a relevant comparison is available. A revealing comparison would be the mean scores on autonomy and supervisory variables at comparable organizations in the same industry. Unfortunately, this is often not possible unless researchers have used the same measuring instruments frequently and reported their scores in the research literature. Comparisons among different groups, departments, and hierarchical levels within the organization itself are always possible, however, and this will at least indicate where in the organization the problems may be better or worse and, therefore, where to focus the efforts at improvement. If the supervisory styles and the employee autonomy are apparent causes of the turnover in this organization, but if they are already very high (good) in general, then there is little that can be done to improve them. Management should then focus efforts on the weaker areas of the organization where the most improvements can be made with the least cost or effort.

As I noted, one must decide how to evaluate the project before starting it, and this almost always means that a pretest of the relevant variables must occur. Fortunately, the diagnosis instrument can often also serve as the pretest, but if this is not the case, then the evaluater must decide on pretests before it is too late. *How* to evaluate the project also means what type of experimental or quasi-experimental design to use. Organizational psychology informs us that a true field experiment would be best if implemented in the local situation. If not, then one should use the best possible quasi-experimental design. This might mean finding a way to have a comparison group (if not a true, randomly chosen, control group), considering the potential threats to the validity of the results based on the nature of the comparison group, the nature of the project to be implemented, and the nature of the organization, industry, and environment. This takes insight into organizations, research, and the particulars of the local site.

Figure 10.1 shows that after these decisions are made, then finally the actual project can begin, whether this would be altering the job to introduce more autonomy in some departments where the diagnosis indicated that was needed, for example, or changing the supervisors' procedures. This implementation would, if successful, change the needs of the organization by reducing them.

Finally, the project is evaluated according to the plan. One makes comparisons of posttest scores both with the pretest scores and those of comparison groups. The evaluater then judges the degree of success of the project. One should take the posttest measurements immediately after the project and again, more than once, at later dates. The Griffin (1991) study, for example, found that some important variables improved right away but did not last, while others did not improve at all until a later time. An arrow goes from the evaluation box in Figure 10.1 back to organizational psychology research and theory, because the evaluation *is* organizational psychology research and because it contributes to theory if it is written and published for others to read and learn. Many organizational psychologists in practice do such writing and have contributed to the broader field. This helps us all to know more and to apply our knowledge more appropriately.

The dotted arrow from project evaluation to diagnosis (Figure 10.1) acknowledges that the final measurements in the evaluation project also constitute a new diagnosis, because the same variables are usually measured. The evaluation includes both the outcome variables that might have been the stimulus of the whole project to begin with, for example, turnover rates, but it also includes the potential causal variables, such as the supervisory style and autonomy. The psychologist should also measure and evaluate them, or it would not be clear what the project had actually done. It should have changed these variables as well as the outcome(s). Assessing changes in these presumed causal variables is comparable to a "manipulation check" in experimental psychology. It lets us know whether we really manipulated the independent variable(s) that we intended to.

If the new diagnosis is still not satisfactory, then the process can begin again, with a new program of change implemented. In fact, organizations are continually changing, although sometimes very slowly, and planned changes such as those based on organizational psychology research are only one type. Because the elements of the organization do not stay the same forever anyway, we should expect that a periodic assessment might help most organizations. Occasional measurements of such variables might even let the organization's decision makers catch problems in their early stages before they would have become apparent otherwise.

CONCLUSION

There are many applications of organizational psychology principles, and we have used the term *organization development* in a general sense to label all of them. While the historical roots of these applications are seen in the use of employee questionnaires (especially for survey feedback to organizational families) and T-groups, modern day organizational development encompasses a wide variety of techniques—in fact, any application derived from any principles based on research and theory in the entire field. This includes practices at all three levels: individual, group, and organizational.

The four basic values of organizational psychology are apparent in its applications. The individual is indeed as important as the organization, as one can see from the interventions, which sometimes singly and certainly in combination, can attempt to improve both of these parties' welfares. As the chapters on individual and organizational outcomes noted, it is sometimes possible to change outcomes for one without affecting the other, and perhaps even to improve the outcomes of one side while adversely affecting the other. The ideal intervention in organizational psychology, however, helps both sides simultaneously. These outcomes become the criteria by which one judges the effectiveness of the intervention.

Organizational psychology strongly values interpersonal activities, as one can see in the historical applications using T-groups and organizational families. The entire array of intervention techniques at the group level all concern interpersonal activities (in the groups). The interpersonal processes of organizational members are often considered important, if not for themselves, then because they are theoretically linked to individual and organizational outcomes. At the organizational level, many interventions also have interpersonal processes as an inherent part of them. This is readily apparent in the examples I offered in this chapter. Sociotechnical systems approaches consider the social system as one of the main components of the organization, and relationships among people are primary ingredients of such systems. The same applies to the cultural and intergroup change techniques. At the individual level, if there is a common, unexpected, and undesired outcome, it is probably related to a failure to adhere enough to this principle. The interrelationships between people and their jobs, for example, was important in the problems resulting from the job redesign intervention of Lawler et al. (1973).

The third organizational psychology value, that people tend to have high abilities and are trustworthy, is also apparent in many of the interventions and techniques used in applying organizational psychology principles. At the individual level, the heavy emphasis on autonomy and variety in job redesign makes this readily apparent, because we would not give more responsibility to people whom we did not trust or who have little ability. This principle is not as apparent in organizational behavior management interventions, however, although there is sometimes some effort to enlist the help of and suggestions of the organization's members themselves in determining the nature of the reinforcement they will implement. At the group and organizational levels, there is a similar effort to introduce various types of group participation and cultures involving participative management.

The final value of organizational psychology, that research and theory have value, arises at many points in the implementation of organizational psychology principles. In the first place, these practical interventions in organizations are based upon research and theory that the field itself developed. The nature of the interventions and the techniques come from the decades of research results in the literature. In addition, two particular activities in organizational applications (see Figure 10.1), are diagnosis and evaluation. Diagnosis often comes with the principles and trappings of the scientific side of the field, namely psychological measurement. One often undertakes organizational diagnoses with the use of surveys, although not always. In using such surveys, the quality of the diagnosis is particularly dependent on such very basic scientific principles as reliability and validity of measurement, without which the diagnosis would be useless. The evaluation of the effectiveness of the project is also primarily a research activity. The principles of experimental and quasi-experimental design are important considerations if one is to believe the results of the evaluations. A common weakness, which I noted in this chapter and many other organizational psychologists have observed, is that scientific principles are not used enough in evaluations of organization development. Problems of credibility occur when this basic principle of research and theory having value is compromised. There is a need for better diagnosis and evaluation of organizational psychology applications. It seems clear that our applications do not work every time, but only better evaluation can allow us to determine which interventions work best in which situations.

REFERENCES

Campbell, J. P., & Dunnette, M. D. (1968). Effectiveness of T-group experiences in managerial training and development. *Psychological Bulletin, 70,* 73–104.
Cook, T. D., Campbell, D. T., & Peracchio, L. (1990). Quasi Experimentation. In M. D. Dunnette & L. M. Hough (Eds.), *Handbook of industrial and organizational psychology,* Vol. 1 (2nd ed.) (pp. 491–576). Palo Alto, CA: Consulting Psychologists Press.
Dalton, G. W., & Lawrence, P. R. (1971). *Motivation and control in organizations.* Homewood, IL: Irwin-Dorsey.
Eden, D. (1985). Team development: A true field experiment at three levels of rigor. *Journal of Applied Psychology, 70,* 94–100.
Griffin, R. (1991). Effects of work redesign on employee perceptions, attitudes, and behaviors: A long-term investigation. *Academy of Management Journal, 34,* 425–435.
Hackman, J. R., & Oldham, G. R. (1980). *Work redesign.* Reading, MA: Addision-Wesley.
Lawler, E. E. III, Hackman, J. R., & Kaufman, S. (1973). Effects of job redesign: A field experiment. *Journal of Applied Social Psychology, 3,* 49–62.
Liebowitz, S. J., & DeMeuse, K. P. (1982). The application of team building. *Human Relations, 16,* 1–18.
Mann, F. C. (1961). Studying and creating change. In W. Bennis, K. Benne, & R. Chin (Eds.), *The planning of change* (pp. 605–613). New York: Holt, Rinehart, & Wintson.
Neumann, G. A., Edwards, J. E., & Raju, N. S. (1989). Organizational development interventions: A meta-analysis of their effects on satisfaction and other attitudes. *Personnel Psychology, 43,* 461–489.
O'Hara, K., Johnson, C. M., & Beehr, T. A. (1985). Organizational behavior management in the private sector: A review of empirical research and recommendations for further investigation. *Academy of Management Review 10,* 848–864.
Porras, J. L., & Robertson, P. J. (1992). Organizational development: Theory, practice, and research. In M. D. Dunnette & L. M. Hough (Eds.) *Handbook of industrial and organizational psychology,* Vol. 3. (2nd ed.) (pp. 719–822). Palo Alto, CA: Consulting Psychologists Press.
Schein, E. A. (1987). *Process consultation,* Vol. II. Reading, MA: Addison-Wesley.

NAME INDEX

Abraham, L. M., 76, 93
Ackerman, P. L., 64, 65
Alderfer, C. P., 54, 55, 65, 126, 142, 177–181, 186
Allport, G. W., 2, 26
Arvey, R. D., 76, 93

Bales, R. F., 21, 26
Bandura, A., 140, 142
Barnard, D. I., 16–18, 26
Barrow, J. C., 35, 49
Bass, B. M., 78, 93
Beehr, T. A., 7, 37, 49, 57–59, 66, 67, 71, 74, 79, 86–94, 98–100, 108, 117, 118, 223, 240
Bell, C. H. Jr., 25, 27
Bell, N. E., 75, 95
Benne, K. D., 21, 26, 34, 142, 240
Bennis, W. 240
Berkowitz, L., 167
Berlo, D. D., 162, 166
Bhagat, R. S., 90–93
Bion, W. R., 132–133
Black, R. H., 136, 142
Blood, M. R., 57, 67
Bonacich, P., 164, 166
Borgatta, E. A., 55, 66

Borman, W. C., 117
Bouchard, T. J., 76, 93
Boyatzis, R. E., 55, 67
Brass, D. J., 163, 166
Brayfield, A. H., 22, 26
Brett, J. M., 169, 186
Brown, N., 114, 117
Brown, R., 145–166
Brief, A. P., 75, 93
Buckley, M. R., 75, 95
Burke, M. J., 75, 93
Byosiere, P., 88, 95

Cammann, C., 34, 49
Campbell, D. T., 38, 40, 49, 219, 232, 235, 240
Campbell, J. P., 219, 240
Campion, M., 137–142
Capwell, D. F., 22, 27
Carey, E. G., 13, 27
Cartwright, D., 20, 26, 120, 142
Chavez, C., 73
Chin, R., 240
Clark, I. A., 75, 95
Clausen, J. A., 75, 95
Colarelli, S. M., 98–100, 117
Cook, T. D., 38, 40, 49, 235, 240

SUBJECT INDEX